FLORIDA STATE
UNIVERSITY LIBRARIES

JAN 15 2001

TALLAHASSEE, FLORIDA

Cognition, Rationality, and Institutions

Springer
*Berlin
Heidelberg
New York
Barcelona
Hong Kong
London
Milan
Paris
Singapore
Tokyo*

Manfred E. Streit · Uwe Mummert
Daniel Kiwit (Eds.)

Cognition, Rationality, and Institutions

With 14 Figures
and 11 Tables

 Springer

Prof. Dr. Manfred E. Streit
Dr. Uwe Mummert
Dr. Daniel Kiwit
Max-Planck-Institute for Research into Economic Systems
Kahlaische Strasse 10
07745 Jena
Germany

ISBN 3-540-67446-2 Springer-Verlag Berlin Heidelberg New York

Library of Congress Cataloging-in-Publication Data
Die Deutsche Bibliothek – CIP-Einheitsaufnahme
Cognition, rationality, and institutions: with 11 tables / Manfred E. Streit ... (ed.). – Berlin; Heidelberg; New York; Barcelona; Hong Kong; London; Milan; Paris; Singapore; Tokyo: Springer, 2000
 ISBN 3-540-67446-2

This work is subject to copyright. All rights are reserved, whether the whole or part of the material is concerned, specifically the rights of translation, reprinting, reuse of illustrations, recitation, broadcasting, reproduction on microfilm or in any other way, and storage in data banks. Duplication of this publication or parts thereof is permitted only under the provisions of the German Copyright Law of September 9, 1965, in its current version, and permission for use must always be obtained from Springer-Verlag. Violations are liable for prosecution under the German Copyright Law.

Springer-Verlag is a company in the BertelsmannSpringer publishing group.
© Springer-Verlag Berlin · Heidelberg 2000
Printed in Germany

The use of general descriptive names, registered names, trademarks, etc. in this publication does not imply, even in the absence of a specific statement, that such names are exempt from the relevant protective laws and regulations and therefore free for general use.

Hardcover-Design: Erich Kirchner, Heidelberg

SPIN 10724826   42/2202-5 4 3 2 1 0 – Printed on acid-free paper

Preface

Most of the contributions of this volume are revised versions of papers that have been presented at an symposium organized by the Max-Planck-Institute for Research into Economic Systems in Jena (Germany). The editors gratefully acknowledge the support of Werner Mussler and Uta Lange who took over most of the burden of organizing the conference. Many thanks are due as well to Ulrike Schleier for her devoted effort to make one layout out of several. The same is true for Stephan Schwarzkopf who provided valuable assistance by searching for mistakes and missing references.

Tragically, László Csontos died toward the end of the conference. We recognized him as a very inspiring economist and warm-hearted colleague. This volume is dedicated to his memory.

Jena, February 2000   *Daniel Kiwit, Uwe Mummert and Manfred E. Streit*

Contents

Preface V

Cognition, Rationality and Institutions - Introduction and Overview 1
Daniel Kiwit, Uwe Mummert, Manfred E. Streit

Part I: Institutions and Cognition

Suboptimality and Social Institutions: The Relationship 11
Between Cognition and Context
Jack Knight

Comment
Piet de Vries 27
Daniel Kiwit 33

Patterned Variation. The Role of Psychological Dispositions
in Social and Institutional Evolution 39
Ekkehart Schlicht

Comment
Brian Loasby 55
Uwe Mummert 61

Legal Design and the Evolution of Remorse 65
Steffen Huck

Comment
Thomas Brenner 87

Part II: Cognition and Rationality

Rent Leaving 97
Bruno S. Frey, Iris Bohnet

Comment
Heiko Geue 111
Andreas Ortmann 121

Reasoning in Economics and Psychology: Why Social Context Matters.............131
Andreas Ortmann, Gerd Gigerenzer

Comment
Markus Pasche 147
Birger P. Priddat 153

Decision Making and Institutionalized Cognition 161
Gernot Handlbauer

Comment
Renate Mayntz 181

Part III: Rationality and Institutions

Rationally Transparent Social Interactions..189
Bruce Chapman

Comment
Thomas S. Ulen 205

Verstehen, Ideal Types and Situational Analysis 213
for Institutional Economics
John Finch

Comment
László Csontos...233

Learning and its Rationality in a Context 239
of Fundamental Uncertainty
Hansjörg Siegenthaler

Comment
Horst Hegmann 255
Thráinn Eggertsson 263

List of Authors...267

Cognition, Rationality, and Institutions - Introduction and Overview

Daniel Kiwit, Uwe Mummert, Manfred E. Streit

Institutions impose social constraints on individual behaviour. They are shared rules that are supported by various enforcement mechanisms. Cognition refers to the process of how human beings perceive and process information, whereas rationality as a heuristic concept refers to the way in which human cognition is modelled in the social sciences. The analysis of institutions is a growing field within economics. But the growth of the literature on institutional economics is accompanied by a growing scepticism towards extending the conventional economic frame of analysis to institutions. In particular, the notion of perfect rationality is increasingly questioned. Perfect rationality may be justified as an „as if" concept to explain human choice within rules. But this heuristic concept becomes highly questionable when applied to the emergence or change of institutions. At the same time human cognition has become a major field of research in psychology. Therefore, it has to be asked whether institutional economics can learn something from cognitive psychology regarding the proper modelling of rationality.

Institutions reduce uncertainty by constraining human action. Thereby, they enable economic actors to form reliable expectations about the actions of others. Due to information costs and to the limited human capacity to perceive and process information, institutions facilitate cognitive processes. However, being part of the cultural environment they also influence the individual's perception of information: It is assumed that the human mind creates cognitive models interpreting the environment. These cognitive models act like filters and influence the perception of information (Hayek 1952, North 1990, Denzau/North 1994). The cognitive models are assumed to be influenced by the process of socialisation. During the process of socialisation institutions are internalised, i.e., external enforcement mechanisms are increasingly supplemented by internal ones (see e.g. Piaget 1932, 1952, Loevinger 1976, Kohlberg 1969, Deci/Ryan 1985). In this way, the institutional environment shapes the cognitive models of human actors. However, the systematic interrelationship between institutions and cognitive models is far from being sufficiently explored. Thereby an understanding of cognitive processes is of fundamental importance for the understanding of human behaviour.

This holds especially true for explaining institutional change. Cognitive processes have a direct impact on individual decision making. Individual decision making is not only about goods. It also involves the choice between accepting or not accepting institutions as constraints. The same is true for decisions on propagating new potential rules. Taking into account the relationship between institutions and cognition, the process of institutional change holds fundamental puzzles: For institutions to reduce complexity their stability is a necessary prerequisite. At the same time, however, institutional change is necessary for the successful adaptation of an economic system to changes in the economic environment. Persistent institutions can hamper economic development (North 1990). One reason for the persistence of institutions is their internalisation by the economic actors. Socialisation within an institutional environment can result in similar cognitive models. But if actors form cognitive models in accordance with the existing institutions, what are the factors that drive human minds to produce institutional innovations, i.e., to create institutional change?

If the limitedness of the human mind is taken seriously, the process of how individuals acquire and process information becomes the centre of attention. In order to get a well-founded concept of rationality - and thus better explanations of the emergence and change of institutions - it seems indispensable to take the phenomenon of cognition explicitly into account. This necessity is further supported by the findings of descriptive decision theory, that human beings can systematically deviate from Bayesian logic (see as a classical reference Kahneman/Tversky 1974). However, new approaches which focus on the simulation of processes of learning in the economy (e.g. Arthur 1992, 1993, Kirman/Salmon 1995) or on the impact of institutions on cognition (Denzau/North 1994) do not provide sufficient answers to the questions of how institutions and cognitive processes are related and of how they can be modelled. In cognitive psychology as well as in the fields of brain theory and artificial intelligence, a growing number of approaches regarding the question of how information is perceived and processed by the human mind are developed (e.g. Gigerenzer 1993, 1994, Holland et al. 1986, Tooby/Cosmides 1992). The question is how this scientific knowledge can be used to develop a model of man that allows for better explanations and predictions of economic behaviour.

In conventional neoclassical economics, human beings are modelled as perfect processors of perfect information. Even the economics of information still presupposes the observing scientist to be perfectly rational and perfectly informed. In assuming that either the marginal utility of information or the underlying probability distribution of information is well-known, it leaves the reference frame of perfect rationality untouched. However, if institutions help to economise on information it is also necessary to concede that human behaviour is shaped by a constitutional lack of knowledge in a systematic way and that perfect rationality neglects important features of human action. Consequently Simon 1955 develops a model of man, which takes the human cognitive limitations into account. Optimising behaviour is substituted by other heuristics, e.g. by "satisficing".

Another question is how institution-guided behaviour can be explained by an economic model of man. One possibility to integrate institutional constraints is to extend the subjective expected utility concept. Such an approach is still one of optimisation. However, Furubotn 1994 demonstrates that logical inconsistencies arise when some traditional assumptions, e.g. zero transaction costs, are rejected while others are retained.

Even more problems arise when the analysis is shifted from a comparative static perspective to an evolutionary one. Economic behaviour is guided by subjective cognitive models of the environment. Due to an ever changing environment, it is not guaranteed that these subjective models will approach reality. The knowledge about this environment might depreciate faster than new information is gathered. Therefore subjective knowledge might remain far from perfect. It was Simon (1978) who tried to take this into account by introducing a concept of „procedural rationality": Because of the limitations of knowledge and computing power, man is incapable of making objectively optimal choices. According to Simon, procedural rationality refers to methods of choice that are as effective as man's decision-making and problem-solving means permit. In spite of this attempt, a consistent general theory of bounded or procedural rationality is not in sight so far. Furthermore, the concepts of Simon still neglect an important feature of cognition, namely the creativity of the human mind. Cognition is not only a process of running after new information about changes of the environment. It is also a process by which new opportunities of action are created (Lachmann 1984, Shackle 1972).

To summarise, there is a fundamental need for research into the interplay of cognition, rationality, and institutions. The following papers and comments gathered in this volume shed light on the outlined issues from quite different perspectives.

The first part of the volume which approaches the relationship of *institutions* with human *cognition* begins with a general discussion by Jack Knight of the extent to which explanations of suboptimal economic and political performances of societies rest on the respective conceptual position taken. Knight confronts different positions of social outcome with different conceptualisations of the relationship between cognition, rationality and institutions. Furthermore, he emphasises the necessity to scrutinise those processes that shape the emergence and change of institutions in order to explain the existence of comparatively suboptimal products.

Piet de Vries in his comment criticises the lack of a clear definition of optimality in Knight's paper. Furthermore, he argues that the existence of an optimum is incompatible with explanations based on variations in a social context. If applying such an approach variation in a social context does not deliver the explanation of suboptimality differences but presents rather a description of what happened.

Daniel Kiwit distinguishes between Knight's broad concept of culture and institutions. He elaborates in more detail on mental models and discusses the issue of path dependence. In particular, he critics D'Andrades concept of culture, that has been applied by Knight, for raising more questions than answering it.

Ekkehart Schlicht criticises institutional economics for being primarily based on concepts of blind evolution that allow for any random variation to occur. By contrast, concepts of organic evolution recognize that variations are patterned by the already existing. Schlicht sees fundamental analogies between processes of organic evolution in nature and society and consequently proposes to apply the concept of patterned variation as well in the social sciences. He argues that in particular classical Gestalt psychology allows to identify those basic human regularities that pattern innovations.

In his comment Brian Loasby agrees with the view that social evolution operates within the constraints of human psychology. He proposes to focus on the constraints imposed by the characteristics of human cognition. How we acquire knowledge sets the limits to what each of us can know. In particular in the study of the evolution of organization he sees an promising field of application for such theories.

Uwe Mummert acknowledges the view of patterned variation as well, however, rejects Schlicht's criticism of the predominant use of concepts of blind evolution in institutional economics. Furthermore, he argues that even the concept of patterned variation does not allow for any predictions of what kind of variations will occur. Therefore, in order to explain evolutionary processes he proposes to focus rather on those constraints that shape the process of selection.

Steffen Huck studies how legal institutions affect feelings of remorse. In a principal-agent game individuals may feel guilty in case of betrayal or unjustified distrust. Changes in the legal design have short-run effects on behavior and long-run effects on preferences. To solve the evolutionary game he relies on sets of neutrally evolutionarily stable strategies and introduces a new refinement concept which guarantees asymptotic stability under various dynamics. Finally, he presents an experimental implementation that shows whether and how the theoretical predictions can be validated by empirical data.

Thomas Brenner agrees that institutions have an effect on individual preferences. In his comment he focuses in particular on the link between institutions and preferences, i.e. cognitive processes of learning. He discusses concepts adopted from biological evolution to describe learning processes and clarifies that the applicability depends on specific conditions.

The second section of this volume is devoted to the implication of experimental evidence on *cognition* for models of *individual rationality*.

Bruno S. Frey and Iris Bohnet argue that ample evidence can be found for rent leaving, i.e. actors refrain from exploiting all feasible opportunities because of some intrinsic motivation. They argue that often such intrinsic motivations have beneficial effects for the society as a whole. Furthermore, they point to the danger of crowding out such motivations by designing institutional settings without taking them into account.

Heiko Geue explains that moral behavior had been already been an issue of classical economics. He reinterprets the concept of intrinsic motivation in Smith's terms and discusses the impact of competition on the likelihood of crowding out such motivations.

Andreas Ortmann rejects almost all hypotheses put forward by Frey and Bohnet. He sees only little evidence for both that rent leaving can be explained by intrinsic motivation and for crowding it out by external interventions. He pleads in general for more concern of how experimental data is generated.

Andreas Ortmann together with Gerd Gigerenzer continue this line of argumentation in their paper in which they present experimental evidence on deviations from standard rational choice predictions. They argue that many anomalies are actually due to both a false application of Bayesian logic and in particular the abstract design of experiments abandoning the social context of interaction. Many anomalies vanish when the test persons are confronted with the same tasks, yet, presented in a familiar context

Markus Pasche acknowledges that there is ample experimental evidence showing deviations from rational choice theory. However, he argues that traditional models of rationality nevertheless may serve as a useful benchmark for measuring the relative performance of simple heuristics. Furthermore, he remarks that so far only little effort has been put on an economic explanation of why such empirically confirmed patterns of reasoning and decision making do exist.

Birger P. Priddat agrees with Ortmann's and Gigerenzer's proposition that content and context matter. However, he disagrees with the epistemological approach taken. He criticises that they do not apply an approach that takes communication into account since content is also language-dependent.

Finally, at the end of this section Gernot Handlbauer analyzes the interrelationship of decision making, cognition and institution. He interprets human decision making in the way, that actors attempt to develop sensible but not necessarily rational concepts of action in an uncertain environment. Since the ways in which individuals attempt to attribute meaning to different actions are quite heterogeneous Handlbauer proposes to drop the idea of a homogenous concept of rationality.

Renate Mayntz criticises Handlbauer's very broad definition of institutions that include cognitive structures as well. She confronts this view with one distinguishing between cognition and institutions and elaborates on the comparative advantage of such an approach.

In the final section of this volume the methodological issue of how *institutions* can be integrated into models of *rationality* is discussed.

John Finch investigates the suitability of situational analysis as a method for conducting research within institutional economics. He argues that situational analysis easily translates into single exit modeling. The consequences of aligning situational analysis with the scientific methodology of single exit modeling are outlined, as are possibilities for broadening objectives to consider the development of institutions.

László Csontos in his comment offers a conceptual analysis of two types of deductive-nomological explanations and highlights the role of situational logic in supplementing these types of explanatory arguments.

Bruce Chapman focuses on the issue of cooperation of rational actor in a prisoner's dilemma context. He takes Gauthier's „solution" of modeling individual actors as constrained maximizers as the starting point. Since this concept is based on the assumption that actors can identify the kind of counterparts they face, Chapman discusses whether full or only partial transparency presents a reasonable assumption in this context.

In his discussion Thomas S. Ulen points out that Chapman misses to tackle the decision process a rational actor goes through in deciding which frame to adopt. Furthermore, he argues that both social norms and unconsciousness inducements may present a neglected explanation for explaining cooperation in the context of prisoner's dilemma.

Hansjörg Siegenthaler focuses on the impact of economic crisis on rationality. He argues that economic crises confront the individual actors with fundamental uncertainty. The individual actor will loose confidence in those cognitive rules which hitherto served to relate expectations to observable facts. In this context a collective process of learning through communication will result in shared experience. Thus, communicable experience tends to become institutionalized in the sense that it affects the further accumulation of knowledge and thus future economic and institutional development.

Horst Hegmann raises some objections to Siegenthaler's hypothesis. He expresses his doubts that all participants will remain in a state of fundamental uncertainty for the whole time of communication. Therefore, he proposes to replace communication by collective actions aiming at the production of knowledge.

Thráinn Eggertsson also expresses his doubts regarding Siegenthaler's notion of radical uncertainty. He proposes that in general it is reasonable to assume that actors will loose all their models of reality. Nevertheless, Eggertsson stresses as well the necessity to pay attention to shared experience.

The articles of this volume approach the interrelationship of cognition, rationality and institutions from quite heterogenous perspectives. Clearly, this volume is no more than a beginning into the exploration of the implications of cognitive science for economics. However, it is shown that there are many different avenues on which it is valuable to proceed.

References

Arthur, W. B. (1992): *On Learning and Adaptation in the Economy*; Institute for Economic Research, Discussion Paper #854, Queen's University, Kingston, Ontario.

Arthur, W. B. (1993): On Designing Economic Agents That Behave Like Human Agents; *Journal of Evolutionary Economics*, 3(1), 1-22.

Deci, E. L. and R.M. Ryan (1985): *Intrinsic Motivation and Self-Determination in Human Behavior*, New York: Plenum Press.

Denzau, A. T. and D.C. North: Shared Mental Models: Ideologies and Institutions; *Kyklos*, 47(1), 3.-31.

Furubotn, E. G. (1994): *Future Developments of the New Institutional Economics: Extension of the Neoclassical Model or New Construct?;* Lectiones Jenenses, 1, Max-Planck-Institute for Research into Economic Systems: Jena.

Gigerenzer, G. (1993): The Bounded Rationality of Probabilistic Mental Models; pp. 284-313 in: K.I. Manktelow and D. E. Over (eds.), *Rationality: Psychological and Philosophical Perspectives*, London: Routledge.

Gigerenzer, G. (1994): Rationality: Why Social Contexts matter; in: P.B. Baltes and U.M. Staudinger (eds.), *Interactive Minds: Life-Span Perspectives on the social Foundation of Cognition*, Cambridge: Cambridge University Press.

Hayek, F. A. (1952): *The Sensory Order - An Inquiry into the Foundations of Theoretical Psychology;* Chicago: University of Chicago Press.

Holland, J. H., K. J. Holyoak, R.E. Nisbett and P.R. Thagard (1986): *Induction. Processes of Inference, Learning, and Discovery,*: Cambridge (USA) and London: MIT Press.

Kahneman, D. and A. Tversky (1974): Judgement Under Uncertainty: Heuristics and Biases; *Science*, 185, 1124-1131.

Kirman, A. and Mark Salmon (1995): *Learning and Rationality in Economics*, Oxford (UK) and Cambridge (USA).

Kohlberg, L. (1969): Stage and Sequence - the Cognitive-Developmental Approach to Socialization; in: D.A. Goslin (ed.), *Handbook of Socialization Theory and Research*, Chicago: Rand MacNally.

Lachmann, L.M. (1984): *Marktprozeß und Erwartungen. Studien zur Theorie der Marktwirtschaft*, München: Philosophia Verlag.

Loevinger, J. (1976): *Ego Development*, San Francisco: Jossey-Bass.

North, D.C. (1990): *Institutions, Institutional Change, and Economic Performance*, Cambridge (USA): Cambridge University Press

Piaget, J. (1932): *The Moral Judgement of the Child*, New York: Free Press.

Piaget, J. (1952): *The Origins of Intelligence in Children*, New York: Free Press.

Shackle, G.L.S. (1972): *Epistemics and Economics: a critique of economic doctrines*, Cambridge: Cambridge University Press:.

Simon, H. (1955): A Behavioral Model of Rational Choice; *Quarterly Journal of Economics*, 69, 99-118.

Simon, H. (1978): Rationality as Process and as Product of Thought; *American Economic Review*, 68, 1-16.

Tooby, J. and L. Cosmides (1992): The Psychological Foundations of Culture; in: J. Barkow, L. Cosmides and J. Tooby (eds.), *The Adapted Mind. Evolutionary Psychology and the Generation of Culture*: New York, Oxford: Oxford University Press, 19-136.

PART I

Institutions and Cognition

Suboptimality and Social Institutions: The Relationship Between Cognition and Context

Jack Knight

The motivating theme of this symposium is the interplay among rationality, cognition and institutions. This relationship is a complex one and there is much about it that we do not yet understand. There are a few basic ideas that generate the interest in this relationship and that structure the growing body of research. They can be stated simply as a set of causal relations: cognition affects rational decisionmaking, rational decisionmaking affects the development of institutions, institutions affect rational decisionmaking, institutions affect cognition, institutions affect social outcomes. These beliefs about the reciprocal causal relations have led many to the conclusion that in order to understand institutional change and the resulting effects on social change, we need to develop a better understanding of the relationship between cognition and rationality on the one hand and social institutions on the other.

This is an important insight and the effort to analyze the cognition-institutions relationship is a significant and valuable one. But in the rush to turn our attention to cognition, it is important that we not lose sight of what we already know about social institutions. In our attempts to explain the effects of institutions on social life, we already know a lot about the causal effects on social outcomes. To illustrate this, I focus here on a particular question: how do we explain Suboptimality in political and economic performance in a society? Here my primary focus is on those categories of social explanations that emphasize (1) intentional (usually rational and often strategic) action and (2) the cognitive effects of institutions and other social factors on that action.[1] This is an especially relevant question for research on the cognition-institutions relationship because much of the interest in cognition has emerged out of a concern about the inability of standard rational-choice approaches to adequately explain the persistence of inefficient institutions.[2]

After setting out some initial claims about the basic logic of explanations of suboptimality, I motivate the analysis with a brief review of a claim about institutional effects on economic performance offered by Douglass North. North identifies important connections among rational decisionmaking, cognition and social

---

[1] See Knight (1992), Knight and Sened (1995) and Eggertsson (1990) for more comprehensive reviews of this literature.

[2] See Knight and North (forthcoming) for a general discussion of this point.

institutions and suggests that these connections plausibly identify major sources of suboptimality. Then I briefly review existing research on cognition and identify three ways of conceptualizing the relationship among these factors. They are distinguished by the extent to which they integrate the cognition and rationality of individual actors with their social context (culture, social institutions, etc.).

These alternatives imply varying ways of explaining the suboptimality of social outcomes. They allow us to distinguish two general approaches to the problem. First, there are the explanations that see suboptimality as a function of problems at the level of the individual actor. For example, the explanation focuses on problems with the process of learning or with cognitive abilities and capacities. On these accounts the suboptimality is primarily a problem of individual cognition: the inability of social actors to properly incorporate contextual information into their decisionmaking process. Second, there are the explanations that understand suboptimality as a function of the social context. By connecting cognition to social context, these account identify a number of sources of explanation in the nature of a society's culture and social institutions. Central to these accounts are the social processes by which institutions emerge and change.

In the concluding section I argue that the logic of the relationship between cognition and social institutions implies that the second approach is the more fruitful way of explaining suboptimality in political and economic performance. This is the case even when cognition plays an explicit role in the analysis. This focus on social context emphasizes how the genesis of social institutions serves as a primary source of explanation of suboptimality. I conclude with a brief review of one account of institutional emergence and change that illustrates how we can explain suboptimality directly in terms of the genesis of these institutions.

The Sources of Suboptimality

What exactly are we attempting to explain when we focus on the suboptimality of social outcomes?[3] More specifically, what is the logic of the analysis from an

---

[3] Criticisms of an earlier draft of this paper focused on the analytical and measurement problems related to concepts such as optimality and efficiency. The basic thrust of these criticisms took the following form: optimality and efficiency are highly contested concepts, about which there is considerable disagreement in any society, and, thus, it is impossible to conceptualize and measure them in such a way as to allow for meaningful analysis. I have two responses to this criticism. First, I agree with the view that these concepts are contestable and that any societal effort to achieve "optimality" or "efficiency" should involve a prior discussion over the content of these goals. Furthermore, I agree that these concepts are contestable among social scientists, resulting in considerable disagreement as to what constitutes efficient or optimal behavior. On this point, see, for example, the cogent discussion of efficiency in Hardin (1993). But, second, from this it does not follow that people, either as economic and political actors or as social scientists, do not act as if these disagreements can be resolved to

individual choice perspective (where social outcomes are the product of a set of individual decisions)? It is important to keep in mind that whenever the question arises, it always implies a comparison and an analysis of variation. Consider two types of comparisons that may be implied by the question. First, questions about suboptimality may imply a comparison of actual choices and outcomes with their hypothetical alternatives (some standard of efficiency, optimality or rationality constructed by theory.) The identification of suboptimality on this comparison rests on the deviation of actual outcomes from the measures of optimality derived from theoretical analysis. Second, questions of suboptimality may imply a comparison of two or more patterns of actual choices and outcomes. Here the question actually constitutes a focus on the relative efficiency of the outcomes produced by the different set of choices. The comparison implied by the question could either be between the present choices and outcomes and the past performance of one set of actors or a comparison of the actual choices and outcomes of two or more groups.

In each case the explanation of suboptimality rests on the explanation of the variance among the compared patterns of behavior. In seeking an explanation of suboptimality in terms of comparisons, it is crucial to identify those features of the different choice histories that might do the work in the explanation. Here variation is again crucial because it is only those factors that vary among the comparison groups that will serve as a possible explanation of the deviation. The first type, possibly the most common in the social sciences, is the basis for many assertions of suboptimality in analyses of both individual choice and group decisionmaking. The focus is on explaining deviation from theoretical constructs of either rational decisionmaking or Pareto-optimal and/or socially efficient group outcomes. The second type is fundamental to much of the research in the area of political and economic performance. This is the logic of comparative empirical analysis that seeks to explain why some groups do better than others on various measures of performance. What I want to focus on in this analysis is what this logic of comparison implies for the possibility that the explanation will rest in the complex relationship among rationality, cognition and social institutions.

To make this problem more concrete, consider the claim by Douglass North that the cognition-institutions relationship is central to understanding economic performance. North emphasizes the fundamental role of political and economic institutions in explaining economic performance of societies over time. Social institutions play a fundamental role in structuring the choices of economic actors:

> "Institutions exist to reduce the uncertainties involved in human interaction. These uncertainties arise as a consequence of both the complexity of the problems to be solved and the problem-solving software (to use a computer analogy) possessed by

---

the extent necessary to make such analyses meaningful. Social actors act as if efficiency and optimality are meaningful concepts and social scientists analyze their actions as if it were the case. Thus, my analysis here seeks to investigate the logic of explaining social performance and to identify the difficulties in doing so, holding aside the additional difficulties involved in actually measuring these concepts.

the individual. ... uncertainties arise from incomplete information with respect to the behavior of other individuals in the process of human interaction. The computational limitations of the individual are determined by the capacity of the mind to process, organize, and utilize information. From this capacity taken in conjunction with the uncertainties involved in deciphering the environment, rules and procedures evolve to simplify the process. The consequent institutional framework, by structuring human interaction, limits the choice set of the actors." (North 1990, 25)

While institutions simplify the process of rational decisionmaking (especially in respect to establishing expectations about the behavior of other individuals), they do not resolve all of the problems that might produce suboptimal social outcomes:

"Incremental change comes from the perceptions of the entrepreneurs in political and economic organizations that they could do better by altering the existing institutional framework at some margin. But the perceptions critically depend on both the information that the entrepreneurs receive and the way they process that information. If political and economic markets were efficient (i.e., there were zero transaction costs) then the choices made would always be efficient. That is the actors would always possess true models or if they initially possessed incorrect models the information feedback would correct them. But that version of the rational actor model has simply led us astray. The actors frequently must act on incomplete information and process the information that they do receive through mental constructs that can result in persistently inefficient paths. Transaction costs in political and economic markets make for inefficient property rights, but the imperfect subjective models of the players as they attempt to understand the complexities of the problems they confront can lead to the persistence of such property rights." (North 1990, 8)

Given this conception of the fundamental relationship between cognition and inefficient institutions, North proposes a central role for cognition and rationality in a future research agenda of the role of institutions in economic performance:

"cognitive scientists have been preoccupied by research exploring the way in which the mind and brain attempt to 'make sense' out of the environment. Making sense consists of learning from experiences that generate the mental models that individuals possess and that therefore are the sources of the choices that individuals make. Different experiences will generate different mental models and hence different choices. However, there is a complex (and little understood) interplay between the cultural heritage that is the source of much early learning, the formation of consequent models, and the particular institutions that will result. If we accept the proposition that institutions exist to reduce uncertainty in human interaction, they are clearly an extension of the mental constructs the human mind develops to interpret the environment of the individual. Clearly there is a connection; research on the nature of that connection would be a major step in understanding more about the formation of institutions." (North 1995, 25)

Two questions arise here that are especially relevant for this analysis. First, how should we treat the relationship between cognition and social context (social institutions, culture, etc.)? North argues that we know very little about the nature of this relationship. As I suggested above, we can distinguish alternative answers to this question in terms of the extent to which they integrate cognition into social context. One way of thinking about this question is in terms of North's use of the concept of "mental models." In Denzau and North (1994) they discuss the evolution of mental models. Within this discussion they are somewhat ambiguous as to where these models, the fundamental mechanism of cognition in their analysis, are located. Compare the ambiguous passage on page 4 ("The mental models are the internal representations that individual cognitive systems create to interpret the environment; the institutions are the external (to the mind) mechanisms individuals create to structure and order the environment. Some types of mental models are shared intersubjectively. If different individuals have similar models they are able to better communicate and share their learning. Ideologies and institutions can then be viewed as classes of shared mental models.") with the passage on page 22 ("The path dependence of the institutional development process can be derived from the way cognition and institutions in societies evolve. Both usually evolve incrementally but the latter, institutions, clearly are a reflection of the evolving mental models.") The first passage implies that some mental models may be embedded in the social context, external to the minds of the individual actors. But the second passage implies that mental models are inside the mind and separated from the world of culture and institutions. We can find in the literature on cognition differing approaches that rest on each of these conceptions.

Second, what evidence can we draw on from research on rationality and cognition that will help us to explain the role of institutions in the production of suboptimal social outcomes? I will develop the implications of the differing conceptions of cognition and rationality in the next sections of this paper. Here I merely want to highlight the general thrust of my analysis to emphasize the relevance of this particular formulation of the question. An understanding of cognition and rationality is obviously fundamental to any explanation of social outcomes that is grounded in intentional (or, more specifically, rational) action. If our underlying conceptions of rationality and cognition are flawed and unrealistic, then they will often cause us to mistake the causal mechanisms that are central to the explanation of suboptimality. This is especially relevant if we are asking questions of suboptimality that are grounded in the first type of comparison (between actual behavior and theoretical constructs of rationality), because the theoretical constructs themselves are derived from these conceptions. But, if we are asking questions of suboptimality and relative efficiency that are grounded in the second type of comparison (between two or more patterns of actual behavior), then the evidence that we need to answer such questions must emphasize the variation that we find in the compared cases. As for the specific research on the relationship among rationality, cognition and institutions, the most fruitful evidence in these cases will be that which identifies variation in properties relevant to the cognitive processes within the different groups.

Cognition and Rationality

Now I want to turn to the existing research on cognition and rationality. The question here is, how will this research further our understanding of the cognition-institutions relationship? Although this research is quite diverse, I think that we can accurately categorize it in terms of how different approaches conceptualize the relationship among rationality, cognition and social context. There are three basic conceptions that can be aligned on an internal/external dimension insofar as they differ in how they treat the role of social context in the cognitive process. At one end of the dimension we can identify an approach to cognition and rationality that situates all of the real work inside the heads of the individual actors, leaving little, if any, role for social context in the explanation of rationality. The two other approaches emphasize the importance of contextual factors, but differ in the extent to which they integrate cognition into social processes.

The first approach to questions of rationality and cognition that I want to consider is a widely prevalent conception in the social sciences. In fact, I take it to be so widely known that I will spend little time discussing the logic of the conception and proceed directly to a discussion of its implications for the questions under consideration here. It is a limiting case on the internal/external dimension of cognition and context, the individualistic conception of rationality and cognition. It is the conception that underlies standard psychological research on cognition and rational decisionmaking (see, e.g., the work of Kahneman, Slovic and Tversky 1982) This research primarily focuses on the behavior of individual actors when they are removed, as much as is possible, from the details and influences of their social context.

On this account cognition takes place inside the heads of the actors and rationality is a concept primarily divorced from the specifics of social context. This is not to say that institutions and social context do not matter in a broader theory of knowledge (a plausible interpretation of some versions of this conception is that it treats context as the source of content of our thoughts, somewhat similar to the second conception to be discussed below), but just that the cognitive work is done at the individual level. Similarly, assessments of the rationality of individual decisions are made in reference to a conception of rationality that is theoretically constructed (usually, as an axiomatic definition of consistency, etc.) Given this focus, deviations from predicted rational behavior are attributed to failures of cognition and rationality by the individual actor.

As for the general question of how we understand the relationship among rationality, cognition and social institutions, this conception places the emphasis on the internal workings of the mind, yet relies mainly on evidence of experimental behavior to draw inferences about these internal activities. To the extent that external factors enter into the analysis it is to see how the individual assimilates information prior to decisionmaking. Here I think that it is important to note that the role of the external factors is, in a sense, merely procedural. By this I mean that there is nothing about either the particular substantive content of these factors or their organizational structure that affects the assessment of cognitive ability or rationality. The definition of rationality is theoretically derived independent of social context; cognition is assessed in terms of the ability of the mind to assimilate the information correctly (as defined by the outside observer). Given its lack of attention to the role of social context in the cognitive process, there is little that this research alone can tell us about the specific role of social institutions in the cognitive process.

As for the specific question of what evidence we can draw from research grounded in this individualistic conception that will help us explain the role of institutions in the production of suboptimal social outcomes, there are two main implications. First, to the extent that we are persuaded that cognition works primarily in the heads of individual actors, evidence from this type of research may cause us to revise the basic assumptions about individual decisionmaking that form the basis of our social explanations. This is a general explanatory issue with no special relevance to explanations of suboptimality. This goes to the question of the realism of our models and the plausibility of the causal mechanisms that we identify as the source of our explanations.

Second, as to the specific question of explaining social suboptimality, there are two issues. Assuming that we accept the individualistic conception of cognition and rationality, then we would find relevant evidence of the following forms. If we are focusing on comparisons of the first type, then evidence from this research may be relevant to explaining suboptimality in terms of the deviation of actual individual choices from theoretical constructions of individual rationality. On this account, the deviation of group outcomes from a theoretically defined measure of optimal performance might be explained by failures of rationality at the individual level. If, however, we are focusing on comparisons of the second type, then evidence from this research will only be relevant to explanations of suboptimality if there is variation in the basic cognitive capacities of the different groups. And here it is important to note that the evidence of variation in cognitive capacities cannot come from variation in some measure of efficiency of group performance because it is the latter phenomena that is the very thing that we seek to explain. In most social situations, this is a very difficult standard to achieve.

This individualistic conception of cognition has dominated much of the thinking about rational decisionmaking in the social scientists. But, given the underlying logic that seeks to abstract cognition and rationality from social context, it is unclear how this conception can successfully enhance our fundamental understanding of the cognition-institutions relationship. In order to better investigate the reciprocal relationship among cognition, rationality and institutions, we need both a conception and research program that explicitly accounts for institutional context. The next two alternatives that I want to consider offer such a conception. These conceptions are drawn from work in the field of cultural anthropology. While they both insist on a fundamental role for culture and social institutions in their analyses of cognition, they vary in the extent to which they deviate from the individualistic conception. The first of these two might be read as compatible with the previous discussion, while the second explicitly rejects this conception.[4] Consider first a conception that emphasizes the importance of culture for understanding cognition and individual action, but maintains the primary focus inside the head of the individual actor. D'Andrade's work (1995) in cognitive anthropology offers a thoughtful example of this conception. The key to understanding his approach can be found in the way that D'Andrade situates culture in a cognitive analysis: "culture has both a public and private aspect" (italics in original) (1995, 246). On the one hand, D'Andrade argues against a conception of culture that is limited to internal mental structures:"[i]t is not that one can not define culture so that it consists of just mental structures. ... The point is that such a definition legitimizes the study of mental structures but leaves unlegitimized the study of external structures." (1995, 146) On the other hand, in his general analytical framework culture's role in the cognitive process rests primarily in its effect on individual mental units: "[i]f culture is placed in the mind, then the organization and limitations of the mind can be used to find cognitively formed units - features, prototypes, schemas, propositions, theories, etc. This makes possible a particulate theory of culture; that is, a theory about the "pieces" of culture, their composition and relations to other things (1995, 246). The emphasis on "pieces" of culture highlights D'Andrade's view that culture's place in the cognitive process is to provide the substantive content of individual thoughts:

> "[a]t this point my own solution is to use the term culture to characterize the entire content of a group's heritage, corresponding to Tylor's earlier use of the term, and to try to be specific when talking about things cultural, specifying cultural schemas or understanding as against material culture, cultural practices, cultural talk, etc." (1995, 146)

D' Andrade bases his anthropology on a conception of individual cognition that is grounded in the logic of parallel-processing: "Cognitive representations - properties, prototypes, schemas, models, theories - make up the stuff of culture in the mind. These representations are adaptive in simply being representations; that is, in providing maps of the world. Such a function is not trivial, since effective action requires an understanding of how the world is organized. But cultural representations do more than provide maps. ... under certain conditions cultural representations have significant effects on perception, memory, and reasoning." (1995, 182) Within this framework D'Andrade envisions the effect of culture as extending beyond the cognitive realm: "[t]he individual psyche appears to consist of several interrelated systems. The cognitive system - reasoning, memory, and perception - are all tightly linked together by the requirements of problem solving. Similarly, personality is a system because of the requirements involved in doing what personality does (which is to guide us around in such a way as to insure that we maintain a good relation to our social and physical environment). This requires not only a problem solving system, but also an emotional system to let us know

---

[4] See Ensminger and Knight (1997) and Allio, Dobek, Mikhailov and Weimer (1997) for recent attempts to assess the relative explanatory power of the different existing theories

how we are doing and a motivational system to provide a structure of goals so that we are directed to do what heeds to be done" (1995, 251).

Yet, for all of D'Andrade's insistence on the important and complex role of culture, we can see that his conception remains primarily individualistic. The cognitive work goes on inside the individual head. D'Andrade's emphasis on culture is mainly part of an intellectual strategy to accentuate an independence of the physical and cultural world from mental processes. His research is, in part, a reaction to what he describes as a dominant conception in anthropology since the 1950's that treated culture "as a purely mental phenomena" and treated "structures that exist in the physical world as objects and events" as "a reflection of these mental cultural structures" (1995, 146). He distinguishes his approach from this alternative through its emphasis on the reciprocal causal relationship between external and internal structures in the cognitive process: "[o]n one hand, the external forms which are physical representations depend on a cognitive system to give these representations meaning. On the other hand, the cognitive system cannot express and communicate meanings without the external forms of talk, writing, ritual, etc., to convey these meanings" (1995, 146). "[C]ognitive anthropology has demonstrated that the psyche is influenced by the representations it learns as part of the human cultural heritage. Cognitive anthropology has also tried to show that the cultural heritage itself is influenced by the inherent capacities and limitations of the human cognitive system - that the influence between cultural representation and cognitive process is reciprocal" (1995, 252).

When we consider the implications of the D'Andrade conception for explanations of suboptimality, we see that it differs markedly from the individualistic conception. D'Andrade explicitly incorporates the content of beliefs into the cognitive process. This highlights one important mechanism by which institutional rules can affect the production of social outcomes: the content of the rules determine the incentives facing rational actors. To explain suboptimality, therefore, we can focus on variation in the content of these rules.

The third conception that I want to consider provides for a more fundamental role for culture in the cognitive process and, thus, suggests an additional source of explanation for suboptimal performance. Hutchins (1995) argues that we cannot adequately understand cognition without accounting for the fact that "culture, context and history ... are fundamental aspects of human cognition and cannot be comfortably integrated into a perspective that privileges abstract properties of isolated individual minds" (1995, 354). The basic logic of this conception involves the interrelationship of cognition and culture in a dynamic process: "I hope to show that human cognition is not just influenced by culture and society, but that it is in a very fundamental sense a cultural and social process" (1995, xiv).

For Hutchins cognition is a process of computation. He claims that he has no commitment to any particular statement about the nature of computations that go on inside individuals "except to say that whatever happens there is part of a larger computational system" (1995, 49). This larger computational system is located in the culture of a society. "Human beings are adaptive systems continually producing and exploiting a rich world of cultural structure. ... This heavy interaction of internal and external structure suggests that the boundary between inside and outside, or between individual and context, should be softened. ... Instead of conceiving the relation between person and environment in terms of moving coded information across a boundary, let us look for processes of entrainment, coordination and resonance among elements of a system that includes a person and the person's surroundings" (1995, 280).

On this account culture facilitates cognition though its organizing and coordinating functions: "[f]rom this perspective, what we learn and what we know, and what our culture knows for us in the form of the structure of artifacts and social organizations, are these hunks of mediating structure. Thinking consists of bringing these structures into coordination so that they can shape and be shaped by one another. The thinker in this world is a very special medium that can provide coordination among many structured media - some internal, some external, some embodied in artifacts, some in ideas, and some in social relationships" (1995, 316). Here an understanding of cognition entails an understanding of the social division of labor that cultural creates: "[w]hen computational tasks are socially distributed, there are two layers of organization to the activity: the computational organization, as defined by the computational dependencies among the various parts of the computation, and the social organization, which structures the interaction among the participants to the computation" (1995, 185). But the fact that "[t]he larger system has cognitive properties very different from those of any individual" (1995, 228) does not imply that these properties will always be positive. In addressing the question of the effects of social organization on individual cognitive defects, Hutchins concludes that "some ways of organizing people around thinking tasks will lead to an exacerbation of the maladaptive aspects of this property of mental states, whereas other forms of organization will actually make an adaptive virtue on the group level of what appears to be an individual vice" (1995, 240).

Hutchins' conception of culture as process emphasizes the reciprocal nature of the cognition-context relationship: "Culture is not any collection of things, whether tangible or abstract. ... It is a human cognitive process that takes place both inside and outside the minds of people. It is the process in which our everyday cultural practices are enacted. ... Culture is a process, and the 'things' that appear on list-like definitions of culture are residue of the process" (1995, 354). The implications of Hutchins' conception of the relationship among rationality, cognition and social institutions are more significant than those of the previous two approaches. Consider first the general question of the relationship between cognition and social context. Hutchins' conception constitutes a significant departure from the individualistic conception of cognition and rationality. While maintaining a role for internal factors, Hutchins places significant weight on external factors in the cognitive process. Cognition is conceived of as an interactive process involving the internal dynamics of the individual mind and the physical and cultural resources found in the social context. This highlights a potentially important cognitive role for social institutions.

One aspect of this role is consistent with, but broader than, the D'Andrade account: institutional rules as cultural tools that guide activity through the prior knowledge that their content embodies. Here the rules do more than give content to thought, they also structure the cognitive process in time-tested ways. But Hutchins envisions an even more significant aspect: the effect of social institutions on the organization of the social division of cognitive labor. This entails a research agenda for the cognition/institutions relationship that cannot be accomplished in an experimental setting, but rather requires an investigation of what Hutchins calls "cognition in the wild." Implicit in this agenda is the idea that we cannot assess the rationality of individual action without taking account of the institutional and cultural context in which everyday decisions are made.

When we turn to the specific question of the explanation of suboptimality, Hutchins' process conception implies many of the same claims about the importance of external factors as is implied by D'Andrade's content account. But he adds one significant addition, especially for questions of suboptimality and relative efficiency involving the second type of comparison: differences in the organization of cognitive tasks across societies. Hutchins emphasizes the importance of these differences: "if groups can have cognitive properties that are significantly different from those of the individuals in them, then differences in the cognitive accomplishments of any two groups might depend entirely on differences in the social organization of distributional cognition and not at all on differences in the cognitive properties of individuals in the two groups" (1995, 177-178).

The Cognitive Effects of Social Institutions

What do these three conceptions of the relationship between cognition and institutions imply for explanations of suboptimality in political and economic performance? On the question of the relationship between cognition and context, the different conceptions of this relationship imply substantially different agendas for research into the role of social institutions in human cognition. The first two approaches, the individualistic and the content conceptions, sustain a continued focus on cognition and rationality as processes removed from the influences of social context. To the extent, however, that we accept the arguments that cognitive activity is dependent in a fundamental way on the cultural and institutional context, research on cognition must move beyond the walls of experimentation and pay greater attention to the mechanisms of everyday cognition in social life. Here the issue is not merely the role of institutions in providing the content of our beliefs. Hutchins' emphasis on the reciprocal effect of cognition and culture insists that cognitive processes themselves are shaped by interaction with the external world. The basic implication here is the following: if external factors have priority for rationality and cognition, then the analysis of the role of institutions in affecting cognition is central to more than our understanding of economic performance and suboptimality. It becomes central to the understanding of cognition and rationality per se.

On the specific question of the role of the cognition/institutions relationship for explanations of suboptimal social outcomes, my analysis of the three conceptions leads to the following conclusion: explanations that understand the suboptimality of social outcomes as a function of social context should be given priority over explanations that seek to explain it in terms of failures of individual cognition and rationality. The important point to note here is that this should be the priority even in those cases in which the beliefs of the actors (and thus issues of cognition) are a central feature of the explanation. And I think that the point can be sustained regardless of which of the three conceptions we choose to endorse.

I justify this conclusion by reference to the logic of comparison that underlies explanations of suboptimality. Only those factors that vary across the patterns of behavior to be compared will serve as a basis for our explanations. For the reasons that I offered in the discussion of the individualistic conception, individual cognitive differences are unlikely to provide the necessary basis for explaining differences in group performance. For such an explanation to be persuasive, there must be evidence of variation in the basic cognitive capacities shared by the members of the different groups. Even if we set aside the question of how we can acquire this evidence without inferring from the very behavior that we seek to explain, we are still left with the question of how we might explain variance in cognitive capacities without referring to properties of social context, given the fact that the members of the different societies are all subject to the same basic conditions of evolutionary development.

This leaves external factors as the primary source of variation for our explanations. To the extent that we base our explanations on variation in the properties of the social context, we should focus on those factors that are shared within the membership of the different communities. This returns the analysis to the effects of social context (culture, social institutions, etc.) on the beliefs of social actors. Both of the last two conceptions endorse the basic idea that social context has an important role to play in belief formation. On both of these accounts, central to the analysis of variation in beliefs is an analysis of why different societies have different sets of beliefs.

This highlights the continued importance of understanding the genesis of social institutions and culture. It is important not only for understanding incentive structures, but also, as we can see from this analysis, for understanding processes of cognition and rationality. The problem with much of the existing literature is that it relies on a functionalism that fails to explain adequately the variation in the nature of culture and social institutions that exist in different societies. We can see this by returning briefly to the accounts of cognition offered by D'Andrade and Hutchins.

On both accounts the reciprocal effects between cognition and cultural context are primarily explained with a functionalist logic. For D'Andrade, culture is explained by its problem-solving effects. However, having adopted a particulate conception of culture and, in doing so, rejected more holistic conceptions, D'Andrade must explain the functional prerequisites of the diversity of cultural models:

> "Each cultural model is a "thing-like," but all the models together do not form any kind of thing. ... There are theories of culture that make sense out of this situation. If culture is seen as socially inherited solutions to life's problems ... then the forces that make for system or structure are the constraints and interdependencies found within these problem-domains. The cultural solutions to life's problems do form systems of various sorts; systems of social relationships, systems of economic exchange, systems of government, etc., but these systems (each made up of a complex of cultural models, roles, activities, etc.) are as various as the problems are. There is no one problem of human life to which culture is a solution" (1995, 249-250).

This leads to the following research agenda for cultural analysis: " ... one can study in a scientific way the elements of culture, but to find out why cultural elements exist and how they fit together one has to step outside the concept of culture and look for whatever it is that creates and organizes these elements, such as the problem of biological reproduction, or the problem of getting food out of the environment, or human cognitive limitations, or personality needs, or whatever."

Similarly, in Hutchins' account, we see the characterization of culture in the service of human problem-solving: "Culture is an adaptive process that accumulates partial solutions to frequently encountered problems" (1995, 354). Expressed in terms of his analysis of the cognitive tasks found in ocean navigation, Hutchins concludes that: "[t]he setting of navigation work evolves over time as partial solutions to frequently encountered problems [that] are saved in the material and conceptual tools of the trade and in the social organization of the work. The development of the practice takes place over centuries. The very same processes that constitute the conduct of the activity and that produce changes in the individual practitioners of navigation also produce changes in the social, material, and conceptual aspects of the setting ... the microgenesis of the cultural elements that make up the navigation setting is visible in the details of the ongoing practice" (1995, 374).

This reliance on functionalism to explain the content of culture raises questions about the ability of these accounts to adequately shed light on suboptimality. To see this, consider a question of the relative efficiency of two different societies, an instance of the second type of comparison. How will D'Andrade's functionalism account for the necessary variation in the content of the institutional rules across these societies? Or Hutchins' for the differences in the nature of cognitive organization in the two societies? They might account for it in terms of differences in the prior functional requirements of the two societies. But to attempt such an argument requires evidence of societal diversity that is usually lacking in such functional accounts. Instead, they might offer an explanation similar to the one that D'Andrade offers to explain intra-society diversity in cultural knowledge: "The difficulties in cultural transmission and formation of various kinds of subgroups also create variation within a culture. ... The result is that the cultural heritage tends to divide into two parts - one part a high consensus code which everyone is expected to share; the other a proliferating number of distributed knowledge systems. The issue is not 'how shared is culture', but rather how to understand both distributed and high consensus aspects of cultural knowledge" (1995, 216). Differences in the mechanisms of cultural transmission is a plausible source of variation, but transmission alone may not be enough to explain the variation in the organizational structure or content of social institutions.

But the basic point here is that one can be committed to these conceptions of the content and organizational roles of institutions in the cognitive process without being committed to their functionalist account of institutional genesis. If we can provide a plausible explanation of why there is variation in either the substantive content or the organizational structure of the relevant social institutions, then we have a promising source of explanation for differences in the relative efficiency of societal performances. Given the appropriate set of social conditions, there are a number of mechanisms that might produce these institutions (Knight 1995).

In Knight (1992) I developed a theory of institutional emergence and change that emphasized one such mechanism: bargaining over the distributional effects of social institutions. On this bargaining account, social institutions are a by-product of strategic conflict over substantive social outcomes. By this I mean that social actors produce social institutions in the process of seeking distributional advantage in the conflict over substantive benefits. In some cases they will create institutional rules consciously; in other cases the rules will emerge as unintended consequences of the pursuit of strategic advantage. In each case the main focus is on the substantive outcome; the development of institutional rules is merely a means to that substantive end.

On this account, institutional development is a contest among actors to establish rules which structure outcomes to those equilibria most favorable for them. As in any bargaining situation, there are a number of factors that distinguish the actors and thus influence the bargaining outcome in favor of one of the parties. One of the primary factors that can resolve bargaining over social institutions is the asymmetry of resource ownership in a society. The main thrust of the argument is that asymmetries in resource ownership affect the willingness of rational self-interested actors to accept the bargaining demands of other actors. Here the asymmetries of resource ownership serve as an ex ante measure of the bargaining power of the actors in a social interaction. In explaining the establishment of particular social institutions, bargaining demands become claims about commitments to particular rules of behavior. The relevant question becomes: what will cause a social actor to accept the commitment of another actor to a particular course of action and thus a particular social outcome?

Through its emphasis on asymmetries in resource ownership, the approach grounds its mechanism of rule selection in an important feature of many social interactions: social actors suffer significant costs for the failure to coordinate on equilibrium outcomes, yet those costs need not be suffered uniformly. When social actors are aware of these differentials, this awareness can influence the credibility of certain strategies. Those who have either fewer alternatives or less beneficial ones will be more inclined to respect the commitments of those who have them. In this way, the existence of resource asymmetries in a society can significantly influence the choice of rules of behavior.

If successful commitments are achievable by strategic actors, then they face the second half of the task of institutionalization: the generalization of these constraints as rules governing the community as a whole. If institutions are going to arise out of bargaining interactions, then we would anticipate the following emergence process. Individual bargaining will be resolved by the commitments of those who enjoy a relative advantage in substantive resources. Through a series of interactions with various members of the group, actors with similar resources will establish a pattern of successful action in a particular type of interaction. As others recognize that they are interacting with one of the actors who possesses these resources, they will adjust their strategies to achieve their best outcome given the anticipated commitments of others. Over time rational actors will continue to adjust their strategies until an equilibrium is reached. As this becomes recognized as the socially-expected combination of equilibrium strategies, a self-enforcing social institution will be established.

This bargaining mechanism provides a basis for explaining the institutional variation necessary to undertake the comparisons implied by questions of suboptimality. Consider the two types of comparisons in turn. As for the first type (comparisons between actual behavior and theoretical constructs), a bargaining approach can explain why the existing institutions in a particular society are suboptimal or inefficient. On this account both the content and organizational structure of social institutions will reflect the interests of those actors who have the bargaining power to establish their preferred outcomes. To the extent that the institutional interests of these dominant actors diverge from the optimal or efficient institutions, there are opportunities for the establishment of suboptimal and inefficient institutions. As for the second type of comparison (between two or more patterns of actual behavior), the bargaining approach offers a framework for explaining the variation in the substantive content and organizational structure of institutions across societies. Possible sources of such explanation can be the variation in the interests of dominant actors and variation in the distribution of bargaining power among institutional interests.

I offer this concluding discussion of the bargaining mechanism merely as an illustration of how existing theories of institutional genesis can complement the emerging work on the cognition-institutions relationship.[5] One can accept a conception of this relationship that integrates cognition into social context without adopting a functionalist approach to institutional and cultural evolution. The bargaining approach demonstrates how existing theories of institutional emergence can assist in the explanation of the variation in beliefs that is at the heart of the relationship between cognition and institutions. Cognition is an important feature

---

[5] See Ensminger and Knight (1997) and Allio, Dobek, Mikhailov and Weimer (1997) for recent attempts to assess the relative explanatory power of the different existing theories.

of intentional explanations of economic and political performance. But one of the primary lessons of the renewed attention to cognition is the fundamental importance of the social context in which rational decisions are made.

References

Allio, Lorene, Mariusz Mark Dobek, Nikolai Mikhailov and David L. Weimer (1997): Post-communist Privatization as a Test of Theories of Institutional Change; in: David L. Weimer (ed.), *The Political Economy of Property Rights, Cambridge*: Cambridge University Press, 182-204.

D'Andrade, Roy (1995): *The Development of Cognitive Anthropology, Cambridge*: Cambridge University Press.

Denzau, Arthur and Douglass North (1994): Shared Mental Models: Ideologies and Institutions; in: *Kyklos* 47, 3-31.

Eggertsson, Thrainn (1990): *Economic Institutions and Behavior*, Cambridge: Cambridge University Press.

Ensminger, Jean and Jack Knight (1997): Changing Social Norms - Common Property, Bridewealth, and Clan Exogamy; *Current Anthropology*, 38, 1-24.

Hardin, Russell (1993): Efficiency; in: Robert Gooding and Philip Petit (eds.), *A Companion to Contemporary Political Philosophy*, Oxford: Blackwell.

Hutchins, Edwin (1995): *Cognition in the Wild*, Cambridge, MA: The MIT Press.

Johnson, James (1991): Symbol and Strategy; Ph.D. Dissertation, University of Chicago.

Kahneman, Daniel, Paul Slovic and Amos Tversky (eds.) (1982): *Judgment Under Uncertainty: Heuristics and Biases*, Cambridge: Cambridge University Press.

Knight, Jack. (1992): *Institutions and Social Conflict*; Cambridge: Cambridge University Press.

Knight, Jack and Itai Sened (1995): *Explaining Social Institutions*; Ann Arbor, MI: The University of Michigan Press.

Knight, Jack and Douglass C. North: Explaining Economic Change: The Interplay Between Cognition and Institutions; *Legal Theory*, forthcoming.

North, Douglass C. (1990): *Institutions, Institutional Change and Economic Performance*; Cambridge: Cambridge University Press.

North, Douglass C. (1995): Five Propositions about Institutional Change; in: Jack Knight and Itai Sened (eds.), *Explaining Social Institutions*, Ann Arbor, MI: The University of Michigan Press.

Comment on Jack Knight

Piet de Vries

Jack Knight's paper delivers a broad perspective on the research agenda of social sciences. Knight shows that the interpretation of a handful of concepts, such as cognition, rationality and social context, has profound consequences for the research on the causes of suboptimal social outcomes of political and economic processes. It is the substance of social outcomes and the processes of cognition, rationality and context which are brought together in Knight's paper. He elaborates the claim that the explanation of the (suboptimal) product of social interaction is determined by the conceptual position taken in the theme of cognition, rationality and social context. This claim is not new, indeed, as Knight acknowledges. It underlies the work of North, and North and Thomas (North 1990; North & Thomas 1973). However, it is the virtue of Knight's paper to confront different positions of social outcomes with different conceptualizations of the relationship among cognition, rationality and social context/institutions. It concerns three suboptimal social outcome comparisons which might be faced with four kinds of conceptualization.

On the one hand, three suboptimalities are identified by a comparison of a theoretical standard with an actual outcome, a comparison of the present and past performances by the same actors, and finally a comparison of actual outcomes of different groups. Knight focuses on the comparison of theoretical-actual outcomes, and of actual outcomes of different groups. On the other, 'three basic conceptions ... can be aligned on an internal/external dimension insofar as they treat the role of social context in the cognitive process' (16). The internal dimension refers to cognition and rationality as situated in the head of the individual actor, whereas the two external dimension leaves little, if any, role for the individual and identifies cognition and rationality as determined by the social context. The two latter approaches represent compromises in the individual-social context dilemma. The 'content' approach perceives the 'elements of culture' as content and building blocks for the rationality and cognitive processes of individuals. '[T]he content of the rules determine the incentives facing rational actors' (19). The 'process' approach stresses the interaction between and the interwovenness of human mind and social context. It is important to notice that in two of these conceptualizations more or less significance is given to factors external to the individual. The confrontation of these distinctions can be depicted in the following matrix.

	Conceptualizations		
Suboptimality	individualistic	content	Process
theoretical-actual	individual	context	Context
present-past	x	x	x
group$_i$-group$_j$	individual	context	Context

A major issue in Knight's paper is that the explanations of suboptimality may differ fundamentally. It is the erroneous behavior of the individual actor which, left of the thick line in the matrix, explains the suboptimality, or differences in suboptimality. Right of this thick, dividing line there is an extending, explaining role 'of the social context in which rational decisions are made' (26).

Towards the individualistic explanation of suboptimalities (first column) Knight raises a fundamental problem. If we assume no variation in human capacities, computational abilities and individual rationality between different groups or between groups in different time periods, it is basically impossible to find an individualistic explanation for suboptimality differences. Knight stresses that the evidence of variation in human capacities will not be found in a cross-section comparison. Therefore, '[I]n order to better investigate the reciprocal relationship among cognition, rationality and institutions, we need both a conception and research program that explicitly accounts for institutional context' (17). As a consequence, revealing the processes of the genesis of institutions is the main task of social sciences which aim to explain suboptimal social products. These constitute the central conclusions of Knight's paper, which are in line with North's analyses.

These conclusions and the analysis described raise some, more or less interrelated questions. A major theoretical problem is caused by the concept(s) of suboptimality as the main explanandum in social sciences, and by the central position of this explanandum in Knight's analysis. If it is the main task of social sciences to bare the genesis of social institutions and social culture there is no a priori necessity to be occupied with suboptimality. For example, this is a fortiori valid in the evolutionary approach of this genesis problem. However, if suboptimality is at issue, there must first be a clear definition of optimality. It is hard to see the possibility of a time-series comparison of suboptimalities or a cross-section comparison (third row) if the optimality definition, as a point of reference, lacks.[6] This benchmark is evidently present in the first suboptimality comparison (first row).

---

[6] Optimality and efficiency are highly contested concepts', Knight admits. Nevertheless, 'social actors act as if efficiency and optimality are meaningful concepts' (footnote 3). As a consequence, Knight might claim that it is inappropriate to stress to importance of an optimality definition, as a point of reference. It might be argued that in reality social actors make social-outcome comparisons. However, Knight addresses

The optimality benchmark in the first row of the matrix adds another theoretical problem to Knight's analysis. This is caused by the assumed existence of a defined optimum. Such a definition is theoretical by nature. In economic theory, which is highly involved in social outcomes, welfare economics distinguishes two optimum options. On the one hand, there is the Bergsonian, ethical approach of the optimum definition. On the other, there is the Paretian. The Bergsonian option is less relevant in this respect as this optimum is not directly related to the problems of suboptimality, individual behavior and social context. The Bergsonian welfare function which describes the welfare variables in a normative way is empirically empty, and has no relation to the mundane problem of suboptimal social outcomes. Contrariwise, it is the Paretian optimum which produces (non-normative) criteria to detect suboptimalities. Therefore, this definition is the appropriate point of reference in the analysis at hand. Moreover, this optimum fits in with Knight's analysis due to its methodological individualistic base. It is this individualistic foundation of social sciences in general, and of economic theory in particular which is the source of the individual-social context issue. This necessity of the Pareto optimum is in contrast with Knight's dismissal of the individual as an explaining variable in the analysis of suboptimality. As a consequence, Knight has to formulate a non-individual-based social optimum definition. However, it must be stressed that the problem at hand demands that this social-context-based optimum is positive and empirically meaningful. It is meaningless to analyze suboptimalities if the optimum defined omits empirical content. The empirical content is produced by the conditions of the optimum. The formulation of these conditions is the challenge of Knight's social- context explanation. This will be a tour de force as society, to which the optimum refers, consists of individuals with preferences. It is illusive, as Arrow has demonstrated, to expect a consistently formulated social-outcome definition to succeed if it is not aimed at denying individual preferences. Individuals return in the analysis of social outcomes by means of their preferences. If it is valid to honor individual preferences, other individual differences should also be taken into account. Therefore, it turns out to be invalid to exclude differences in abilities relevant for social outcomes. At the same time, Knight seems to be occupied with the individual-social-context issue throughout his paper, as it deals with the effect of social context on the individual-oriented concepts of cognition and rationality.

It is not quite clear why Knight pays attention to the effect of social context ('culture, social institutions, etc.') on rationality, cognition and the beliefs of social actors. In Knight's perspective social contexts will certainly differ. Consequently, it is not interesting to know what the social context impact on the individual abilities of rationality and cognition is when it is claimed a priori that these abilities do not differ in different societies.

---

the theoretical issue of considering different approaches to social outcomes. In this theoretical setting it is indispensable to apply well-defined (optimality) concepts.

The individual-social context issue is also a central theme in modern economic theory. This may be shown by the post-War development of neo-institutionalism. For that matter, Knight refers to North, who is a representative of neo-institutional economics. North presents a transaction cost explanation of the history of institutions. Such an explanation deals with the individual-social context theme, but it is straightforwardly individual-based. Property rights and transaction cost theory explain the function of (social) institutions for individual actors who face their bounded rationality and informational problems. These individual actors recognize their limited abilities and informational problem as a consequence of the optimum definition. Moreover, without purpose, such as an optimum, there is no meaning in the behavior. There must be criteria for behavioral choices. Therefore, the Pareto optimum is a starting point in the analysis at hand. It delivers the criteria for the empirical evidence of the substantial problem of suboptimality, and it is the stepping stone for the theme of individual-versus-context processes, analyzed in neo-institutional economics. The dismissal of the individual basically excludes any intended rational involvement of individual actors in the creation of institutions. This position implies the dismissal of individual responsibility for individual as well as group suboptimality. Moreover, it may be inferred that microeconomic analysis is in vain and fruitless. At the same time, Knight points out that the analysis of the genesis of institutions and culture is important 'for understanding incentive structures'. However, if the individual does not play a role in the explanans of suboptimality the incentive structures do not have any significance.

In the 'bargaining account' the contrast between Knight's context position and the individual-based explanation of institutions recurs. On the one hand, Knight stresses the appropriateness of social-context explanations. On the other, he seems to embrace the 'bargaining account of institutions', in which rational self-interested actors 'will continue to adjust their strategies until an equilibrium is reached' (25).

Knight's context-based analysis reflects the problem of embeddedness. His emphasis on institutions, culture and belief formation may result in an 'oversocialized conception' by which social sciences 'is all about how people don't have any choices to make' (Granovetter 1992, 56). This embeddedness increases going from the content position towards social practices as explanation. Apart from the unanswered question which context position is preferable, it may be inferred that the extreme external position of social practices certainly results in the Panglossian problem. This implies that the context position cannot explain suboptimalities at all. Habits, rules and institutions evolve as social practices, and given these practices, the social outcome is determined. Consequently, variation in social context does not deliver the explanation of suboptimality differences, but forms a description of what happened. Suboptimalities do not exist. This inference may be illustrated by a short excursion to cultural theory, which also represents the extreme social-context position. Cultural theory claims to offer an explanation for human behavior concerning 'making ends meet' -this will entail a social outcome- which is alternative to the traditional scarcity approach of economic theory

(Thompson et al. 1990, Ch. 2). Cultural theory distinguishes different ways of life, such as individualistic, hierarchical and egalitarian, which systematically determine individual behavior. Everyone is happy with his way of life and its corresponding social outcome. We live in the best possible, Panglossian world.

In his Institutions and Credible Commitment North tells a short 'institutional/cognitive story of long run economic change'. Different physical environments entail 'different languages and, with different experiences, different mental models' will be developed to explain the world (North 1993, 16). This is a story of the genesis of institutions. As shown, the analysis of this genesis is claimed to be highly relevant. However, North's story brings about a final point. According to North, institutional variation and differences in mental models trace back to differences in physical environment. In respect of an explanation of suboptimalities these physical differences will be very important, indeed. These differences may directly explain the social outcome differences. At the same time, it is difficult to understand how to deal with these physical differences in a (cross section) suboptimality comparison. The physical environment differences result in relative optima. As a consequence, the suboptimality comparison needs a value judgment. North's genesis story is even more troublesome to the time series (2nd row) comparison. It will take an unimaginably long time to ascribe institutional differences to variation in physical environment. Or, a new genesis story might be applicable. Finally, it is impossible by definition to apply any genesis story to the theoretical-actual comparison (1st row). It is a fallacy to pose that 'in the world of instrumental rationality' -in this world a (Pareto) optimum is perceivable- 'institutions are unnecessary' (North 1993, 16). The definition of an optimum certainly presumes a strictly defined institutional setting, as can readily be seen in the strictly held private property rights and in an institution such as the Walrasian auctioneer.

Knight's paper offers a broad perspective on modern developments in social sciences, such as institutional theories, cultural theory and evolutionary approaches. However, it raises some questions from an economic point of view. Predominantly, these questions come down to the lack of the optimum definition. At the same time, it is shown that the existence of an optimum is incompatible with the explanation preferred, which is based on variation in social contexts.

References

Granovetter, Mark (1992): Economic Action and Social Structure: The Problem of Embeddedness; in: Mark Granovetter, Richard Swedburg, *The Sociology of Economic Life*, Boulder: Westview Press, 53-81.

North, Douglas C. (1990*): Institutions, Institutional Change, and Economic Performance*; Cambridge: Cambridge University Press.

North, Douglas C. (1993): Institutions and Credible Commitment; *Journal of Institutional and Theoretical Economics*, 149, 11-23.

North, Douglas C. and Thomas Robert P. (1973): *The Rise of the Western World: A New Economic History*; Cambridge: Cambridge University Press.

Thompson, Michael, Richard Ellis, Aaron Wildavsky, (1990): *Cultural Theory*; Boulder: Westview Press.

Comment on Jack Knight

Daniel Kiwit

In economics the term institutions is used to denote rules which are supported by an enforcement mechanism. Institutions affect economic processes in several ways: Firstly, they cognitively relieve the individual actor. This is the information function of institutions. Secondly, they set incentives to take or avoid certain actions or a range of actions. This is the incentive function of institutions. The definition just given shows that the concept of institutions is much more restricted than that of culture which often comprises elements like of language, ideas, beliefs, customs, codes, tools, techniques, works of art, rituals, ceremonies, and so on. My reason for stressing the difference between both concepts is that Jack Knight for large parts of his paper is not so much concerned with the interplay between cognition and institutions as with that between cognition and culture or cognition and context. This broader perspective promises both advantages and disadvantages. The main advantage lies in facilitating an interdisciplinary exchange of ideas with those disciplines whose principal focus of research is culture not only in its institutional but in all aspects. Specifically the author seems to pin his hopes on cognitive anthropology as he spends much time discussing the ideas of Roy D'Andrade (1995) and Edwin Hutchins (1995), both anthropologists with a special interest in the linkages between cognition and culture. The possible disadvantage, on the other hand, can be seen in the danger that the findings are not or at least not directly applicable to institutional questions.

It is Jack Knight declared interest to inquire into the question of „how [...] we explain suboptimality in political and economic performance in a society". The author introduces a distinction between different understandings of suboptimality, of which only one serves him constantly throughout the whole paper. This definition rests on an empirical comparison between the performance of different groups. A group performs suboptimal if there is another group that does better „on various measures of performance" (13). But how are we to interpret the reference to various measures of performance? Are these measures exclusively economic in nature or do they include some non-economic standards as well. Notwithstanding which standards are used Knight concentrates on the concept of relative efficiency within the bounds of a comparative institutional or cultural analysis. His impression is that much of the answer to why some groups outperform others lies in the relationship between cognition and culture or more specifically between cognition and institutions. And he finds a basis for that supposition in the work of Douglass

North (i.e. 1990) who found several reasons for possible inefficiencies in institutional change[7], namely transaction costs of economic and political markets and the subjective mental models of the individuals. Knight concentrates on the last reason „because it attributes inefficiency in performance to issues of cognition and rationality„.

Because it is the introductory paper of our conference it seems especially important to make concepts clear. Even at the risk of repeating many of the things Jack Knight tells us in his paper I will therefore take the liberty to present the idea of mental models in my own words again. In cognitive psychology this concept is discussed under the term of representations. The basic train of thought is as follows: Individuals build up a hierarchical classification system with which they interpret their environment. The internal representations of the environment can be differentiated according to their level of abstraction. Scripts are representations with a comparatively low level of abstraction because they tell the individual how to behave in specific recurring situations. An example is the script that tells us how to behave as a participant of a scientific conference. More abstract in the sense of not being oriented towards specific situations are schemata. These are cognitive structures which represent the internal model of the environment an individual holds in form of beliefs, opinions, and practical or theoretical knowledge. These cognitions are not separately stored but become tied by associations in semantic networks (see Rumelhart and Norman 1981). How these schemata interact with the environment is shown in the following chart (see Neisser 1976).

The emergence of internal cognitive representations (schemata) in the interaction with the environment

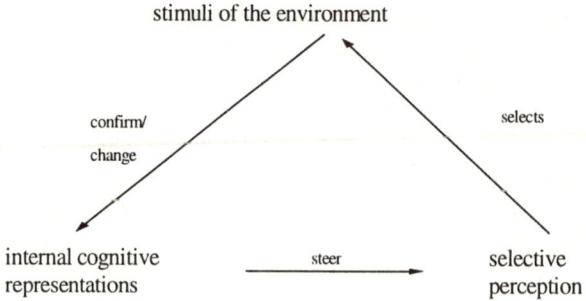

---

[7] It remains somewhat vague whether North's understanding of inefficiency as adaptive inefficiency (see North 1990, p. 80 ff.) can be related to Knight's distinction between three types of suboptimality.

The aforementioned parallels the nature of sensory perception as analyzed by Friedrich August von Hayek in his early work "The Sensory Order" (1952) long before institutions or even cognition became fashionable in the economic discipline. Hayek came to the conclusion that sensory perception represents an interpretative act on part of the individual (Hayek 1952, p. 142). Groups of stimuli establish linkages between neurons and constitute a "semi-permanent structure provid[ing] the framework within which [...] the impulses proceeding at any time are evaluated" (Hayek 1952, p. p. 115). Each act of perception is the creation of theories about the environment based on experiences made in the past.

These findings can be translated into a concept which Jack Knight also mentions but probably has not the time and place to delve into more deeply, namely path-dependence. Path-dependence in the emergence of schemata requires that we can make out self-reinforcing elements of the mental process. And that is clearly the case: Experimental learning, cultural transmission of social norms and further stimuli give rise to mental representations which in turn act as preselectors in subsequent decision processes. In this way early mental models shape the path for later perception. The decisive question is then, how difficult it is to leave the path. I will pick up that topic later.

Let me return to the paper and the question how internal representations or individual cognition and institutions or more generally culture interact. The author in trying to answer this question divides his paper into four sections each one devoted to a special kind of approach. The organizing principle of this division is how the approaches differ in treating "the role of social context in the cognitive process" (16). The author finds two extremes and two approaches that he classifies as in between.

One extreme approach is grounded on psychological research in the laboratory. Knight considers it as extreme insofar as individual cognition is isolated to a very high degree from social context. He mentions the research of Kahneman, Slovic and Tversky (1982) as an example. As a more convincing example Jack Knight could have mentioned the psychological research of Kohlberg on the development of moral judgement that has been rightly criticized for capturing "nothing more than what is commonly called the 'idealism of youth'" (Scott 1971, p. 161) because it does not take account of social factors. Other examples include opinion polls in which people are asked for instance, whether they support wage cuts or not. Typically, social consequences of either choice are not mentioned in such cases so that it is not surprising at all that almost everyone rejects cuts. What are the consequences of such an approach concentrating exclusively on individual cognition isolated from social context? Knights general conclusion is that such an approach „can tell us [little] about the specific role of social institutions in the cognitive process„ (17). And concerning the specific question of relative economic efficiency he rightly emphasizes that an approach concentrating on individual cognition can explain differential economic success of groups only "if there is variation in the basic cognitive capacities of the different groups" (17).

At the other extreme we find an approach that stresses only social context and sees individual cognition completely determined by social practice[8]. Because I conjecture that the participants of this conference share a similar view with regard to the conception of "Homo sociologicus" I simply jump to the more promising approaches being located in between the two extremes.

One approach is that of Roy D'Andrade. For him culture as well as cognition consist of pieces that work together in solving problems. Culture interacts with individual cognition in a reciprocal way. The cognition of the individuals is influenced by culture insofar as culture gives content to the representations individuals develop internally without, however, changing cognitive capacity as such.. And culture is influenced by cognition because only individual cognition can give culture a meaning. In trying to relate the hypotheses of D'Andrade to institutional matters Jack Knight argues that social institutions give content to the rules that affect rational decisionmaking. Let us take a typical institution to see whether the idea of D'Andrade helps us in understanding anything about the emergence, the function or the change of institutions. A typical institution is the rule that you shall not steal which is normally not only backed by legal sanctions but also by religious and social forces. With D'Andrade we would conjecture that the rule that you shall not steal gives "content to the rules that affect rational decisionmaking". I have the impression that this raises more questions than insights. How is rational decisionmaking defined? How is it affected by the rule not to steal? How does the rule come into existence at the first place? Is it rational to obey the rule or not? What if a critical mass of individuals does not obey the rule? Does the rule need enforcement by the state or is it sufficient to have private enforcement mechanisms? The passages which Knight quotes from D'Andrade do not provide an answer to any of these questions. What is left then is the general idea that institutions influence cognition somehow. That is not much to build upon and certainly less than the institutional theory of Douglass North has to offer. The implication Knight draws from D'Andrades approach seems to confirm this judgement. The implication of D'Andrades work for the specific question of suboptimality is that the group that performs suboptimal did not have the right institutions. I do not want to discuss the difficulties here which Jack Knight himself sees in such an explanation of suboptimality because the concept does not tell us much about institutions even if these difficulties did not exist.

References

D'Andrade, Roy (1995): *The Development of Cognitive Anthropology*, Cambridge: Cambridge University Press.

---

[8] This used to be the typical anthropological position which attributed every aspect of human behavior to culture. For a detailed critique see Shore (1996).

Hayek, Friedrich August (1952): *The Sensory Order: An Inquiry into the Foundations of Theoretical Psychology*, London: Routledge.

Hutchins, Edwin (1995): *Cognition in the Wild*, Cambridge: Cambridge University Press.

Kahneman, Daniel, Paul Slovic and Amos Tversky (eds.) (1982*): Judgment Under Uncertainty: Heuristics and Biases*, Cambridge: Cambridge University Press.

Neisser, Ulric (1976): *Cognition and Reality*, San Francisco: Freeman.

North, Douglass C. (1990): *Institutions, Institutional Change and Economic Performance*, Cambridge: Cambridge University Press.

Rumelhart, David E. and D. Norman (1981): Analogical processes in learning, in: J.R. Anderson (ed.), *Cognitive Skills and their Acquisition*, Hillsdale, NJ: Erlbaum.

Scott, John Finley (1971): *Internalization of Norms: A Sociological Theory of Moral Commitment*, Engelwood Cliffs: Prentice-Hall.

Shore, Bradd (1996): *Culture in Mind: Cognition, Culture, and the Problem of Meaning*, Oxford: Oxford University Press.

Patterned Variation. The Role of Psychological Dispositions in Social and Institutional Evolution

Ekkehart Schlicht[1]

Introduction

The new institutional economics has one of its roots in evolutionary thinking.[2] The idea is that there is competition between organizational forms. Some organizational forms spread faster than others and thereby displace and eventually destroy the less well adapted forms. In the end, the most "efficient" organizational formation will survive, where "efficiency" is a social analogue for biological fitness. The process is predominately envisaged as a process of what I am going to term "blind evolution": A combination of random variation and selection.[3]

One task of this essay is to put into question the idea that is indeed *random* variation which drives evolutionary processes. It will be argued that this idea of random variation is of rather limited value for purposes of social analysis. In order that evolution can work successfully on complex organism or organisations it is necessary that variation occurs in a patterned fashion with systematically correlated changes[4].

Once the importance of patterned variation is established, it must be asked where the patterns come from. It will be argued that, for the purpose of social sciences, these patterns are generated by psychological regularities, both cognitive and emotional.[5]

---

[1] I thank Ariane Breitfelder, Andreas Gösele, Dieter Grimm, Gisela Kubon-Gilke, Brian Loasby, Florian Mayer-Haßelwander, Peter Mücke, Uwe Mummert, Andreas Nicolin and Eric Leyers, for helpful comments on an earlier draft.
[2] Alchian (1950, 211-221).
[3] I use the term "blind evolution" in analogy to Campell's (1974, 421) "blind variation and selective retention".
[4] Related views, as pertaining to the social sciences, may be found in Hallpike (1986, 81-145) and Kubon-Gilke (1997, 470-478).
[5] I interpret, thus, the term "cognition" in the theme of this conference as referring in a psychological, rather than in a logical or rationality sense-whatever the latter two meanings way involve.

The argument about patterned variation will be presented in the first three sections. Sections four to six illustrate patterning processes in biological evolution, social evolution, and learning. These processes exhibit surprising parallels. The subsequent sections elaborate on the nature of social and institutional evolution, as conceived from the psychological perspective outlined in the paper.

1 Two Types of Evolution

In order to set the stage for the argument, two types of change may be contrasted. They will be termed "blind evolution" and "organic evolution", respectively.

Blind evolution. A predominant view of evolution, frequently invoked in institutional economics, is as follows. Evolution occurs by the joint action of random variation and survival of the fittest. This idea is applied to explaining not only the evolution of biological species, but also the evolution of human societies. It has even been applied to psychology, where behaviourists have depicted individuals as emitting random behaviours that are than selected by the environment.

In institutional economics, institutions are explained by random variation and competitive selection. There is institutional variation, which may come about for sundry reasons. Personal preferences, coincidences, idiosyncratic convictions of some individuals, or even superstitious beliefs may entail such institutional variation. Many variations will fail and disappear, but occasionally a variant may be generated that is able to survive and spread by outcompeting other institutional solutions. In this way, new institutions may come into being.

Organic evolution. Another vision of the evolutionary process emphasises the internal tendencies, regularities, and constraints which govern the grow of an organism or institution, or the way it responds to new exigencies. The most prominent example for this organic evolution (as it may be termed) is the development of the system of law.

In law, new cases are treated in analogy to old cases, and inconsistencies in the body of the law are removed by refining definitions, classifications, and delineations. If changing circumstances require changes in the law, these changes are introduced such as to conform with the principles underlying the body of the law as a whole, which constraints possible changes. Ideally, such processes are driven by legal reasoning alone. The actual process of evolution of law is, however, not exclusively propelled by pure reason, but is subject to quite mundane and often quite distortive interests of interfering parties.

Other cases of organic evolution are even more extreme in their reliance on organic rule-guided growth. Some branches in pure mathematics seem to evolve entirely on their own, driven by their internal logic. This is not to say that selection processes do not play any role; rather the selection processes themselves reflect both the internal logic of mathematics and the social pressure prevailing within the mathematical community. The referees of mathematical journals decide about publication by following this logic, and the appointments to professorships are influenced by similar evaluations. It seems, however, entirely misleading to describe the growth of mathematics as governed by the two unrelated elements of random variation and competitive selection. Rather, the logic of mathematics guides the generation, the evaluation, and the selection of new results.

In drawing a distinction between blind and organic evolution, I do not want to suggest that the received arguments in institutional and evolutionary economics fit nicely into the one or the other category. My purpose is rather to draw attention to an important distinction and to some arguments surrounding this distinction which may help to sharpen our ideas about social and institutional evolution. These issues are typically left unmentioned. Hayek (1945, 528) simply says, for instance, that man had "stumbled" upon the price system without understanding it. Other writers, like Alchian (1950) with his "chance" model, stress the blind elements in evolution quite explicitly. Still others, like List (1837) and Marshall (1920) allude more to organic patterns, but these arguments are presented in an *ad-hoc* fashion in the context of discussing specific problems.[6] My purpose is to face the general issue head on.

2 Fitness Landscapes

It will be argued in the following that blind evolution is not a useful mechanism for generating change of complex organisms or institutions, and that variation must be organic (in the sense outlined above) in order to produce change in any relevant sense. Blind evolution can only serve to locally adapt in a small way.

The major obstacle posted to blind evolution is well illustrated by the following example from engineering. With the advent of the computer arose the possibility for using the mechanism of random variation and selection for optimising computer programs. The attempt was made. Certain computer programs - simple programs by current standards - were subjected to random disturbances in their code. It was hoped that among the many failures and crashes to be expected, some variants with improved performance would emerge. This was, however, not the case. There was no way to improve a computer program in this manner. The attempt was a complete failure.[7]

The reason for this failure is straightforward. A computer program may be described as a sequence of digits of a certain length. Consider all conceivable sequences of digits of equal length. This set describes all possible computer programs of given lengths. The "fitness" of one particular program may be measured by the speed it needs for performing the required operation. Each member of the set of programs may thus be characterised by a certain fitness. In the case of com-

---

[6] For a variety of usages of "evolutionary economics", see Hodgson (1996).

[7] Eden (1967, 11). The argument carries over to biological organisms where - even for the genom of a simple bacterium - the age of the world would not have been sufficient to generate the appropriate gene frequencies randomly (Küppers 1983).

puter programs, the 'fitness landscape' covering the plane of possible programs has a very jagged profile.[8] Nearly all programs have zero fitness. The plane is sprinkled sparsely with a few isolated pinnacles characterising the positive fitness of workable programs.

Blind evolution cannot work on such a jagged fitness profile. It works best on smooth fitness surfaces with bell-shaped hills. Blind evolution can easily find the path of steepest ascend and reach the point of maximum fitness quickly under such circumstances. Rolling fitness landscapes of this kind must implicitly be presupposed in all models which employ ideas about blind evolution or adaptive learning.

Complex organisms or organisations are, however, characterised by functionally correlated traits. Changing one attribute without simultaneously changing some others in a certain way is doomed to failure. A larger organism requires a larger respiratory system, for instance, or a change of one trait in a computer program requires a correlated change in other traits such that the program remains functional.[9] In terms of fitness landscapes, correlated traits induce ridges and canyons. Evolution in such ridged landscapes requires strategies other than blind trial and error in order to succeed. In particular, variation must be kept within certain limits and must occur not randomly, but in a correlated fashion.[10]

3 Patterned Variation

For complex organisms, blind evolution is, therefore, not a feasible mechanism for evolution and adaptation. Because random variation cannot produce evolution of complex organisms, variation must be structured and patterned. Biologists have speculated that such patterned variation is itself the outcome of evolutionary processes, and have established theoretically and experimentally that patterned variation will occur as a result of selection processes. Those genes which generate a good pattern must be expected to outcompete others.[11] This argument ties the

---

[8] Biologists use the twin concepts of 'adaptive landscapes' and 'fitness landscapes', see e.g. Eldrege (1989, 19-21)

[9] Wagner (1984a) argues that these problems become important if more than *three* independent characters contribute to the variation of a functionally constrained system.

[10] Accordingly, the evolutionary strategy for optimising technical systems, as initiated by Rechenberg (1973), employs a further optimisation of step-width and direction.

[11] See Wagner (1984b; 1986) for the idea of 'Evolution der Evolutionsfähigkeit' - the evolution of the possibility to generate evolution - in biology. What I term patterned evolution variation here is closely related to ideas about 'canalisation' and 'developmental constraints' in biology. Economists may find this congenial. The economist Kenneth Boulding (1992, 183) asks whether 'it is possible to have a genetic mutation that increases the rate of mutation'. (The answer is 'yes'.) Boulding relates this to the

nature of variation - its particular patterning - to the nature of the universe of organisms or organizations explored in the past. Empirically, this patterning shows up in the phenomenon of 'morphological integration': Variations in functionally interrelated traits are, as a rule, more strongly correlated than variations in functionally independent traits.[12]

In other words, *if* evolution starts in a blind way, the emerging evolutionary strategies will eventually be patterned according to their relative evolutionary success. Subsequent evolutionary processes must be conceived as patterned, even if evolution has started 'originally' in a blind fashion. The argument does not necessarily imply that evolution was in fact 'originally blind'. There is no necessity to argue the nature of initial evolutionary processes. What matters are the later stages, where variation must be assumed to be patterned anyway. This pertains certainly to humans and social institutions.

4 Evolutionary Patterning in Biology

Patterned variations will give rise to directed, rather than blind evolution, in the sense that changes are controlled by internal constraints. Such variation may be conceived as generating new forms of organisms as constructed according to certain rules and principles which govern variation. Successful trials are then selected by competition. In other words: Evolutionary developments create new possibilities and shape new constraints, thereby channeling further developments in particular ways. Here are some examples of evolutionary processes studied in biology, which may be understood as the outgrowth of patterned variation.

Channeling by Constraints. Patterned variation may be interpreted as variation within constraints. In biology, such 'constraints' are conceived as 'features of ontogenetic mechanisms and morphogenetic design which limit the power of selection to mould phenotypic traits.'[13] Constraints are sometimes structurally given. Gastropod shells can, for instance, assume only certain forms because of the way they grow. There cannot be gastropods with square shells.[14] In this sense, developmental constraints limit the kinds of change that can occur - they pattern variation. Other constraints may arise at higher levels. Reptiles cannot accommodate to

---

'extraordinary phenomenon of acceleration in social and economic systems, especially in the last few centuries'. In another context, the economist Kaushik Basu (1996, 749) has argued that groups that never breed non-cooperating mutants may outcompete groups that do.

[12] Wagner (1986, 136)
[13] Stearns (1982)
[14] The above follows Maynard Smith (1982, 142). See also the discussion of constraints in Wagner (1984b, 102). The importance of constraints, in particular the laws of physics and chemistry, has been stressed by Köhler (1960). See also Kubon-Gilke (1996) for pertinent discussion.

arctic climates, because their metabolism depends on external sources of heat. This constrains possible adaptations. Such phenomena may be envisaged as brought about by evolution working on jagged fitness landscapes, rather than being a direct consequence of physical constraints. The effect - the patterning of variation by genetic constraints - amounts to much the same as the patterning of the gastropod shells by structural or physical constraints.

Hitchhiking. Correlation of changes gives rise to the possibility that certain features emerge without any reason in terms of fitness. If two new traits A and B emerge conjointly, where trait A improves fitness and trait B is neutral or even slightly detrimental for fitness, trait B may spread in a population because it is coupled with the successful trait A. Trait B survives and spreads not because of its own fitness, but because it is hitchhiking with the successful trait A. It is, ultimately, the structural coupling of traits A and B which generates the effect.[15]

Radiation. Evolution is, in Darwin's classic phrase, "descent with modification". Newly emerging niches will, accordingly, be filled by new organisms which derive from existing organisms, rather than develop anew in an "optimally adapted" way. In this sense, history channels future possibilities. Marsupial evolution in Australia affords the classic example for such radiation. Marsupials occupy a wide variety of ecological niches in Australia and Tasmania. Some developments among them have coincidentally paralleled developments in placental mammalian evolution elsewhere, Tasmanian wolf, for example, resembles placental wolves in the northern hemisphere in many ways.[16] Such phenomena of radiation illustrate how constraints emerge in biological evolution. Certain features, like a marsupium, once developed, create conditions and pose constraints for further developments; they pattern variation.

Founder effects. Radiation and irreversibility work conjointly to produce 'founder effects'. New organisms will contain traces of older organisms. In particular, some crucial features present in the parent population may provide the starting point for further developments and canalise these developments in a particular and irreversible way, just as the marsupium is maintained in the diverse Australian marsupials, and no mammals have developed from them.[17]

Irreversibility. Consider an organism with different organs. All organs are subject to evolution. Further, each organ constitutes a part of the environment of the other organs. Thus, any change in one organ induces changes in the other organs,

---

[15] Wagner (1986, 140). A closely related effect is related to "feedback selection". An organism may outcompete another organism B simply because it can accommodate faster to new circumstances, even if the latter type of organism can achieve better fitness in a (properly defined) long-run sense.

[16] Eldrege (1989, 177).

[17] The "founder effect" or "founder principle" in biology is usually phrased in a less extreme form by simply stating that the gene pool of an isolated population may differ from that of the parent population. This entails different selective conditions for the individuals in the peripheral group. Such differences may induce drastic genetic restructuring (Mayr 1982, 600-6, E.B.1995).

and further repercussions on the changing organ. Each adaptive step dismantles the conditions under which the other organs have developed and destroys, in this way, the bridges to the past. All organs will, therefore, exhibit traces of their history, but the route of return will be disbanded.[18]

Functional shifts. One of the great problems in biology relates to the emergence of novelties. It has been asked, for example, how a rudimentary wing can be enlarged by natural selection before it enables its processors to fly. One answer given by biologists is that the rudimentary wing may first evolve to serve some other function. Once it is large enough, it can be used as a wing. This induces a shift in function. In this way, the new feature builds on another, perhaps functionally unrelated, feature.[19]

Evolutionary detours. Complex adaptations are envisaged as accruing through a series of intermediary stages. Such developments may not necessarily progress in a uni-directional way, but may entail various evolutionary detours. Functional shifts of various kinds may be required to bring about complex matrix of new features. Each channel starts, so to speak, from previous channels, and there is no over-arching integrating force which enforces a coherent overall direction on the processes. Locations A and B may, so to speak, be situated fairly closely to each other, but evolution from A to B may involve a detour through a remote place C.[20]

Punctuation. It has been argued that variation is often patterned in such a way that jerky (or punctuational) rather than gradual evolution is generated.[21] This punctualist thesis refers to a special case of patterning which may be important both in biology and in the social sciences. According to these theories, blind evolution may play a role in locally optimising a certain type of organism, but the evolutionary jumps involved in the development of new types of organisms are brought about by channeled changes, i.e. by patterned variation.[22]

---

[18] This paraphrases Wagner (1984b, 108). A formal proof is supplied in Wagner (1982).
[19] Mayr (1982, 610).
[20] Eldrege (1989, 210).
[21] See Eldrege and Gould (1971), Gould (1977), Eldrege (1985; 1989)
[22] The discussion about punctuational evolution remains unsettled in biology, in part because it ties back to the unexplored features of the underlying fitness landscapes, in part because the qualitative difference between "fast" and "slow" changes remains controversial. This discussion is reminiscent of the discussion around Marshall's "long" and "short" periods, or Piaget's "assimilation" and "accommodation". Note, however, that palaeontologists have other time scales in mind, with "fast" punctuation taking place within 5000 to 50,000 years, and "slow" stasis persisting for 5 to 10 million years (Eldrege 1989, 66, 78).

5 Evolutionary Patterning in the Society

Patterns processes in social evolution exhibit strong similarities to those occurring in biological evolution. The following remarks illustrate this parallelism.

Channeling by Constraints. Constraints are obviously of the outmost importance in social evolution. At any given point in time, society is swamped with customs and laws and characterised by an amalgam of knowledge and superstition. All this channels change by preventing certain developments while easing others. In this way, the existing constraints, as brought about by evolution, channel future developments and structure the fate of society.[23] Similar observations pertain to the evolution of organizations within society. Each single firm is characterised by a set of behavioural patterns, routines and convictions which ease cooperation while constraining and channeling change.[24]

Hitchhiking. Hitchhiking phenomena seem readily conceivable in the social sciences. Some inefficient aspects of the personal computer (like the unnecessary SysRq key) are spreading along with the item to which they are attached. Similarly, technical standards, languages, and habits may survive because they are coupled with competitively successful features, and changes in one feature of an organisation may induce some slightly dysfunctional changes in somewhat unrelated dimensions. Schumpeter (1942) has argued, for instance, that capitalism will, by its very success, generate attitudes and preferences that undermine the moral foundations of market processes.

Radiation. There is, again, a strong case for radiation to be made in the social sciences. Many dissemination and diffusion processes may be envisaged as phenomena of radiation. The Western alphabet derives from Phoenician precursors, technologies or fashions spread, and some radically new inventions may be blocked by the presence of existing technologies which render it possible to solve new problems according to prevailing patterns.

Irreversibility. The argument about irreversibility can easily be applied to social processes. Newly emerging institutions will, for instance, entail changes throughout society, and thereby dismantle the conditions which gave birth to them. This entails irreversibility. The argument about irreversibility of evolutionary processes is obviously of immense importance for the social sciences. It sketches a way to outdo the simple view that society selects its institutions by taking the best specimen from a pre-conceived book of blueprints, given the environmental conditions and the state of technology.[25]

Founder effect. Founder effects can be observed on a large scale in many societies. The most prominent case in point is provided by the Hartz thesis according to which the societies of Australia, South Africa, Canada, or Latin America still

---

[23] Vanberg (1996) has emphasised the importance of constraints for social evolution recently.
[24] See Schlicht (1997, Ch.13).
[25] North and Thomas (1973).

carry the strong imprint of features of the parent societies prevailing at colonization.[26] Similarly, many features of western countries can be traced back to Roman or Celtic roots.

Functional shifts. Again, we must take account of functional shifts in many dimensions of society. The origin of money has, for example, been traced back to religious practices. In other words, functionality has switched from the sacred to the profane. It would be illuminating to comb history texts from this perspective.

Evolutionary detours. As in biology, we should expect (and seem to observe) evolutionary detours in social evolution. In a sense, a development going from democracy in Athens to modern democracy seems more straightforward than the actual course of history, involving the backlash of the dark ages. Likewise, it seems straightforward to conceive the modern firm as growing directly from the guild system, but the modern corporation has not developed in such a way. Rather, the intermediate step of putting-out system was required, apparently because there was no way to produce the necessary adaptations - legal and otherwise - by starting from the guild directly. Similarly, our modern alphabet has not been developed directly by associating certain elementary sounds with some elementary symbols, as a behaviourist might have expected. Rather, alphabetic characters have grown out of syllabic signs, and these developed from pictorial representation of sound, which in turn derived from picture symbols denoting certain objects or ideas, which were developed quite independently of their pronunciation. Modern Japanese kanjis illustrate these earlier stages. In the European case, the invention of twenty-six symbols required a detour of several millennia, which is a considerable time span.[27] It seems nearly impossible to account for such occurrences without resorting to patterned variation.

Punctuation. A discussion of punctuation in economics has hardly commenced.[28] The idea of punctuation in economics has, however, a long and venerable history. While some economists (most notably Alfred Marshall) have stressed the element of continuity and gradual progress, others (like Karl Marx) have envisaged discontinuous revolutionary shifts in the overall character of society. Sometimes, these discussions carry a religious flavour, but this does not mean that the issue is settled in a theoretically compelling fashion. Modern arguments in system theory have pointed again to the possibility of both continuos *and* discontinuous change on the system level.[29]

---

[26] Hartz et. al. (1964).
[27] Asch (1987:109).
[28] Mokyr (1990), Jones (1995), Boulding (1992).
[29] Eger and Weise (1993), Weise (1996, 719). Kuran (1995, Ch. 15-18) offers a theory of society-wide punctuation processes.

6 Psychology and Social Evolution

In a formal way, the argument about patterned variation carries over to social processes: Without patterning, there would be no discernible evolution; once evolution starts, the processes of variation themselves are moulded by evolutionary forces. If evolutionary processes are relevant on the level of society, they must be patterned.

The argument is, however, not entirely satisfactory, because basic traits of human nature have remained invariant throughout history. These features must be taken as givens for purposes of social analysis. As social processes emerge from the joint action of individuals, the patterning of individual behaviour should not itself be considered as brought about by social evolution. Rather, the patterning of social evolution is engendered by the way individuals behave.

With regard to the behaviour of individuals, however, the biological argument about patterning applies with full force in the sense that this behaviour must indeed be assumed patterned from the outset. The starting-point for social evolution is, then, provided by those patterned features of human behaviour, thinking, and feeling, that remain unaffected by processes of social evolution. The theory of social evolution, unlike the theory of biological evolution, can start with these givens.

These givens comprise basic regularities of pattern recognition, routine formation and thinking, but also emotional and behavioural dispositions. Classical Gestalt psychology has focused on these fundamental aspects of human nature, and modern cognitive and social psychology continue this tradition. Theories about social evolution may benefit from using the knowledge accumulated in these fields.[30]

The parallelism between biological and social patterning mentioned in the previous sections is supplemented by a number of similar features of learning processes. Without going too much into psychology, the following illustrates this correspondence.

Channeling by constraints. People act from strategies, rules, or habits acquired in the past. This channels and constrains their future behaviour. [31]

---

[30] I have related various aspects of economic behaviour regarding custom, property, the law, the firm, and the market, to these psychological regularities, see Schlicht (1997). In similar way, Kubon-Gilke (1997) has analyzed the (often implicit) psychological premises of institutional economics.

By the way, the rationality assumption used in economics may be interpreted as a device for generating behavioural patterns, in the sense that 'rational' behaviour can be distinguished from erratic behaviour by obeying some constraints posed by rational calculation.

[31] Recent theorising about the role of "mental models" in institutional analysis starts from this observation, see North and Denzau (1994).

Hitchhiking. As people act from reasons and strategies, they treat "similar" cases similarly. This may entail maintaining dysfunctional aspects of otherwise functional behaviour.
Irreversibility. People will develop new behaviours by means of old behaviours. If the old behaviours are forgotten, they cannot be reached again. Various stage theories of language learning illustrate such irreversibility.
Radiation. People learn by imitation.
Founder effects. First impressions loom large and influence later developments strongly.
Novelty and functional shifts. Many phenomena of insight are due to restructuring a given problem in an appropriate way.
Evolutionary detours. Teaching practices, e.g. in musical education, rely heavily on certain detours.
Punctuation. Certain learning phenomena, especially those related to "insight learning" exhibit strong discontinuity.[32]
What seems to be required, then, is a theory which derives the social patterning from the psychological patterning in a systematic way.

7 Organic Growth

Up to now, the discussion has focused on the nature of variation: Variation must be assumed patterned, rather than random. But variation is only one element in the process of evolution; the other is selection.

With regard to selection, biologists stress the importance of competition, and this element of competitive selection is undoubtedly of central importance not only in biology, but also in the analysis of social processes.[33] Sometimes, however, competition is not available as a selective force. Think about isolated societies on remote islands, or society-wide institutions like legal systems, kinship

---

[32] Maynard Smith (1989, 149) challenges the punctional position in remarking that" one does not know whether one is studying the rates of evolution of real organisms, ore merely the habits of the taxonomists who gave the names to the fossils." Such a position suggests not that punctuation does not occur, but that may arise not in the fossil records themselves, but in the way people perceive the world. The fact that humans *perceive* the world in punctuational terms may be of even greater significance for the social sciences than "real" punctuation in the fossil record. Eldrege (1989, 134) has reversed Maynard Smith's argument when observing: 'Many "trends" singled out by evolutionary biologists are ex post facto renderings of phylogenetic history: biologists may simply pick out species at different points in geological time that seem to fit on some line of directional modification through time.' This would, again, hint at the structuring force of human perception, albeit in another direction.

[33] The phrase "survival of the fittest" was actually invented by Spencer, not Darwin, see Hallpike (1996, 682-3).

systems, or languages.[34] For such institutions, the mechanism of external competitive selection may be absent. Evolution of such institutions must be conceived as generated by patterned variation on the level of the elements of such systems, with changes selected by the conditions prevailing in the system as a whole. Such systems, seen from the outside, will exhibit organic growth, i.e., patterned variation unchecked by any kind of selection.[35] (Returning to the earlier example of mathematics, alternative approaches for solving certain problems within mathematics are selected by their success within mathematics.)

Further, patterned variation restrains certain alternatives from evolving, and variants may survive simply because no superior variants are generated by variation. Under such circumstances, competition cannot act as a selection device either. Change (or stasis) will be brought about by the interaction of internal factors.

8 Constraints and Institutions

In an abstract sense, any evolutionary argument can be described as follows: There is a set of feasible alternatives, and there is a selective mechanism which selects among the alternatives. The outcome of the selection process must depend, therefore, on the set of feasible alternatives, and on the mechanisms generating these feasible alternatives. The fact that humans have survived is due to the fact that superior animals - with lesser needs but more power and more aggressiveness - have not emerged. Thus any explanation must rely on theories on what is *not* possible[36]. In other words, it must rely on arguments about canalisation and constraints. It must start from possible patterns. Thus, even within evolutionary arguments, a thorough knowledge of nature cannot be replaced by abstract principles.[37] With regard to social analysis, this abstract argument may be supplemented by saying that the patterning of human behaviour, which is a necessary prerequisite for the emergence of any kind of social structure, must originate in psychology, broadly conceived, and comprising not only cognition, but emotion and habit as well.

It has been said that 'institutions are humanly devised constraints that shape human interaction'.[38] I would prefer to put weights differently. A categorical distinction between human design and social evolution seems problematic. In so far as institutions are 'constraints that shape human interaction', these constraints are

---

[34] Hallpike (1996).
[35] As a matter of terminology, I use "organic growth" as "patterned variation without selection".
[36] Witt (1987, 22)
[37] Selten (1991, 9)
[38] North (1990, 3)

not brought about by human design alone, but are in part reflections of constraints working on the level of individuals. The consistency requirements constraining a firm's compensations policies are, for example, not 'humanly devised' but part and parcel of the way in which humans form fairness perceptions.[39] Human design starts from these givens. As purposeful behaviour is patterned, not random, it generates patterned variation. The collective result of such activity is, however, not fully reducible to human design. Mechanisms of selection and interaction working on the level of society may generate quite unintended consequences. But the statement about institutions as humanly devised constraints is also biased in another way. Institutions are not merely constraints. Sometimes they create possibilities and shape motivations which would otherwise not be available.

References

Alchian, A.A. (1950): Uncertainty, Evolution, and Economic Theory; *Journal of Political Economy*, 58(3), 211-221.

Asch, S. (1987): *Social Psychology*, second edition, Oxford-New York-Tokyo: Oxford University Press.

Basu, K. (1996): Notes on Evolution, Rationality, and Norms; *Journal of Institutional and Theoretical Economics*, 152(4), 739-50.

Boulding, K.E. (1992): Punctuation in Societal Evolution; in: A. Somit and S. Peterson (eds.), *The Dynamics of Evolution*, Ithaca and London: Cornell University Press, 171-186.

Eden, M. (1967): Inadequacies of Neo-Darwinian Evolution as a Scientific Theory; in: P.Moorhead and M. Kaplan (eds.), *Mathematical Challenges to the Neodarwian Interpretation of Evolution*, Symposium Monograph 5, Philadelphia: Winstar Int. Press 1967, 5-19.

Eger, T. and P. Weise (1993): Economic Transformation Process: Political Possibilities and Social Limitations; in: H.-J. Wegener (ed.), *On the Theory and Policy of Systematic Change*, Heidelberg: Physica, 51-65.

Eldrege, N. (1985): *Time Frames: The Rethinking of Darwinian Evolution and the Theory of Punctual Equilibria*, New York: Simon and Schuster.

Eldrege, N. (1989): *Macro-Evolutionary Dynamics*, New York: Mc Graw-Hill.

Eldrege, N. and S.J. GOULD (1972): Punctuated Equilibria: An Alternative to Phyletic Gradualism; in: T.J.M. SCHOPF (ed.), *Models of Paleabiology*, San Francisco: Freeman, Cooper, pp. 82-115. (Reprinted in Eldrege 1985).

Encyclopaedia Britannica (1994): Founder Principle; *The New Encyclopaedia Britannica*, 15th. edition, Vol.4, Chicago: Encyclopaedia Britannica, 902.

Gould, S.J. (1977): *Ontogeny and Phylogeny*, Cambridge (Mass.): Harvard University Press.

---

[39] See section above. As another quite obvious instance, property is not a human invention, see Schlicht (1997, Ch. 11)

Hallpike, C.R. (1986): The Principle of Social Evolution, Oxford: Clarendon
Hallpike, C.R. (1996): Social Evolution; *Journal of Institutional and Theoretical Economics*, 152, 682-689.
Hayek, F.A: (1945): The Use of Knowledge in Society; *The American Economic Review*, 35(4), 519-530.
Hartz, L. et al. (1964): *The Founding of New Societies*, San Diego-New York-London: Harcourt Brace Jovanovich.
Hodgson, G.M. (1996): The Challenge of Evolutionary Economics; *Journal of Institutional and Theoretical Economics*, 152(4), 697-706.
Jones, E. (1995): Technology, the Human Niche and Darwinian Explanation; in: E.Jones and V. Reynolds (eds.), *Survival and Religion. Biological Evolution and Cultural Change*, Chinchester-New York-Brisbane-Toronto-Singapore: John Wiley and Sons, 163-186.
Köhler, W. (1960): The Mind-Body Problem; in: S. HOOK (ed.), *Dimensions of Mind*, New York: New York University Press, 3-23, reprinted in M. Henle (ed.), *The Selected Papers of Wolfgang Köhler*, New York: Liveright 1971, 62-82.
Kubon-Gilke, G. (1996): Institutional Economics and the Evolutionary Metaphor; *Journal of Institutional and Theoretical Economics*, 152(4), 723-38.
Kubon-Gilke, G. (1997): *Verhaltensbindung und die Evolution ökonomischer Institutionen*, Marburg: Metropolis.
Küppers, B.O. (1983): Zufall oder Planmäßigkeit. Erkenntnistheoretische Aspekte der biologischen Informationsverarbeitung; *Biologie in unserer Zeit*, 13(4).
List, F. (1837): *The Natural System of Political Economy*, translated and edited by W.O.Henderson, London: Cass.
Maynard Smith, J (1989): *Did Darwin Get it Right?*, New York and London: Chapman and Hall.
Marshall, A. (1890): *Principles of Economics*, eighth edition, London: Macmillian 1920.
Mayr, E. (1982): The Growth of Biological Thought, Cambridge (Mass.): Harvard University Press.
Marx, K. (1873): *Capital. A Critical Analysis of Capitalist Production*, vol.1, translated from the third German edition by S. Moore and E.Avelling and edited by F.Engels, with a supplement edited and translated by D. Torr, London: George Allen and Unwin 1946.
North, D. (1990): *Institutions, Institutional Change and Economic Performance*, Cambridge: Cambridge University Press.
North, D.C. and A.T. Denzau (1994): Shared Mental Models: Ideologies and Institutions; *Kyklos*, 47(1), 3-31.
North, D.C. and Thomas, R.P. (1973): The Rise of the Western World, Cambridge: Cambridge University Press.
Piaget, J. (1967): *Biologie et Connaissance*, Paris: Gallimard.

Rechenberg, I. (1973): *Evolutionsstrategie: Optimierung technischer Systeme nach Prinzipien der biologischen Evolution*, Stuttgart-Bad Cannstadt: Friedrich Frommann Verlag.

Schlicht, E. (1979): The Transition to Labour Management as a Gestalt Switch; *Gestalt Theory*, 1:54-67.

Schlicht, E. (1997): *On Custom in the Economy*, Oxford: Oxford University Press.

Schumpeter, J.A. (1942): Capitalism, Socialism and Democracy, New York: Harper

Selten, R. (1991): Evolution, Learning, and Economic Behaviour; *Games and Economic Behaviour*, 3, 3-24.

Stearns, S.C. (1982): The Role of Development in the Evolution of Life Histories; in: J.T. Bonner (ed.), *Evolution and Development*, Berlin-Heidelberg-New York: Springer Verlag, 237-258.

Vanberg, V. (1988): Rules and Choice in Economics and Sociology; *Jahrbuch für Neue Politische Ökonomie*, 7:1-22, Tübingen: Mohr.

Vanberg, V. (1996): Institutional Evolution Within Constraints; *Journal of Theoretical and Institutional Economics*, 152, 690-696.

Wagner, G. P. (1982): The Logical Structure of Irreversible Systems Transformations: A Theorem Concerning Dollo's Law; *Journal of Theoretical Biology*, 96, 337-346.

Wagner, G.P. (1984a): Coevolution of Functionally Constrained Characters: Prerequisites for Adaptive Versality; *BioSystems*, 17, 51-55.

Wagner, G.P. (1984b): Evolution der Evolutionsfähigkeit; in: A. Dress, H. Hendrichs und G. Küpper (eds.), *Selbstorganisation. Die Entstehung von Ordnung in Natur und Gesellschaft*, München-Zürich: Piper, 121-147.

Weise, P. (1996): Evolution and Self-Organisation; *Journal of Institutional and Theoretical Economics*, 152(4), 716-22.

Witt, U. (1987): *Individualistische Grundlagen der evolutorischen Ökonomik*, Tübingen: J.C.B.Mohr (Paul Siebeck).

Witt, U. (1988): Emergence and Dissemination of Innovations: Some Principles of Evolutionary Economics; in: R.H.DAY and P. CHEN (eds.), *Nonlinear Dynamics and Evolutionary Economics*, Oxford: Oxford University Press, 91-100.

Witt, U. (1996): A"Darwinian Revolution" in Economics?; *Journal of Institutional and Theoretical Economics*, 152(4), 707-15.

Comment on Ekkehart Schlicht

Brian Loasby

Patterned Variations: Evolution, Psychology and Economic Institutions

1. Professor Schlicht's proposition that evolutionary explanations "must presuppose regularities which are not themselves subject to the processes studied" may be subsumed under the general principle, which was stated in the course of conversation by Professor Van de Ven of the University of Minnesota, that we can not even recognize change unless there is something which does not change. Everything may be subject to change, but not everything can change at once. In the study of institutions and evolution, this principle implies that we may seek, as Professor Schlicht does here, to explain the evolution of institutions in a context of unchanging psychological dispositions; on another occasion we may choose instead to explain on a shorter time-scale the evolution of behaviour within a specific and unchanging institutional environment, or, on a larger time-scale, the evolution of the underlying psychological dispositions. As with Alfred Marshall's time-period analysis, different time-scales are appropriate for the analysis of different kinds of change.

Our theoretical choice of what to told constant for a particular analytical purpose will necessarily constrain the conclusions which it is possible to draw; what is less often acknowledged is that it will also affect the acceptability of those conclusions among the various audiences to which they are presented. This choice of what to vary and what to hold constant may be crucial in determining the success of both commercial and intellectual innovation. Indeed, all evolutionary change is similarly constrained by the requirements for compatibility with the relevant environment. In every context the success of a new variation is dependent on "good continuity" and what particular configuration of regularities must be preserved in order to maintain good continuity in each context is therefor an important topic for investigation. We shall return to this principle in Section 4 of this commentary (though it is implicit throughout), and conclude this section by agreeing that psychological regularities of cognition and motivation provide the basis for the patterns which govern the successful emergence of detailed variations in economic and social systems. Though it lies beyond the scope both of Professor Schlicht's paper and this commentary, we should record that terms like "compatibility", "success", and indeed "fitness" do not imply that any particular change is an improvement: that requires different criteria.

2. The processes which Professor Schlicht explicitly wishes to consider in his paper do not include biological evolution. For his purposes, only the consequences of biological evolution matter; and that makes it unnecessary to discuss the importance of patterned evolution within biology. As Adam Smith observed, the generality of a connection principle enhances its rhetorical power, and so Professor Schlicht is naturally attracted to the possibility that patterned evolution may be a principle which connects biological, psychological, and institutional development. However, patterned evolution in biology is a disputed issue; and we do not at present need to become involved in this dispute. Richard Dawkins has argued that blind evolution, through a long series of local adaptations, is all that is needed for "climbing mount improbable". But, as Dawkins points out, what apparently makes possible the development of highly complex structures without the aid of patterned variation is the biological timescale of 50-500 million years; it is not easy to see how similar step by step changes could create "improbable institutions" within a few hundred, or even a few thousand, years. In explaining the evolution of institutions, as often in the study of economic evolution, the biological model is oft doubtful relevance to modelling strategy; and since it is currently disputed, as well as unnecessary, it is better left out of the argument.

Cosmides and Tooby (1996) have attempted to demonstrate a pathway along which altruism might have developed by a series of incremental adaptations, but this is a conjectural history, about which we can remain agnostic. Altruism may affect the viability of some institutions, and it may itself be encouraged or discouraged by particular institutions, as demonstrated in the paper of Professor Frey and Dr. Bohnet. The acceptability of altruism as a motivator within economics is clearly discouraged by North American conceptions of rationality, as shown by Dr. Ortmann's response to that paper; Oliver Williamson's reliance on opportunism is far more congenial to North American patterns of economic analysis, as shown by the ineffectiveness of Coase's cogent objections to opportunism as the organising principle of transaction cost economics. But whether altruism arises from patterned variation or incremental adaptation presumably has no effect on its acceptability in this discussion. Altruism is presumably included in the set of motivations which Professor Schlicht would wish us to consider among the possible "psychological regularities ... concerning motivation" (page 1): it may be sufficient to agree that motivations help to explain the patterns of behaviour, without enquiring into their origins. In this particular study of evolution, psychological regularities provide the unchanging setting within which the changes in which we are interested take place.

3. Social evolution clearly must operate within biological constraints, and in particularly the constraints of human psychology. In these comments I propose to focus on the constraints imposed by the characteristics of human cognition. How we acquire knowledge - both knowledge of facts and relationships, and the skills of physical and mental performance - sets the limits to what each of us can know. It is because for every individual the range of cognitive potential is wide but the scope of what any single individual can encompass is narrow that the division of

labour, in both practical and intellectual activities, is so important for human progress. As Professor Schlicht suggests on page 9, "the main source of patterning is the human mind"; and specialisation encourages the emergence of distinctive patterns which shape or may even constitute the experience of each category of specialists (Kelly 1963). Adam Smith offered a psychological explanation of the urge to impose patterns, using examples from the history of astronomy, on which Kuhn also drew in explaining his theory of scientific paradigms, and Popper remarked on the apparent determination of people to find patterns even when there are none to be found. We create patterns, we generate variations within these patterns, and we normally reject variations which threaten to violate these patterns. As Professor Schlicht remarks in a footnote on page 7, Maynard Smith' suggestion that punctuation in the fossil record may be an artefact of perception rather than a natural phenomenon indicates the significance of perception in the social sciences - both as a subject of study and as a major influence on the professional behaviour of social scientists. Given the asymmetric costs of error in many human situations, this apparent bias towards pattern-making may be efficient; with only a few million years of human existence to judge by it is probably too early to say. However, it is easy to imagine that skills in pattern-recognition have long been major contributors to the fitness of both predators and their prey, and that surviving species - not least the primates - have brains which are particularly suited to the formation and linking of patterns. The evolution of the human brain, it is important to note, predates the emergence of conscious thought. It is not, therefore surprising that conscious thought appears to rest on the ability to structure problems unconsciously before beginning to reason about them. Such a need for pre-analytic structure has been used by Choi (1993) to explain why we are so ready to accept conventions, without subjecting them to the rational choice procedures which economists officially identify as the core of their discipline. Choi's reliance on Smith's *Theory of Moral Sediments* indicates that his argument is relevant to the theme of this conference.

4. A major reason why patterned variation in economic evolution does not depend on patterned variation in biology is that in human affairs selection is ex-ante as well as ex-post. We are guided by rules not only in deciding what to accept but also in deciding what will be tried. As a recently-recruited research chemist, a former colleague of mine was writing down the chemical formulae for some potentially-interesting compounds when his manager came by, stopped to look, and asked "Where's the chlorine, Frank?"; in an organisation which produced more chlorine than it could use, no new product was of interest unless it could absorb some of the excess. Similarly, the research staff at BP Chemicals, at a time when the parent company was brilliantly successful at finding oil but not very good at selling it, were told by their Research Director that their research objective was "to shift crude".

Such patterning of variations which is generated may help an organisation to evolve towards a local optimum, or towards the best of a group of local optima; but if an economy is to move towards a distant, but possibly higher, optimum it requires either some means of jumping over jagged landscapes or a diversity of starting points. Both require a variety of patterns within the system. Schumpeter recognised the difficulty of escaping from well-established routines, and relied on entrepreneurs to create "new combinations"; he respected the principle that not everything can change at once by identifying innovation with the combination, not the pre-existing elements which are combined. Professor Schlicht could increase the effectiveness of his argument by emphasising both the complementarity between pattern-guided variation and the creation of new patterns in the process of economic and social evolution and the problems of encouraging both incremental and discontinuous change within a single environment.

5. Even with the ability to invent patterns by the use of our imagination (which Shackle is quite exceptional inn emphasising), not all transitions are possible. What transitions, what kinds of patterns and what kinds of variations within patterns, are compatible with any particular set of institutions is a seriously under-developed theme in economic theory and policy; one needs only to glance at the quality of advice given by eminent economists to the governments of "economies of transition", or to the reliance on convergence criteria, a cloned Bundesbank and a stability pact to guide the transition to European Monetary Union - particularly when some of the potential members are determined to manipulate the convergence criteria, prevent the cloning of the Bundesbank, and neutralise the effects of the stability pact. This is also a substantially underdeveloped theme in business strategy, which has swung from the management of a portfolio of business to the exploitation of core competencies with little thought for the institutional requirements of either recipe, let alone for the institutional requirements of the transition between them. Some companies, it should be noted, have recognised the issue: the senior management of Cadbury, which included several members of the founding family, went to considerable trouble to present their transition from a paternalistic to a market-focused company as an updating of their founder's principles. Others have only begun to glimpse the difficulties when their institutions have proved disastrously defective.

6. Firms constitute the class of patterned variation which might have been expected to be of most obvious interest to economists - expected, that is, by those who are not aware of the assumption of individual rational choice on which so much economic analysis is based. This assumption leads either to an analytical world in which there are no firms as organisations, which was Coase's original problem, or to an ideal conception of the economy as a single firm. Professor Schlicht's reminder, that in formal theory the integrated firm can achieve whatever the equivalent set of independent firms can achieve - *and more* echoes the familiar comparison of planning and markets; and riposte echoes Hayek's riposte, which is now widely accepted as a policy proposition, though it is still not thoroughly incorporated in theory. Professor Schlicht's example of different payment systems is, however, not the most apt to the theme of this conference, or even to his own general argument. For that we should look to the differences between activities in the most efficient patterning of behaviour (Richardson 1972), which create diverse

optima between which transition is not easy, and therefore (inter alia) hinder the movement of both workers and employers between labour markets which would otherwise eliminate the wage differences which Professor Schlicht cites. This argument can be cast in terms of specific human capital, but in a conference which is explicitly seeking cognitional foundations for economic analysis the cognitive imperative to organise knowledge around an array of differentiated patterns is more appropriate. The human capital is not necessarily worse (or better), but it is in important respects different, and the expression of those differences in different patterns of analysis offer increased possibilities of improving the total of our understanding.

7. For these cognitive reasons, the growth of knowledge, whether within a discipline or within an industry, should not be very closely co-ordinated. Conformity within a small system is often a condition of efficiency; but non-conformity enhances the chances of discovery. In an unpublished paper on the units of selection, Levinthal (1996, p.11), noting that organisations generally seem unable to tolerate much diversity, points to the advantages of local autonomy in increasing the variety that is needed in order for even the most efficient selection mechanism to do much good. But he also identifies an important opportunity cost of local autonomy: His argument is that the smaller the unit, the greater the likelihood of significant effects across its boundaries, and therefore the greater the chance of "attribution bias" - the false identification of an internal cause for good effects and of an external cause for bad effects. Such a bias may be expected to affect the interpretation of each firm's experiments with its own patterned variation, and therefore its contribution to the range of alternatives on which external selection processes can work. The role of institutions is important here, and must not be assumed to be always beneficial; moreover, since actual Pareto improvements are rare, and potential Pareto improvements offer a dubious criterion, we should always ask for whom a change is beneficial.

8. Though the case for patterned-governed variation and for the creation of new patterns is convincing, Professor Schlicht's comparison with "blind evolution" may cause confusion among some readers. For it has been argued in the philosophy of science literature that "blind" does not necessarily mean random, but can be extended to cover the "bold conjectures" advocated by Popper (which go well beyond the available evidence), since scientists have no means of knowing which of these will be corroborated and will indeed expect the great majority to be falsified. In this sense "blindness" is compatible with direction - only certain kinds of conjecture will be offered - but it is opposed to "design", as in the Pareto-optimal planned economy, Bayesian learning, or the currently-fashionable "rational expectations". Without this degree of blindness - and this falsibility of attempts at design - there is no role for selection, nor for unintended consequences, both of which seem to be essential components of institutional economics. In relation to this paper, the point is semantic, not substantial - except that, as Professor Schlicht would be the first to point out, the patterns that we impose have substantial results.

9. One substantial result of the imposition of patterns both bon what is tried and what is accepted, which is properly seen by Professor Schlicht as an essential part of his analysis, is path-dependency, which is interpreted as the accumulation of constraints, not as a justification for single-exit models. However, we should not forget that humans do have a limited possibility of escape from such dependencies. Extinct species cannot be recreated, but discarded ideas which are still on record can be at least partially retrieved: if "the past is another country: they do things differently there", these differences can be observed and sometimes adapted. A firm may find it more difficult to escape from its past than an individual, because the escape must be collective and in a direction which is mutually acceptable; but if the institutions of an industry permit diversity then transition may be possible for some of its members, and even though some firms may disappear the people who worked for them may be able to fit into new patterns. As an illustration, we may note that the revival of the moribund British car industry was initiated by incoming Japanese companies, one of which , Nissan, found many of its most productive workers among the discards of another moribund industry, coalmining.

References

Choi, Y.B.(1993): *Paradigms and Conventions: Uncertainty, Decision Making, and Entrepreneurship*, Ann Arbor: University of Michigan Press.

Kelly, G.A. (1963): *A Theory of Personality*, New York: W.W. Norton.

Levinthal, D. (1996): Organisations and Capabilities: The Role of Decompositions and Units of Selection; unpublished manuscript.

Richardson, G.B. (1972): The Organisation of Industry; *Economic Journal*, 82, 883-96.

Tooby, J. and Cosmides, L. (1996): Friendship and the Banker' Paradox: Other Pathways to the Evolution of Adaptations for Altruism; in: W. G. Runciman, J.M. Smith and R.I. M. Dunbar (eds.), *Evolution of Social Behaviour Patterns in Primates and Man* (Proceedings of the British Academy, 88), Oxford: Oxford University Press for the British Academy, 119-43.

Comment on Ekkehart Schlicht

Uwe Mummert

Ekkehart Schlicht asserts that in institutional economics a view of evolution frequently invoked is that of blind evolution. According to blind evolution every kind of variation may possibly occur. Schlicht rejects this view and contrasts it with a concept of organic evolution. The concept of organic evolution acknowledges that variation is patterned. It is patterned because variation takes place on the basis of the already existing. The existing structure of what is going to mutate constrains the way it will mutate.

Schlicht is right when pointing out that variation takes place on the basis of the already existing and that we observe what he calls patterned variation: A bird will not hatch a dog, but a bird with maybe some slight modifications. But what are the reasons for this? I find two explanations: First, the likelihood of a simultaneous change of all genes or bits - or whatever is to mutate - is very low. It is even lower for creating a new viable mutant. And this leads to a second reason: we do not know what kind of variations are immediately discarded because the mutant is simply not viable. However, this implies that variation is not patterned by itself, but because of a very low likelihood of massive mutation to create a fundamentally new and viable species. Therefore, we can simply not know whether variation is indeed by itself patterned or whether we only observe some structure because what we see has already been subject to a process of selection. Nonetheless, we indeed observe patterns in variation.

However, before commenting more elaborately on the possibilities created by the concept of patterned variation for social science, I would like to take a critical look at Schlicht's assertion that the "view of evolution, frequently invoked in institutional economics" is that of a blind evolution. I would like to learn more about the authors Schlicht is referring to. In particular because in institutional economics we already find a developed theory of "organic evolution", namely the theory of pathdependence (e.g., Arthur 1988, 1989; David 1985). Douglass C. North (1990) draws deeply on this concept to explain particular constraints to institutional change. Honestly, I fail also to see the concept of blind evolution in the main body of literature on institutional economics. Already Alchian (1950) in his famous article argued that many innovations take place on the basis of what is already existing. For him one major source of innovation is the attempt of individuals to imitate others, and by doing this "innovate by unwittingly acquiring some unexpected or unsought unique attributes" (Alchian 1950, 218f.). Nelson and Winter as well emphasize that "innovation ... consists to a substantial extent of a recombination of conceptual and physical materials that were previously in existence" (1982, 130). Both are concerned with technological innovations and new routines. Robert Sugden on the other hand focuses on the emergence of new institutions, but he also argues that one feature of new conventions is their relatedness to already existing conventions.[16] Therefore I am at a loss to find evidence for a blind evolutionary perspective in institutional economics. If, however, Schlicht's proposal aims at replacing the concept of path dependence with his own concept, I would have liked to learn what comparative heuristic advantages the concept of organic evolution has.

But let us return to the patterness of variation itself. It is important to keep in mind that we observe this pattern only when looking at what evolutionary processes have created in the past. Variation is patterned only in a certain sense: we know that a variation is a change of what is already existing but we do not know what particular kind of change will occur at what point of time.[17] The theory of natural selection is not about the course of evolution but about the process of evolution (Vanberg 1994, 173). Schlicht is somewhat unclear in this regard pointing out that due to the patterness of variation "novelty is never random". We need to distinguish clearly between two meanings of "random": one that involves a total break in the causal chain of explanation and the other that simply means unpredictability. Of course variation is not random in the first sense, but it definitely is in the second sense. We will never know more about patterned variations than that they will be some alteration of what already exists. Therefore I am very much in doubt if concentrating on the patterns of variation is a promising way to proceed. In open and complex systems, it will never be possible to identify as Schlicht proposes "a set of feasible alternatives" between which a selective mechanism might select.

The outcome of the process of selection depends on both variation and the constraints within which variation takes place. As we will never know what kind of variation will emerge, I would suggest rather to focus on the constraints which determine the selective pressure.

Furthermore, I am somewhat uneasy about the methodological status Schlicht ascribes to the concept of evolution when pointing out "that blind evolution is not a useful mechanism for generating change of complex organisms or institutions". This gives the impression that he considers evolution to be an ontological rather than a heuristic concept. However, this is very questionable. This is particular questionable since the idea of evolution was originally developed in the social

---

[16] "If conventions can spread by analogy, then the conventions that are best able to spread are those that are most susceptible to analogy. Thus we should expect to find family relationships among conventions, and not just a chaos of arbitrary and unrelated rules." (Sugden 1989, 93f.)

[17] And even if we would be able to rewind the process of evolution and start it again, the particular variations would be different.

sciences long before Darwin applied it to the natural sciences (Hayek 1973, 22f.).[18]

So far I focused only on the patterness of variation. But one has also to ask what is it anyway that is supposed to vary? What is the respective subject of analysis, and can the concept of evolution be equally applied regardless whether gastropods, law, mathematical solutions or organisational variants like outsourcing are to be analysed? It is unclear what the complement of genes and differential reproductive success in the domain of economics are (Witt 1996, 709). Furthermore, the mechanisms of biological and social evolution are very different. Whereas in biological evolution the decisive factor is the variation and selection of physical and inheritable properties, in social evolution it is about institutions and habits. Furthermore, social evolution does not take place on the individual but rather the group level (Hayek 1960, 59). Therefore the mechanisms of evolution must be very different.

The heuristic value of utilising an evolutionary approach depends critically on the explicit definition of the subject of analysis and the mechanisms by which evolution is to take place. Schlicht identifies three elements of analysis: individual behaviour, organisations and social institutions. But all are subject to different processes. There are fundamental differences between changes of individual behaviour and institutional change. Whereas individual behaviour takes place within a system of rules, institutional change means a change of the rules themselves. Furthermore, we can distinguish two sources of institutional variation: it can be the result of intentional collective action or the unintentional result of individual action. However, the evolutionary features of both processes of variation will be very different.

References

Alchian, Armen A. (1950): Uncertainty, Evolution and Economic Theory; *Journal of Political Economy*, 58, 211-221.

Arthur, W. Brian (1988): Self-Reinforcing Mechanisms in Economics; in: P.W. Anderson, K.J. Arrow and D. Pines (Eds.): *The Economy as an Evolving Complex System*; 9-31; Redwood City: Addison-Wesley.

Arthur, W. Brian (1989): Competing Technologies, Inreasing Returns, and Lock-in by Historical Events; *Economic Journal*, 99, 116-131.

David, P. A. (1985): Clio and the Economics of QWERTY; *American Economic Review*, 75, Papers and Proceedings, 332-337.

Hayek, Friedrich A. (1960): *The Constitution of Liberty*; Chicago: The University of Chicago Press.

---

[18] Yet, the pattern of the evolution of the concept of evolution within social sciences led in another direction.

Hayek 1973: *Law, Legislation and Liberty; Volume 1. Rules and Order*; Reprinted 1993, London: Routledge.

Nelson, Richard R. and Winter, Sidney G. (1982): *An Evolutionary Theory of Economic Change*; Cambridge, Mass., London, England: Harvard University Press.

North, Douglass C. (1990): *Institutions, Institutional Change, and Economic Performance*; Cambridge: Cambridge University Press.

Sugden, Robert (1989): Spontaneous Order; *Journal of Economic Perspectives*, 3, 85-97.

Vanberg, Viktor (1994): Cultural Evolution, Collective Learning, And Constitutional Design; in: David Reisman (Ed.): *Economic Thought and Political Theory*; Boston, Dordrecht, London: Kluwer.

Witt, Ulrich (1996): A 'Darwinian Revolution' in Economics?; *Journal of Institutional and Theoretical Economics*, 152, 707-715.

Legal Design and the Evolution of Remorse[1]

Steffen Huck

1 Introduction

Comparative institutional analysis is a building block of law and economics. To compare different legal rules one analyses how incentives are affected by these rules and how subsequent individual behavior is affected by the induced incentives. Building on the rational actor paradigm, analyses of this kind typically require stable, i.e. exogeneously given preferences. This may cause a fallacy since all behavior can be rationalized by assuming appropriate preferences. However, for a long time economists refused to deal with endogenous preferences arguing that the question where preferences come from should be answered by scholars from other disciplines. Early exceptions are papers by Becker (1976) and Hirshleifer (1977) who argue that preferences are shaped in an evolutionary process. More than a decade later Güth and Yaari (1992) developed a tool to study systematically the evolution of preferences, the *indirect evolutionary approach* which meanwhile has been successfully applied to quite a number of questions[2]. The indirect evolutionary approach is based on two analytical stages: At the first stage individual behavior is determined for given preferences. At the second stage preferences are subjected to an evolutionary process - the material payoff (or, as biologists put it, the *fitness*) being derived via the solution of stage one. The line of reasoning can be illustrated in the following (biological) way: Individuals are endowed with preferences. Given any situation (say a market or a game) preferences determine behavior and thereby an allocation of goods. Consumption of goods yields not only happiness (or utility) but also fitness, i.e. it determines the expected number of offspring. If the offspring inherits the preferences of the parents those preferences will spread which made individuals successful in terms of material payoffs.

---

[1] I have to thank Sebastian Keim and Michael Knörzer for their efforts in conducting the experiment. Financial support of the Deutsche Forschungsgemeinschaft (DFG) is gratefully acknowledged.

[2] See e.g. Ockenfels (1993) who studies the evolution of cooperativeness in a prisoner's dilemma context, Güth and Kliemt (1994) who also adress the evolution of remorse, Bester and Güth (1998) who deal with the evolution of altruism in a market setting, or Huck and Oechssler (1995) who study the evolution of vengefulness to explain behaviour in ultimatum games.

Given this mechanism it is easy to see how it relates to the field of law and economics or, to be more precise, to comparative institutional analysis. Changing institutions means changing the situation in which individuals interact. But such changes not only induce different incentives and behavior but possibly also different preferences whose evolution is linked to behavior.

In an earlier paper (Huck 1996) I illustrated this kind of analysis in a rather simple framework. The present paper presents an extended and more elaborate version of the same model. In this model there is large population in which individuals are pairwisely matched to engage in some kind of principle-agent game. The two individuals are assumed to have performed some joint activity which stochastically yields a certain amount of a consumable resource. However, only one individual sees whether the activity has been successful or not, and in case of success he has the opportunity to betray his partner by telling him the efforts failed. The second individual can check the first one whenever he hears that there was no success, but this is costly and if the first individual is guilty he will only be convicted with a certain probability. In case of conviction the resource is split equally and the first individual has to pay a legal fine.

The model considers three kinds of variables: a) variables defining the value of resources and the probability of success; b) variables reflecting legal institutions, such as private costs of monitoring (or trials), effectiveness of monitoring, and punishment in case of conviction; c) psychological variables reflecting remorse in case of betrayal and in case of unjustified distrust.

In Huck (1996) I analyzed the case in which the first individual may feel remorse in case of betrayal and studied the evolution of this remorse parameter. It showed that when remorse is assumed as endogenous legal design can be more effective in yielding socially desirable states. In particular I showed that punishments which are - in order to achieve a desirable state - required to be *very* large in case of fixed and low remorse can be much smaller when feelings of remorse evolve. In the paper at hand I add another kind of remorse to the model: Also the second individual may feel remorse, namely whenever he checks his partner but does not convict him. Interestingly, such feelings of guilt in case of unjustified distrust can only be evolutionarily stable when monitoring mechanisms are more or less inefficient. Often conviction rates serve as a measure for the efficiency of a legal system. But when the private costs of accessing the legal system are high, good conviction rates may lead to misjudgments since only a small fraction of illegal activities may come to court. In this case the presence of remorse in case of unjustified distrust can be seen as an indicator for an inefficient legal system because such inefficiency is necessary for the evolutionary stability of non-negligible remorse of this type.

A further extension concerns the fitness function. Whereas in the earlier paper fitness is assumed to depend linearly on consumption here I allow for decreasing marginal fitness of consumption. Finally, I also show how the theoretical predictions can be validated by laboratory experiments, and add some data which partly corroborates the theory.

The remainder of the paper is organized as follows: Section 2 carries out the first stage of the indirect approach by solving the (principle-agent) game for all possible constellations of given preferences. Then Section 3 carries out the analysis of the second stage. An evolutionary game is defined and analyzed to study the evolution of both remorse parameters. I will rely on sets of neutrally evolutionarily stable strategies but will also introduce a refinement of this concept which has the property that it contains the *long run survivors* under a fairly general class of dynamics. Section 4 concludes, and Appendix A contains the proofs, while Appendix B presents the experimental part of this study.

2 The interaction model

The extensive form of the basic game is shown in Figure 1. As pointed out in the introduction it is the same game as in Huck (1996) with the only difference that there is an additional remorse parameter for the second mover.

Payoffs reflect nature (w,z), legal institutions (p,c,s) and psychological effects (δ,τ). Whereas all kinds of variables determine utility, fitness is only determined by the former two. To solve the basic game by standard game theory one needs, of course, only utilities[3].

The game can also be described as a stage game.

Stage 1 A chance move determines the actual outcome of joint efforts. The probability of success w with $1 > w > 0$ is commonly known.

Stage 2 In case of success player M (who is the only one who can observe the result of the chance move) decides whether to be honest (move H) or to lie (move L). The choice of H ends the game, and the surplus of 2 is equally split as due to a cooperation contract. In case of failure player M always reveals the truth. (M does not have the opportunity to tell N that the outcome of the chance move was positive, since he simply does not have any resource he can split.)

---

[3] In principle, the utility functions are assumed to be additively separable, such that utility is the sum of fitness and psychological effects. The additively separable utility functions can be written as $\psi = \alpha F + \beta P$ where F denotes fitness and P the purely psychological benefits (or costs). Since one can normalise α to 1 and express $\frac{\beta}{\alpha} P$ by $\tilde{P}$ by we can rewrite the utility function without loss of generality as $\overline{\Psi} = F + \tilde{P}$ where $F = f(x) - \lambda_c c - \lambda_s s$ and $\tilde{P} = -\lambda_\delta \delta - \lambda_\tau \tau$ and where x are consumed resources, $f(x)$ is a concave function of consumption, c denotes monitoring costs, δ and τ are psychological costs and $\lambda_i \in \{0,1\}$ with $i \in \{c,s,\delta,\tau\}$. Since x is either 2, 1 or zero we equate $f(0) = 0, f(1) = 1$, and $f(2) = z$ with $1 < z \leq 2$.

Stage 3 Being informed about the failure of the efforts and the zero-surplus (but not knowing whether this is due to a real failure or to M's move L), player N decides if he wants to check his partner (move K) or not (move $\overline{K}$). The choice $\overline{K}$ ends the game. In case of real failure both parties gain zero-payoffs. If M has been cheating, he gains $z-\tau$ with $1 < z \leq 2$ and $0 \leq \tau \leq 1$. The parameter z reflects that the utility gained by receiving the whole surplus might be - due to decreasing marginal utility of consumption and fitness - less than 2, whereas the parameter τ reflects his remorse for betraying N, who receives nothing. The game ends when N chooses K and the efforts had initially failed.

Figure 1: The basic game in its extensive form.

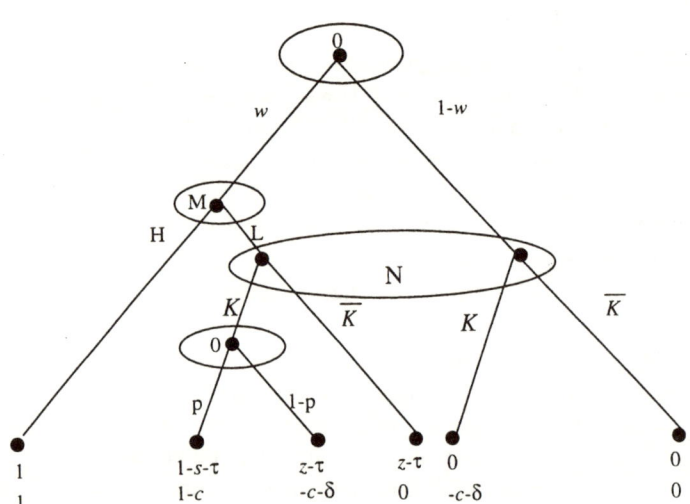

In this case M receives nothing whereas N has to bear the costs of control c and psychological costs δ with $0 \leq c, \delta \leq 1$. The latter can be interpreted as remorse for distrusting M without reason. Thus, N earns in terms of utility $-c-\delta$.

Stage 4 The last stage will only be reached if N checks M after a lie (move L): Then a chance move determines whether monitoring is effective (probability p) or not ($1-p$) with $1 > p > 0$. If not, M receives $z-\tau$, whereas N again receives the negative payoff $-c-\delta$. If monitoring reveals that M has lied, they share the surplus, but M has to pay a legal penalty $s \geq 0$.[4] Thus, his payoff is $1-s-\tau$, whereas N receives $1-c$.

Note that the game is not a signaling game since neither M reports success after a failure nor N checks after reported success. In order to derive the solution of the

---

[4] This interpretation implies the presence of penal law. Another possible interpretation of s is that M suffers a reputation loss after being convicted as someone who betrayed his partner.

basic game I assume that a player always eliminates a (weakly) dominated strategy whenever there is one. Furthermore I assume that the rules of the basic game are always common knowledge, what especially implies that the (δ,τ)-combinations of the two individuals playing the basic game are commonly known.[5] Depending on the psychological variables δ and τ (which are to be endogenously explained by the indirect evolutionary approach), the basic game has four different equilibria in undominated strategies.

1) **'Treason and desperation'**: $\left[\delta \geq \frac{wp-c}{1-wp}\right] \wedge [\tau < z-1]$: In this situation M always tries to hide the successful outcome, and N always does not check. The equilibrium is $\Pi_1 = (L, \overline{K})$.

2) **'Treason and trials'**: $\left[\delta < \frac{wp-c}{1-wp}\right] \wedge [\tau \leq (z-1)(1-p) - ps]$: In this case M betrays, but N checks. The equilibrium is $\Pi_2 = (L, K)$.

3) **'Trust'**: $\tau \geq z-1$: If this condition is satisfied, M always tells the truth, and N does not check. The equilibrium is $\Pi_3 = (H, \overline{K})$.

4) **'Trust, treason and trials'**: $[(z-1)(1-p) - ps < \tau < z-1] \wedge \left[\delta < \frac{wp-c}{1-wp}\right]$: In this last parameter constellation both players, M and N, play mixed strategies. The equilibrium is $\Pi_4 = (r^*(H), q^*(K))$ with $r^* = \frac{wp(1+\delta)-c-\delta}{wp(1+\delta)-w(c+\delta)}$ denoting the probability of strategy H, and $q^* = \frac{z-1-\tau}{p(z-1+s)}$ denoting the probability of K.

It is interesting to note that in case of $wp<c$ player N will not use K regardless of the actual values of δ and τ. The costs of control c are prohibitive, and whether the individuals are in a world of mutual trust (Π_1) or in the desperate world where crime is usual (Π_3), depends only on the value of z-τ, which is the incentive for cheating.

3 The evolution of remorse

The analysis in this section is carried out by means of static evolutionary solution concepts which will be explained below. Their nature, however, is that they describe stable outcomes of large classes of dynamics. I will also refer to this below. An essential difference to Huck (1996) is that the type space is now two-dimensional; an individual is assumed to be characterized by both, a δ- and a τ-

---

[5] For a detailed justification of this assumption see Huck (1996) and Ellingsen (1997).

value. This leads to a more complicated analysis and requires the introduction of a new evolutionary refinement concept.

The underlying assumptions of the analysis are the following:

- There is a large population of individuals who are (repeatedly) randomly matched.
- Each individual is endowed with a certain (δ, τ)-combination.

When being matched an individual becomes player M, or player N respectively, with probability 1/2.

- When two individuals have played the game according to one of the four equilibria they receive resources determining their reproductive success. In other words: When two (δ, τ)-combinations are matched each gains a payoff in the evolutionary game which equals the amount of resources (fitness) gained in the basic game.[6]

Table 1: Reproductive success of players M and N according to the four equilibria.

Φ_r^h	role r	
equilibrium h	M	N
Π_1	wz	0
Π_2	Q	wp − c
Π_3	w	w
Π_4	X	Y

- The psychological variables δ and τ are purely motivational and determine only *pleasure*.[7] They do not have any direct effect on the amount of resources which can be consumed and analogously on the fitness that is received.[8]

Table 1 displays the fitness Φ_r^h which is gained by an individual when playing one of the four equilibria (h) in one of the two roles $r \in \{M,N\}$.[9]

---

[6] Since the population is assumed to be large the payoff a certain (δ, τ)-combination receives against another (δ, τ)-combination can be measured by expected values.

[7] Interestingly, this term which has been so crucial for early utilitarians (Bentham 1817) is also used by modern biologists (Kummer 1992) who are used to distinguish between *pleasure* - measurable only in terms of utility, or *utils* as Edgeworth 1881 suggested - and *fitness*.

[8] For a discussion of this assumption see also Huck (1996).

[9] Deriving the reproductive success is particularly easy when the matched individuals play one of the first three equilibria. One just takes the equilibrium payoffs and sets δ and τ equal to zero. It is a bit more complicated in case of equilibrium Π_4, where

The variables Q, X, and Y are defined as follows:

$$Q = wp(1-s-z) + wz \tag{1}$$

$$X = X(\delta, \tau) = w + (1-w)\frac{\tau(c+\delta)}{p(1+\delta)-c-\delta} \tag{2}$$

$$Y = Y(\delta, \tau) = w + (1-w)\frac{c\delta(1+\tau-z)-c(z-1+s)-\delta(\tau+s)}{(z-1+s)(p(1+\delta)-c-\delta)} \tag{3}$$

where δ belongs to player N and τ belongs to player M.

Table 2 displays which equilibria of the basic game will be played when two particular (δ, τ)-combinations are matched.[10] Typically, the equilibria depend on who is M and who N.

Table 2: Equilibria (k,l) which are achieved if players with specific (δ, τ)-combinations are matched, where k indicates the equilibrium played when player i is M in the basic game.

equilibria	player j					
player i	$\mathcal{A}$	$\mathcal{B}$	$\mathcal{C}$	$\mathcal{D}$	$\mathcal{E}$	$\mathcal{J}$
$\mathcal{A}$	(2,2)	(1,2)	(2,4)	(1,4)	(2,3)	(1,3)
$\mathcal{B}$	(2,1)	(1,1)	(2,1)	(1,1)	(2,3)	(1,3)
$\mathcal{C}$	(4,2)	(1,2)	(4,4)	(1,4)	(4,3)	(1,3)
$\mathcal{D}$	(4,1)	(1,1)	(4,1)	(1,1)	(4,3)	(1,3)
$\mathcal{E}$	(3,2)	(3,2)	(3,4)	(3,4)	(3,3)	(3,3)
$\mathcal{J}$	(3,1)	(3,1)	(3,1)	(3,1)	(3,3)	(3,3)

With these preliminaries the evolutionary game can be defined as a symmetric 2-player game, where the strategy set of each player, $S = [0,1]^2$, consists of two-dimensional strategies (δ, τ).[11] However, for technical reasons I have to rely on a small grid in a special case (Proposition 3), i.e. on a discrete approximation of $S = [0,1]^2$. The actual payoff (fitness) Ω_i of a player i adopting some (δ_i, τ_i) as his strategy in the evolutionary game against another player adopting some other combination (δ_j, τ_j) is a function of both (δ, τ)-combinations and results by computing

---

one has to set δ and τ equal to zero only in the payoffs according to Table 1 but, of course, not in the probabilities r^* and q^*.

[10] To read the table properly you have to wait until a certain division of the (δ, τ)-space is introduced.

[11] In principle it would be easy to relax this assumption of boundedness and to allow $\mathbf{R}_+^2$ to be the strategy set of the evolutionary game. However, this would not add anything to the results.

$$\Omega_i[(\delta_i,\tau_i),(\delta_j,\tau_j)] = (\Phi_M^k + \Phi_N^l)/2 \tag{4}$$

and

$$\Omega_j[(\delta_j,\tau_j),(\delta_i,\tau_i)] = (\Phi_M^l + \Phi_N^k)/2 \tag{5}$$

where $k \in \{1,2,3,4\}$ is the equilibrium that is achieved when player i of the evolutionary game is M in the basic game, and $l \in \{1,2,3,4\}$ is the equilibrium achieved when player j of the evolutionary game is M in the basic game.

Table 3: Representation of the evolutionary game.[a]

EG	player j (d_j, t_j)					
player i (d_i, t_i)	$\mathcal{A}$	$\mathcal{B}$	$\mathcal{C}$	$\mathcal{D}$	$\mathcal{E}$	$\mathcal{J}$
$\mathcal{A}$	$\dfrac{Q+wp-c}{2}$	$\dfrac{wz+wp-c}{2}$	$\dfrac{Y+Q}{2}$	$\dfrac{Y+wz}{2}$	$\dfrac{Q+w}{2}$	$\dfrac{w+wz}{2}$
$\mathcal{B}$	$\dfrac{Q}{2}$	$\dfrac{wz}{2}$	$\dfrac{Q}{2}$	$\dfrac{wz}{2}$	$\dfrac{Q+w}{2}$	$\dfrac{w+wz}{2}$
$\mathcal{C}$	$\dfrac{X+wp-c}{2}$	$\dfrac{wz+wp-c}{2}$	$\dfrac{X+Y}{2}$	$\dfrac{Y+wz}{2}$	$\dfrac{X+w}{2}$	$\dfrac{w+wz}{2}$
$\mathcal{D}$	$\dfrac{X}{2}$	$\dfrac{wz}{2}$	$\dfrac{X}{2}$	$\dfrac{wz}{2}$	$\dfrac{X+w}{2}$	$\dfrac{w+wz}{2}$
$\mathcal{E}$	$\dfrac{w+wp-c}{2}$	$\dfrac{w+wp-c}{2}$	$\dfrac{Y+w}{2}$	$\dfrac{Y+w}{2}$	w	w
$\mathcal{J}$	$\dfrac{w}{2}$	$\dfrac{w}{2}$	$\dfrac{w}{2}$	$\dfrac{w}{2}$	w	w

a) Note that $Y = Y(\delta_i, \tau_j)$ and $X = X(\delta_j, \tau_i)$

Table 3 shows these payoffs of the players in the evolutionary game. Since game and payoffs are symmetric I only indicate the payoffs of player 1.

Tables 2 and 3 rely on the definition of six subsets of the type set $S = [0,1]^2$. These subsets of S are defined as follows:

$\mathcal{A} = [0,\bar{\delta}) \times [0,\bar{\tau}]$ with $\bar{\delta} = \max\left\{\dfrac{wp-c}{1-wp}, 0\right\}$ and $\bar{\tau} = \max\{(z-1)(1-p) - ps, 0\}$

$\mathcal{B} = [\bar{\delta},1] \times [0,\bar{\tau}]$

$\mathcal{C} = [0,\bar{\delta}) \times (\bar{\tau}, \bar{\bar{\tau}})$ with $\bar{\bar{\tau}} = z - 1$

$\mathcal{D} = [\bar{\delta},1] \times (\bar{\tau}, \bar{\bar{\tau}})$

$\mathcal{E} = [0,\bar{\delta}) \times [\bar{\bar{\tau}},1]$

$\mathcal{J} = [\bar{\delta},1] \times [\bar{\bar{\tau}},1]$

Since all strategies of the subsets $\mathcal{A}, \mathcal{B}, \mathcal{C}, \mathcal{D}, \mathcal{E}$ and $\mathcal{F}$ receive the same fitness when being matched against another strategy belonging to the same subset, the (symmetric) evolutionary game may have no strict equilibria.[12]

Analogously, there may be no evolutionarily stable strategy (ESS, see Maynard Smith and Price 1973).[13] Therefore, I have to rely on a weaker criteria. A natural coarsening of evolutionarily stable strategies is that of neutrally evolutionarily stable strategies (NESS) suggested by Maynard Smith (1982). With our notation a strategy (δ_i, τ_i) is neutrally stable if and only if the following two conditions are fulfilled:

$$\Omega_i[(\delta_i,\tau_i),(\delta_i,\tau_i)] \geq \Omega_j[(\delta_j,\tau_j),(\delta_i,\tau_i)] \text{ for all } j \tag{6}$$

$$\Omega_i[(\delta_i,\tau_i),(\delta_i,\tau_i)] \geq \Omega_j[(\delta_j,\tau_j),(\delta_i,\tau_i)] \Rightarrow$$
$$\Omega_i[(\delta_i,\tau_i),(\delta_j,\tau_j)] \geq \Omega_j[(\delta_j,\tau_j),(\delta_j,\tau_j)] \text{ for all } j \tag{7}$$

This means that (δ_i, τ_i) has to be a Nash equilibrium of the evolutionary game. Furthermore, (δ_i, τ_i) must earn against an alternative best reply at least the same as the alternative best reply against itself. Generally, one can expand the concept of evolutionary stability by regarding also the mixed strategy space. To simplify matters I will focus on pure strategies and will use sets of neutrally stable strategies S^{NESS} as the appropriate solution concept.

However, there is some criticism against the concept of neutral stability: Suppose there is a NESS which is not an ESS. Then, there exists at least one other strategy which could enter into the neutrally stable population. Suppose further there is some drift in the new population such that the proportion of the intruding strategy grows. If now another mutant enters the population which fares better against the first intruding strategy than all other types in the population this new type will rapidly spread and the whole population will change.

To avoid this problem one can refine the concept of S^{NESS} by imposing two additional restrictions. First, one can restrict the set of solution candidates to sets of NESSs which are closed under best replies. Second, one can require that all strategies contained in this set are strategically equivalent in the game defined by this set of strategies. A set $S^* \subseteq S^{NESS}$ which meets these conditions will be called a *strongly stable set* (SSS).[14] Formally, the first requirement can be expressed by

$$\beta(\delta_i, \tau_i) \subseteq S^* \subseteq S^{NESS} \text{ for all } (\delta_i, \tau_i) \in S^* \tag{8}$$

---

[12] Table 3 reveals this feature clearly. Suppose any strategy outside $\mathcal{C}$ was an equilibrium strategy, then all strategies within the same subset would be alternative best replies. Hence, the equilibrium could not be strict. Note that this argument does not apply for potential equilibrium strategies within subset $\mathcal{C}$, since the payoff two $\mathcal{C}$-strategies receive depend on their particular δ- and τ-values determining X and Y.

[13] This follows directly from the argument in the preceding footnote.

[14] Note that if the SSS is a singleton it is a strict equilibrium.

with $\beta(\delta_i,\tau_i)$ denoting the set of alternative best replies against the pure strategy (δ_i,τ_i) and S^{NESS} denoting the set of all neutrally stable strategies. Obviously, this implies the following condition

$$\Omega_i[(\delta_i,\tau_i),(\delta_i,\tau_i)] > \Omega_k[(\delta_k,\tau_k),(\delta_i,\tau_i)] \text{ for all } (\delta_i,\tau_i) \in S^* \text{ and for all } (\delta_k,\tau_k) \notin S^*$$
(9)

The second requirement means formally

$$\Omega_i[(\delta_i,\tau_i),(\delta_k,\tau_k)] = \Omega_j[(\delta_j,\tau_j),(\delta_k,\tau_k)] \text{ for all } (\delta_i,\tau_i),(\delta_j,\tau_j),(\delta_k,\tau_k) \in S^* \quad (10)$$

This condition has two nice properties: First, it ensures that S^* is closed under weakly better replies in the sense of Ritzberger and Weibull (1995) and Weibull (1995) and contains no proper subset which is closed under weakly better replies. But this ensures - as Weibull shows - that the strategies contained in S^* are *long run survivors* of a large class of dynamic systems containing the replicator dynamics as a special case, or that S^* is asymptotically stable under these dynamics and contains no asymptotically stable subset. Second, it ensures that there is no selection pressure within S^*, what means that any given probability distribution over the set is stable as long as the set is not exposed to mutations.[15] Hence, *strong stability* in the sense of (8) and (10) is stronger than asymptotic stability.

Figure 2: Evolutionarily stable sets of preferences depending on monitoring costs and incentives for betraying.

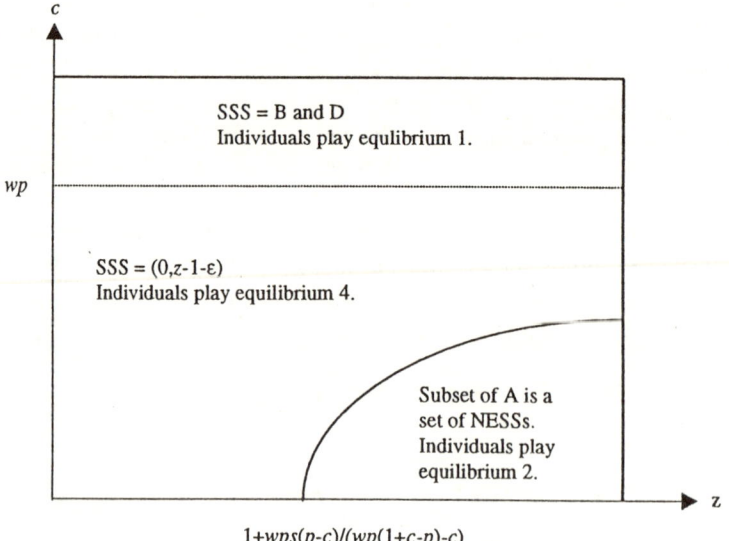

---

[15] Requiring stability within the set in the presence of mutations would lead to a notion of stability similar to Selten's (1983 and 1988) concept of limit evolutionary stability.

Altogether, a SSS can be viewed as a set-wise generalization of strict Nash equilibria in symmetric games.[16] Therefore, it is not very surprising that one can generally not expect existence of a SSS.[17] In the game at hand I always can prove existence of a set of neutrally stable strategies - in two cases the S^{NESS} is also a SSS, once a singleton.

The results of the formal analysis (which is in its main parts relegated to Appendix A) show that the stability of the preference parameters δ and τ crucially depends on the exogenous parameters of which p (effectiveness of trials), c (private cost of trials), and s (penalty in case of conviction) can be influenced by legislators. One can phrase the results in a way in which the relation of monitoring costs and betraying incentives decides about what is evolutionarily stable and what is not (see also Figure 2). The following three propositions, which are proved in Appendix A, summarize the results.

High monitoring costs

Proposition 1 *In case of high monitoring costs $c \geq wp$ there is a unique strongly stable set $S^* = \mathcal{B} \cup \mathcal{D}$.*

In case of prohibitive monitoring costs all mutants of the subset $\mathcal{B} \cup \mathcal{D}$ are neutrally evolutionarily stable and constitute a SSS. The $\mathcal{B}$ and $\mathcal{D}$ types always play equilibrium Π_1, where M lies and N does not check. The value of τ (remorse in case of betraying) has to be smaller than $\bar{\bar{\tau}}$, the value of δ (remorse in case of unjustified distrust) has to be greater than $\bar{\delta}$ (what is always fulfilled). This means that in a world without useful monitoring mechanisms types who feel great remorse in case of betraying ($\tau > z-1$) cannot survive. All other types who have at least a small cheating incentive and refrain from checking their partner will lie and survive, although there is - due to decreasing marginal utility (and fitness) of consumption ($1 < z \leq 2$) - an efficiency loss compared to the world of mutual trust (Π_3).

From a political point of view, this situation cannot be desirable. However, without much knowledge about private interaction this situation might be difficult to detect since in equilibrium Π_1 trials do not take place. One way of identifying such a situation would, of course, be to ask N-players about their beliefs concerning the behavior of M-players. But in the light of this analysis another (and probably more elegant way) could be to elicit values of δ in order to find out whether a society is in this state. If substantial remorse in case of unjustified distrust is common this may serve as an indicator for an inefficient system. And by design-

---

[16] SSS share this property with primitive formations (Harsanyi and Selten 1988), curb sets (Basu and Weibull 1991) and others. An overview of these concepts can be found in Hurkens (1994).

[17] Note that - in contrast to Harsanyi and Selten's (1988) notion of (primitive) formations - the game itself is not trivially a SSS.

Low monitoring costs and high betraying incentives

Proposition 2 *In case of* $z \geq 1 + wps\dfrac{p-c}{wp(1+c-p)-c}$ *there is a unique set of neutrally stable strategies* $S^{NESS} = \mathcal{A} \subset \mathcal{A}$ *which is not a SSS.*

Lemma 13 (see Appendix) shows that high betraying incentives in the sense of $z \geq 1 + wps\dfrac{p-c}{wp(1+c-p)-c}$ imply low monitoring costs in so far as $c < wp\dfrac{1-p}{1-wp}(< wp)$ has to be fulfilled. The proposition shows that at low monitoring costs and high betraying incentives evolution will generate preferences with low δ- and τ-values. Nobody who feels substantial remorse in any of the two situations is able to survive. Everybody with large scruples in case of betraying or distrusting ($\delta \geq \bar{\delta} \vee \tau > \bar{\tau}$) will be exploited by types belonging to the subset of $\mathcal{A}$. Within the stable population equilibrium Π_2 is always played: M betrays, and N checks. Thus, the only difference to the above case of high (i.e., prohibitive) monitoring costs is that now trials take place, which is bad news for those hoping for or believing in a kind world of trust and efficiency. Note, however, that for $p > \dfrac{1}{1+s}$ betraying incentives cannot be 'high' in the sense of Proposition 2.[18] This implies that legislators can always rule out that evolution yields this kind of 'bad' preferences by making trials (or monitoring mechanisms) sufficiently effective (for given penalties) or by imposing sufficiently high penalties $s > \dfrac{1-p}{p}$ (for given efficiency of trials).

Low monitoring costs and low betraying incentives

Proposition 3 *In case of* $c < wp$ *and* $z < 1 + wps\dfrac{p-c}{wp(1+c-p)-c}$ *there is a singleton SSS* $S^* = (0, z-1-\varepsilon)$ *with ε being the smallest interval of a finite grid.*

In case of low monitoring costs and low betraying incentives the evolutionary game has a unique strict equilibrium where individuals do not feel any remorse in case of unjustified distrust but substantial remorse in case of betraying. Interestingly, types who do feel some remorse in case of unjustified distrust will die out since they will - by checking their partners when in the role of N - incur too high costs. This leads the individuals to play the mixed equilibrium

---

[18] Note that $wps\dfrac{p-c}{wp(1+c-p)-c} > \dfrac{ps}{1-p}$. Hence, $p > \dfrac{1}{1+s}$ is sufficient but not necessary for low cheating incentives in the sense of the proposition.

$\Pi_4 = (r^*(H), q^*(K))$ in the basic game with $r^* = \dfrac{wp-c}{wp-wc}$ and $q^* = \dfrac{\varepsilon}{p(z-1+s)}$.
Basically, this implies that anything can happen, but monitoring is extremely seldom. This has been the main result of Huck (1996)]. In general, the probability of monitoring in the mixed equilibrium is $\dfrac{z-1-\tau}{p(z-1+s)}$ which shows that with very large s legislators always have the opportunity to make it very small. Proposition 3 (which can be seen as a generalization of Lemma 3 of Huck 1996) shows that in case of endogenous remorse finite punishments are sufficient to reach such a political aim. In case of really low monitoring costs $c<<wp$, the probability of honesty is also rather high. For $c \to 0$, the probability even approaches 1. This shows that legislators can provide institutional settings where preferences yielding 'nice' behavior do evolve. For very low values of c one would almost always observe behavior as in a world of mutual trust. Accordingly, efficiency can be nearly optimal. Of course, such low monitoring costs may be unachievable. However, to rule out 'bad' preferences according to Propositions 1 and 2, it would be sufficient to provide an efficient monitoring mechanism (efficient trials) with $p > \max\left\{\dfrac{c}{w}, \dfrac{1}{1+s}\right\}$.

When compared with the earlier study, where remorse in case of unjustified distrust and the case of $c > wp$ were not addressed, Proposition 2 is probably most interesting. As can be easily seen in Figure 2 it implies some kind of non-monotonic effects of the monitoring costs c on behavior when z is comparatively high. As long as $c > wp$ types of $\mathcal{B} \cup \mathcal{D}$ will be stable and individuals will play equilibrium Π_1 where crime is usual and nobody ever checks. Then follows a range of c-values in which the mixed equilibrium (Π_4) is played: Monitoring will be extremely seldom, and the probability of betrayal is decreasing in c. Finally, when c becomes smaller than some critical value set $\mathcal{A}'$ will be stable and the probabilities of crime and monitoring jump to 1 (equilibrium Π_2).

4 Final remarks

The previous section has shown that legal institutions may have a substantial impact on preferences of individuals. In particular the study shows a) that the results concerning remorse in case of betrayal which have been obtained in Huck (1996) are robust in a larger setting which also allows for another kind of remorse and for decreasing marginal fitness of consumption; b) that therefore legislation might indeed be more effective when one considers the indirect effects of legal rules on behavior via changes of preferences; c) that substantial remorse in case of unjustified distrust might be an indicator for an inefficient legal system; d) that when betraying incentives are high private monitoring costs have a non-monotonic impact on behavior.

With respect to the general purpose of this paper points b) and d) are probably most important, since it is in them that the indirect evolutionary analysis differs from the usual comparative institutional analysis with fixed preferences. With fixed preferences the influence of the monitoring costs would, of course, not be non-monotonic which can be easily seen in Section 2, and for some cases punishments would have to be infinite to induce nice behavior. Thus, this more elaborate model puts further emphasize on the theoretical and practical relevance of studying how institutions may shape preferences.

The experimental results presented in Appendix B suggest that the theoretical considerations can be empirically validated. Interestingly, they point out to a real world which deselected types feeling remorse in case of unjustified distrust but enabled the survival of remorse in case of betraying. This may indicate that the institutional design of, say, the country in which the subjects grew up, is a rather efficient one.

References

Basu, K. and J.W. Weibull (1991): Strategy subsets closed under rational behavior; *Economics Letters*, 36, 141-146.

Becker, G.S. (1976): Altruism, egoism, and genetic fitness: Economics and sociobiology; *Journal of Economic Literature*, 14, 817-826.

Bentham, J. (1817): *A table of the springs of actions*; London.

Bester, H. and W. Güth (1998): Is altruism evolutionarily stable; *Journal of Economic Behavior and Organization*, 34, 193-209.

Edgeworth, F.Y. (1881): *Mathematical Psychics*, London.

Ellingsen, T. (1997): The evolution of bargaining behavior; *Quarterly Journal of Economics*, 112, 581-602.

Güth, W. and H. Kliemt (1994): Competition or co-operation; *Metroeconomica*, 45, 155-187.

Güth, W. and M. Yaari (1992): An evolutionary approach to explain reciprocal behavior in a simple strategic game; in: U. Witt (ed.), *Explaining Process and Change - Approaches to Evolutionary Economics*, Ann Arbor 1992: University of Michigan Press, 23-34.

Harsanyi, J. and R. Selten (1988): *A general theory of equilibrium selection in games*, Cambridge/Mass.: M.I.T. Press.

Hirshleifer, J. (1977): Economics from a biological viewpoint; *Journal of Law and Economics*, 20, 1-52.

Huck, S. (1996): Trust, treason, and trials: An example of how the evolution of preferences can be driven by legal institutions; *Working Paper*, Humboldt-University.

Huck, S. and J. Oechssler (1995): The indirect evolutionary approach to explaining fair allocations; *Working Paper*, Humboldt-University.

Hurkens, S. (1994): Learning by forgetful players: From primitive formations to persistent retracts; *Center Discussion Paper*, No. 9437.

Kummer, H. (1992): *Weiße Affen am roten Meer*, München.

Maynard Smith (1982): *Evolution and the Theory of Games*, Cambridge.

Maynard Smith , J. and G.R. Price (1973): The logic of animal conflict; *Nature*, 246, 15-18.

Ockenfels, P. (1993): Cooperation in prisoners' dilemma; *European Journal of Political Economy*, 9, 567-579.

Ritzenberger, K. and J.W. Weibull (1995): Evolutionary selection in normal-form games; *Econometrica*, 63, 1371-1400.

Selten, R. (1983): Evolutionary stability in extensive two-person games; *Mathematical Social Sciences*, 5, 269-363.

Selten, R. (1988): Evolutionary stability in extensive two-person games: Corrections and further development; *Mathematical Social Sciences*, 16, 223-266.

Weibull, J.W. (1995): *Evolutionary game theory*, Cambridge/Mass.: M.I.T. Press.

Appendix

A. Proofs

To prove the three propositions I start by proving some lemmas from which the propositions, then, follow immediately.

Lemma 4 *If there is a set $\mathcal{H} \subset S$ with (a) $\Omega_i[(\delta_i,\tau_i),(\delta_i,\tau_i)] > \Omega_k[(\delta_k,\tau_k),(\delta_i,\tau_i)]$ and (b) $\Omega_i[(\delta_i,\tau_i),(\delta_j,\tau_j)] = \Omega_j[(\delta_j,\tau_j),(\delta_i,\tau_i)]$ for all $(\delta_i,\tau_i),(\delta_j,\tau_j) \in \mathcal{H}$ and $(\delta_k,\tau_k) \notin \mathcal{H}$ then $\mathcal{H}$ is strictly stable.*

Proof Inequality (a) implies that there is no best reply against any $(\delta_i,\tau_i) \in \mathcal{H}$ outside $\mathcal{H}$, together with (b) this means that any $(\delta_i,\tau_i) \in \mathcal{H}$ is a Nash equilibrium of the evolutionary game. Furthermore (b) ensures that also the second condition for a neutrally stable type (7) is fulfilled. Hence, $\mathcal{H} \subseteq S^{NESS}$.

Lemma 5 *For all subsets $S \subset S$ with $S \neq \mathcal{C}$ either all types $(\delta,\tau) \in S$ or none belong to a strictly stable set.*

Proof Any two $(\delta_i,\tau_i),(\delta_j,\tau_j) \in S$ with $S \neq \mathcal{C}$ earn the same payoff in the evolutionary game when matched against each other. Accordingly, (δ_j,τ_j) is against (δ_i,τ_i) as good as (δ_i,τ_i) against itself. Thus, if $(\delta_i,\tau_i) \in S^*$ follows $(\delta_j,\tau_j) \in \beta(\delta_i,\tau_i)$ and – due to property (8) - $(\delta_j,\tau_j) \in S^*$.

Lemma 6 *No type $(\delta_i,\tau_i) \in \mathcal{E} \cup \mathcal{J}$ is element of a S^{NESS}.*

Proof Since $z > 1$, all $(\delta_k,\tau_k) \in S \setminus \mathcal{E} \cup \mathcal{J}$ fare better against a $(\delta_i,\tau_i) \in \mathcal{J}$ than an $(\delta_i,\tau_i) \in \mathcal{J}$ against itself. Hence, no $(\delta_i,\tau_i) \in \mathcal{J}$ is a Nash equilibrium of the evolutionary game. Now suppose any $(\delta_j,\tau_j) \in \mathcal{E}$ would be neutrally stable. Then $X(\delta_j,\tau_h) \geq w$ would have to hold. But, since $\delta_j < \frac{wp-c}{1-wp}$ this can never be true. Hence, all $(\ddot{a}_h, \delta_h)$ far better against all $(\delta_j,\tau_j) \in \mathcal{E}$ than these against themselves.

Lemma 7 *In case of $c \geq wp$ the subset $\mathcal{BD}^* = \mathcal{B} \cup \mathcal{D} \in S$ is a SSS.*

Proof For $c \geq wp$ the subset $\mathcal{A} \cup \mathcal{C} \cup \mathcal{E} \in S$ is per definition empty. Furthermore, no $(\delta_k,\tau_k) \in \mathcal{J}$ is a Nash equilibrium of the evolutionary game, since $z > 1$. Additionally, no $(\delta_k,\tau_k) \in \mathcal{J}$ is a best reply against any $(\delta_i,\tau_i) \in \mathcal{BD}^*$; $\Omega_i[(\delta_i,\tau_i),(\delta_j,\tau_j)] = \Omega_j[(\delta_j,\tau_j),(\delta_i,\tau_i)]$ is fulfilled for all $(\delta_i,\tau_i),(\delta_j,\tau_j) \in \mathcal{BD}^*$. According to Lemma 4 $\mathcal{BD}^*$ is then strictly stable.

Lemma 8 *In case of $c < wp$ no type $(\delta_i, \tau_i) \in \mathcal{B} \cup \mathcal{D}$ is element of S^{NESS}.*

Proof Note first that – due to $wp > c$ – any $(\delta_j, \tau_j) \in \mathcal{A}$ would be better off against any $(\delta_i, \tau_i) \in \mathcal{B}$ than $(\delta_i, \tau_i) \in \mathcal{B}$ against itself. Therefore, no $(\delta_i, \tau_i) \in \mathcal{B}$ is then a Nash equilibrium of the evolutionary game. Now, note that $Y(0, \tau_j) = w - \frac{(1-w)c}{p-c} > 0$ for the given assumption. Therefore all types $(0, \tau_k) \in \mathcal{C}$ fare better against all $(\delta_j, \tau_j) \in \mathcal{D}$ than these against themselves.

Lemma 9 *No type $(\delta_i, \tau_i) \in \mathcal{A}$ is element of a strictly stable set.*

Proof To prove this Lemma I show that there is some $(\delta_j, \tau_j) \in \mathcal{C}$ which is better off against some $(\delta_i, \tau_i) \in \mathcal{A}$ than this $(\delta_i, \tau_i) \in \mathcal{A}$ against itself. By Lemma 5 then the claim follows. Both partial derivatives, $\frac{\partial X(\bar{a}_i, \hat{o}_j)}{\partial \bar{a}_i} = \hat{o}_j p \frac{(c-1)(w-1)}{(c+\bar{a}_i - p - p\bar{a}_i)^2}$ and $\frac{\partial X(\delta_i, \tau_j)}{\partial \tau_j} = (1-w)\frac{c+\delta_j}{p(1+\delta_j)-c-\delta_j}$, are for $\delta_i < \bar{\delta}$ always positive. This means that those $\mathcal{C}$-Types with $\tau_j = z - 1 - \varepsilon$ (where $\varepsilon \to 0$) are strongest against any $\mathcal{A}$ Type, while those $\mathcal{A}$-Types with $\delta_i = \frac{wp-c}{1-wp} - \varepsilon$ are weakest against any $\mathcal{C}$-Type. Hence for $\mathcal{A}$ being stable $Q > X(\frac{wp-c}{1-wp}, z-1)$ would have to be fulfilled. But $X(\frac{wp-c}{1-wp}, z-1) = wz > Q$ since $s > 0$ and $z > 1$.

Lemma 10 *In case of $wp\frac{1-p}{1-wp} < c < wp$ or $\left[c < wp\frac{1-p}{1-wp} \text{ and } z < 1 + wps\frac{p-c}{wp(1+c-p)-c}\right]$ the type $(\delta_i, \tau_i) = (0, z-1-\varepsilon)$ with $\varepsilon \to 0$ is a singleton SSS.*

Proof We start by showing that $(\delta_i, \tau_i) = (0, z-1-\varepsilon)$ is the best reply against any $(\delta_j, \tau_j) \in \mathcal{C}$. As shown in the proof of the Lemma 9 the partial derivative $\frac{\partial X(\delta_j, \tau_i)}{\partial \tau_i}$ is always positive for $\delta_j < \bar{\delta}$. Since $p > c$, the partial derivative $\frac{\partial Y(\delta_i, \tau_j)}{\partial \delta_i} = (1-w)\frac{(c-1)(\tau_j(p-c)+c(z-1)+ps)}{(z-1+s)(-p-p\delta_i+c+\delta_i)^2}$ is always negative. Accordingly, a strategy with the highest possible τ-value and the lowest possible δ-value is best reply against any $(\delta_j, \tau_j) \in \mathcal{C}$. The latter is obviously zero. Approximating the continuous strategy space by a finite grid the former is $z-1-\varepsilon$ with $\varepsilon \to 0$. Note that $\lim_{\varepsilon \to 0} X(0, z-1-\varepsilon) = X(0, z-1)$ what can easily be checked. It remains to show that there is no best reply against $(\delta_i, \tau_i) = (0, z-1-\varepsilon)$ outside of $\mathcal{C}$. Taking advantage of the above analysis of the partial derivatives $\frac{\partial X(\delta_j, \tau_i)}{\partial \tau_i}$ and $\frac{\partial Y(\delta_i, \tau_j)}{\partial \delta_i}$ one has to show that (a) $Q < X(0, z-1)$, (b) $Q < X(0, z-1) + Y(0, z-1)$, (c) $Y(0, z-1) > 0$, (d) $w < X(0, z-1)$, and (e) $w < X(0, z-1) + Y(0, z-1)$. For $wp > c$ (c) and (d) follow immediately. Accordingly, (e) follows, and it remains to prove (a). In case of $c > wp\frac{1-p}{1-wp}$ (a) is equivalent with $z > 1 + wps\frac{p-c}{wp(1+c-p)-c}$ what is always fulfilled since $z > 1$. In case of $c < wp\frac{1-p}{1-wp}$ the reserve inequality $z < 1 + wps\frac{p-c}{wp(1+c-p)-c}$ has to hold.

Lemma 11 *In case of* $c \geq wp$ *or* $\left[c < wp\frac{1-p}{1-wp} \text{ and } z > 1 + wps\frac{p-c}{wp(1+c-p)-c}\right]$ *no* $(\delta_i, \tau_i) \in \mathcal{C}$ *is element of a* S^{NESS}.

Proof In case of $c \geq wp$ set $\mathcal{C}$ is by definition empty. The rest follows from the proof of Lemma 10.

Lemma 12 *In case of* $c < wp\frac{1-p}{1-wp}$ *and* $z > 1 + wps\frac{p-c}{wp(1+c-p)-c}$ *a set* $\mathcal{A}' \subset \mathcal{A}$ *is a* S^{NESS}.

Proof From the proof Lemma 9 follows that there are some $(\delta_j, \tau_j) \in \mathcal{A}$ which are not best replies against themselves. Now it is easy to see that for $z > 1 + \frac{ps}{1-p}$ no type of $S \setminus (\mathcal{A} \cup \mathcal{C})$ can be best reply against any $(\delta_i, \tau_i) \in \mathcal{A}$. Since we also know from Lemma 9 that $\mathcal{C}$-Types with $\tau = z - 1 - \varepsilon$ are far better against all $(\delta_i, \tau_i) \in \mathcal{A}$ than all other elements of $\mathcal{C}$, it is clear that if a $(\delta_i, \tau_i) \in \mathcal{A}$ is better off against itself than $(0, z-1-\varepsilon)$ against this (δ_i, τ_i), it will also be better off against itself than any other $\mathcal{C}$-Type against it. Accordingly, only types of $\mathcal{A}$ can be neutrally stable for which $Q > X(\delta_i, z-1)$ is fulfilled. Since $\frac{\partial X}{\partial \delta_i} > 0$ we can simply solve the equation $Q = X(\delta_i, z-1)$ for δ_i. The solution yields then an upper bound δ' for the δ-value of types of set $\mathcal{A}$, $\delta' = \frac{wp(p(z-1+s)+(1-z)(1+c)-sc)+c(z-1)}{(1-z)(1+wp^2-2wp)+wps(1-p)}$. From the proof of Lemma 10 follows that $X(0, z-1) < Q$ holds for the assumed parameters. Hence, $\bar{\delta} > \delta' > 0$. Accordingly, $\mathcal{A} = [0, \delta') \times [0, \bar{\tau}]$ is a S^{NESS}.

Lemma 13 $z > 1 + wps\frac{p-c}{wp(1+c-p)-c} \Rightarrow c < wp\frac{1-p}{1-wp}$.

Proof Define $\tilde{z}(c) = 1 + wps\frac{p-c}{wp(1+c-p)-c}$ and $c^u = wp\frac{1-p}{1-wp}$. Note first that $\tilde{z}(c^u) = \infty$. Then observe that $\frac{d\tilde{z}}{dc} > 0$ for all $c \neq c^u$.

With these Lemmas as preparation the proofs of Propositions 1, 2, and 3 are now very straightforward and, therefore, omitted.

B. Experimental evidence

The experimental data presented in this Appendix has been collected in an experiment conducted in the framework of a seminar about experimental economics at the Goethe-University of Frankfurt/Main. Thus, the participants were all highly experienced subjects familiar with game theory and experimental methods. Here I will only present a small part of the whole data set which is interesting in view of the indirect evolutionary approach.

The participants had to play the basic game twice in order to gain experience with the game and to learn about the population: All choices of the first round were - protecting anonymity - publicly announced.[19] In the repetition the participants did not only have to choose between their two strategies but were also asked to indicate with which probability they expected their opponent to choose one of the two possible strategies and at which critical values $\hat{c}$ and $\hat{s}$ they would change their behavior, i.e. actually M-players had to indicate their critical value $\hat{s}$ while N-players had to indicate their critical $\hat{c}$. Another possibility was to exclude a change of behavior. M had to indicate the expected probability k of N choosing K, N had to indicate his expected probability l of M choosing L.

In case of successful joint efforts the surplus was DM 5 which was either equally split or completely received by a successfully cheating player M (which means that normalizing the experimental payoff parameters yields $z = 2$). The probability of successful joint efforts was $w=0.7$, the probability of successful monitoring $p=0.55$. The experimental (unnormalized) monitoring costs were $c' = $ DM 1, whereas the penalty in case of cheating was $s' = $ DM 2. (The according normalized values are $c = 0.4$ and $s = 0.8$.) Thus, the solution of the basic game (without adding the psychological payoffs) was $\Pi_1 = (L, \overline{K})$.

Using our procedure we can elicit and compute the personal (unnormalized) preference parameters τ^* and δ^* for M, respectively N. Equating the expected payoffs for both choices yields for M:

$$\tau^* = 2.5 - 1.375k - 0.55k\hat{s}$$

and for N:

$$\delta^* = \frac{0.9625l}{0.7l + 0.3} - \hat{c}$$

---

[19] Learning might in this context be a weak substitute for the assumed perfect detection technology which tells a participant which (δ, τ)-combination his opponent has.

In case of stating 'I won't ever change my behavior' one can argue for

Table 4: Decision data and elicited τ^*-values of M-players

subject	Choice	K	$\hat{s}$	τ^*
1	L	0.6	1	1.345
2	L	0.7	2.1	0.729
3	L	1.0	2.05	0
4	L	0.4125	2.5	1.366
5	L	0.75	2.05	0.623
6	L	0.3	3	1.593
7	L	0.825	3	0.004
8	L	0.15	2.05	2.125
9	L	0.35	3	1.441
10	L	0.15	2.5	2.088
11	H	0.6	≤0	≥1.675
12	H	0.15	≤0	≥2.294
13	H	0.1	≤0	≥2.363
14	H	0.4	≤0	≥1.95
15	H	0.5	≤0	≥1.813
16	H	0.75	≤0	≥1.469
	10/6	0.484	1.453	1.429

- M choosing L that he would even lie if the sentence was higher than 2. Thus one knows at least that $\hat{s} \geq 2$.
- M choosing H that he would not lie even if there was no sentence. Thus, one gets $\hat{s} \leq 0$.
- N choosing K that he would check even if the monitoring costs were higher than 1. Thus, we know $\hat{c} \geq 1$.
- N choosing $\overline{K}$ that he would not check even if monitoring was for free. Thus, we know $\hat{c} \leq 0$.

Given the parameters of the experiment and the actual choice one now can compute upper or lower bounds for δ^* or τ^*.

Table 4 shows the decision data of all Ms and the computed values of τ^* while Table 5 shows the N-data including the elicited values of δ^*. To compute the average values I took upper/lower bounds and used them as an exact value.

To get some impression of what real preferences look like we first compute the normalized average δ^+ and τ^+

$$\delta^+ = 0.013$$
$$\tau^+ = 0.572$$

Supposing that the population is rather homogeneous and analyzing only the average values, one gets the result that the population belongs to subset C. (One easily obtains this result by computing the bounds of the six subsets.) However, especially the N - data suggests that there are very different types of preferences - just compare those participants who chose K with the others. Those who monitored have an average $\delta^{+(K)} \leq -0.211$, the others have an average of $\delta^{+(\overline{K})} \geq 0.346$.

Table 5: Decision data and elicited δ^*-values of the N-players

subject	choice	l	$\hat{c}$	δ^*
1	K	0.51	1	-0.253
2	K	0.7	≥ 1	≤ -0.147
3	K	0.8	≥ 1	≤ -0.105
4	K	0.3	≥ 1	≤ -0.434
5	K	0.75	≥ 1	≤ -0.125
6	K	0.6	≥ 1	≤ -0.198
7	K	0.8	≥ 1	≤ -0.105
8	K	0.6	≥ 1	≤ -0.198
9	K	0.4	≥ 1	≤ -0.336
10	$\overline{K}$	0.25	≤ 0	≥ 0.507
11	$\overline{K}$	0.7	≤ 0	≥ 0.853
12	$\overline{K}$	0.25	≤ 0	≥ 0.507
13	$\overline{K}$	0.5	0.999	-0.259
14	$\overline{K}$	0.5	0.1	0.64
15	$\overline{K}$	0.4	0.5	0.164
16	$\overline{K}$	0.55	0.76	0.013
	9/7	0.51	0.709	0.033

Thus, it is not very easy to draw conclusions from the experimental data, but at least they give interesting hints. The surprisingly low $\delta^{+(K)}$-average of the checking participants suggests that there might be even some kind of pleasure in convicting liars. The relatively high values of τ^+ and the, all in all, low values of δ^+ can be viewed as hinting to a real world which deselected types feeling remorse in case of unjustified distrust but enabled the survival of remorse in case of betraying.

Comment on Steffen Huck

Thomas Brenner

1 Introduction

Steffen Huck studies in his mainly theoretical approach the behaviour of individuals in a principal-agent game. In such a game two individuals interact who have different information about the profit to share. One individual (the principal) knows about the amount that is to be shared while the other (the agent) does not. Therefore, the principal is able to betray the agent by holding back profit. The agent, in turn, has the possibility to control the principal although this is costly and not always successful.

There is general agreement on the relevance of the principal-agent problem for economics. Consequently, there is an enormous amount of literature on this topic. Behaviour in games is usually described by the assumption that individuals attempt to maximise their payoff. The payoff is defined by the utility that each outcome gives rise to. In general different aspects of an outcome are relevant. In experiments economists hope that the subjects evaluate the outcomes by their monetary payoffs only. However, this is not necessarily the case. Other aspects may influence their decisions.

For a long period of time economists avoided any discussion about different contents of utility. Utility was regarded as a construct that only can be measured by observing behaviour. Assuming that preferences are constant a preference order or utility function deduced from observed behaviour in the past enables to describe future behaviour. This way, economists have restricted their research to a description of economic behaviour. Furthermore, the validity of this approach is restricted by the condition that preferences have to be constant.

Recently, stimulated by the experimental findings that individual leave greater monetary payoffs, economists started to reflect on the contents of utility. Two reasons for the increased interest in preferences exist. First, in various experiments (e.g. in the prisoner's dilemma game, the ultimatum game, and the principal-agent game) individuals have been found to deviate from maximising monetary payoffs. The most common explanation for the leaving of monetary payoffs is the claim that individuals evaluate outcomes not only according to monetary profit. However, this implies that the evolution of other aspects of evaluation have to be explained. Second, some economists claim that it is important to understand the changes of preferences over time (cf. Witt [1987]). If preferences of individuals change during life, the reasons of these change have to be found within the circumstances of individuals. Institutions, like legal settings, are an important part of the economic circumstances of individuals. Thus, I agree with Steffen Huck when he claims that institutions influence payoffs of actions not only directly but also indirectly by changing preferences. To understand this influence of institutions on individual preferences seems to be an important task. It is related to the general task to understand the evolution of preferences.

Steffen Huck offers one proposal how to deal with the development and change of preferences in his work „Legal design and the evolution of remorse". To this end, he abandons two common assumptions. First, he breaks with the assumption that utilities in a principle-agent game equal monetary payoffs. Instead, he assumes players to assign positive or negative feelings to some of the outcomes in addition to the monetary payoffs. Second, he assumes that these feelings change over time. As a consequence, the preferences of the players change. The abandonment of both these assumptions is necessary if the evolution of preferences is to be understood.

However, these assumptions have to be replaced by assumptions about the dynamics of preferences. An examination of the adequate assumption has been started in the literature in the last few years. Different proposals have been put forward (cf. Witt 1991 and Güth & Yaari 1992). Therefore, I focus on this aspect of Steffen Huck's paper.

Steffen Huck describes the evolution of preferences, in his case the evolution of the feeling of remorse, by the concept of evolutionary stable strategies. He distinguishes three processes. First, individuals are assumed to maximise their payoffs with respect to their preferences at each time. Thus, the individual's preferences determine behaviour. Second, behaviour causes outcomes that are characterised by the payoffs they give rise to. In a biological sense these payoffs lead to a fitness, i.e., to a certain ability to reproduce. The fitness that a behaviour gives rise to depends only on monetary payoffs according to Steffen Huck's approach. Third, biological evolution leads to a selection of the fittest individuals. Since the fitness of individuals depends on their behaviour and therefore their preferences, some types of preferences supersede while others disappear. This way, the evolution of certain preferences is explained.

The concept described requires the validity of some assumptions that will be discussed in the following. In the next section I will focus on the generality of preferences and the validity of an approach that considers one situation only. The third section addresses the question of whether preferences are caused by biological or social evolution. In section four the differences between learning processes and biological selection are discussed. Finally, section five presents some conclusion and some suggestions for further studies of the evolution of preferences.

2 Generality of preferences

Traditionally, preferences are defined on the set of outcomes in economics. One possible state of affair is compared to another possible state of affairs. Such an approach is adequate if preferences are assumed to be constant.

If the evolution of preferences is to be studied, two alternative approaches exist: Preferences may be defined based on states of affairs, as it is done in traditional utility theory, or they may be defined based on certain aspects of states of affairs. To examine the appropriateness of both approaches, the dynamics of preferences have to be understood. However, preferences cannot be directly measured so that. Only the consequences of preferences can be measured so that some assumption must be made followed by an examination of their implication. Two contrary fundamental assumptions about the changes of preferences can be made. First, it might be assumed that two states of affairs exchange their positions within the preference order at a certain point in time while all other parts of the preference order remain constant. This assumption implies that each preferring is independent of the others. Second, it might be assumed that each change of preferences affects the ranking of many states of affairs at the same time. This implies that changes of preferences relate to certain aspects that are common to many states of affairs.

Unfortunately, there are no empirical or experimental studies about the changes of preference orders. Lacking knowledge about the changes of preference I claim the second assumption to be more realistic. This claim is supported by experimental studies on motivational attitudes where it has been shown that motivational attitudes influence behaviour in various situations (cf. Liebrand 1986) which implies that a change of motivational attitudes changes several positions in a preference order simultaneously.

Assuming preferences to change with respect to certain aspects of states of affairs, a definition of preferences based on these aspects seems to be more appropriate. Following the traditional definition of preferences would imply that the relations between the rankings of different states of affairs have to be analysed. Although such an approach can be used it causes unnecessary complications. Therefore, preferences are related to certain aspects in the following. For example higher monetary payoffs are preferred to lower monetary payoffs or not to betray others is preferred to betraying others.

A definition of preferences based on certain aspects of states of affairs faces two obstacles. First, an adequate set of aspects has to be defined. Second, it has to be declared how preferences for different aspects add up (cf. Brenner 1997b for a more detailed analysis). In the case of Steffen Huck's principal-agent game the set of aspects contains monetary payoffs, betrayal, and suspicion. Furthermore, it is assumed that the preferences for these aspects add up mathematically. Such assumptions seems to be plausible and are therefore a good point to start an analysis of the change of preferences. Thus, let me assume these assumption to be correct so that the prerequisites for an analysis of the evolution of preferences are given and attention can be redirected to the changes of preferences themselves.

Preferences are defined for different aspects of states of affairs. Therefore, a study of changes of preferences can be done for each aspect separately. Each aspect of states of affairs generally occurs in various situations. In all these situations the preference for this aspect influences behaviour. The experience made in these situations, in turn, influences preferences. Thus, all situations related to a certain preference play a role for the evolution of preferences.

For example, the feeling of remorse after the betrayal of another individual occurs not only in the situation of a principal-agent game. It influences the behaviour in many different situations. Thus, the evolution of the feeling of remorse is influenced by the experience with all these situations. A consideration of only one kind of game, like the principal-agent game, neglects this aspect. To analyse the evolution of remorse adequately, all situations where a feeling of remorse plays a role have to be identified first. These situations have to be studied simultaneously.

It might be claimed that individuals have a preference related only to betrayal in principle-agent games. As mentioned already, it is difficult to identify the set of aspects building the basis for preferences. In general, however, preferences are related not only to one type of situation and at least not only to one specification of this type of situation. This again points to the importance of identifying the relevant set of situations before the dynamics of preferences for certain aspects can be studied.

3 Preferences, social evolution, and biological evolution

The study of the evolution of preferences is a topic recognised by economists only recently. A clear generally shared concept has not yet been established. Two approaches can be distinguished: Some authors describe the evolution of preferences with the help of biological evolution (cf. Güth & Yaari 1992) while others claim that the evolution of preferences is caused by social evolution (cf. Witt 1991).

The first approach is in line with the concept of socio-biology (see e.g. Barash 1982 for a presentation of the concept of socio-biology). It is claimed that preferences are selected by biological evolution. For example, in the context of altruism such an approach is frequently applied (cf. e.g. Harbach 1992 and references therein). However, the claim that many social attitudes are caused by biological evolution is controversially discussed in the literature (cf. Wuketits 1990 and Symons 1992). Biological evolution of preferences implies two characteristics of these preferences.

First, if preferences are caused by biological evolution, they have to be encoded in the individual's genes. The number of genes is restricted. Consequently, only basic preferences can be determined by genes. Furthermore, genes change very slowly from generation to generation. Thus, genetically fixed preferences change slowly and are the same for large groups of individuals. Populations with the same history (where history includes the previous thousands of years) should share the same preferences. To identify the preferences shared by many individuals, we may go back to the psychological studies of motivation and reinforcement learning. In both research areas psychologists studied needs and reinforcers, respectively, shared by people. The needs or reinforcers found are very fundamental. Preferences that are not shared by all individuals, at least in an adequately defined population, cannot be explained by biological evolution. Therefore, an approach to the evolution of preferences based on biological evolution should be restricted to the fundamental preferences.

Second, biological evolution of preferences implies that preferences remain constant during an individual's life. Furthermore, preferences also remain fairly constant in a population in the short run (in biological times scales, i.e., during periods of thousands of years). This means that preferences remain constant over periods of time relevant in an economic context. Therefore, an explanation of preferences by biological evolution restricts the approach to an explanation of their existence. Changes of preferences cannot be explained by biological evolution, at least not on time scales relevant in economics. Consequently, the impact of institutions on preferences cannot be analysed in the context of biological evolution.

The second approach to the evolution of preferences claims that social evolution is responsible for changes of preferences. Social evolution is based on individual learning processes in a social environment. Thus, according to this approach preferences are learnt during life. This holds for all preferences that are not fixed genetically. According to the above considerations preferences that change during life are the relevant preferences in the context of economic progress. In the following I will focus on these preferences.

To study changes of preferences due to social evolution, the underlying learning processes have to be identified. Learning processes may have very different features. To analyse changes of preferences, it is necessary to identify the features of the learning process that causes the changes in preferences. In the literature this topic is widely neglected (see Witt 1987 and Witt 1991 for some exceptions where this topic is approached theoretically).

Preferring one state of affairs to another can be caused by different individual characteristics. Preferences may be the reflection of needs, desires, or attitudes. All these are subsumed under the label of preferences in economics. However, each of them changes according to a different learning process. Therefore, several assumptions on the features of the evolution of preferences can be justified. I will present three of them in the following.

First, preferences may be claimed to correspond to the psychological notion of reinforcers (cf. Witt 1991). Subsequently, primary reinforcers can be identified with innate preferences while secondary reinforcers correspond to learnt preferences. This implies that preferences are learnt according to classical conditioning.

Second, if preferences are seen as attitudes, the experience with these attitudes and imitation of other individuals play an important role. Individuals change their attitudes either if they have led to harmful results or if they are convinced by others in a process similar to imitation.

Third, aspects of states of affairs might be preferred because individuals believe that these aspects are helpful in the future. In this case preferences are caused by cognitive beliefs (cf. Brenner 1997b). Consequently, cognitive learning processes have to be studied to analyse changes of preferences.

To sum up, genetically determined preferences can be explained by biological evolution. An analysis of changes of preferences in an economic context, however, requires to study the learning processes that cause these changes. The features of these learning processes depend on the definition of preferences. A more detailed analysis of these learning processes is an essential requirement for an analysis of the evolution of preferences.

4 Learning modeled by evolutionary processes

In the recent literature learning is often modelled by evolutionary algorithms (cf. Dekel & Scotchmer 1992, Gale, Binmore & Samuelson 1995, and Dawid 1996a). Such an approach may also be used to describe changes of preferences. Two reasons may be put forward in favour of such an approach. First, the use of evolutionary algorithms or the concept of evolutionary stable states is comfortable and leads to well-defined results as shown in the approach of Steffen Huck. Second, it is repeatedly claimed in the literature that learning processes and evolutionary algorithms lead to the same or similar dynamics (cf. Börgers and Sarin 1993 and Dawid 1996b). If this claim holds, evolutionary algorithms would present a favourable tool to describe the evolution of preferences even in the case of preferences that are developed during life.

In the literature two kinds of learning processes are repeatedly compared to evolutionary dynamics. These are reinforcement learning which is compared to the replicator dynamics (Börgers and Sarin 1993 as well as Brenner and Witt 1997 have shown that the dynamics of reinforcement learning is at least similar to the replicator dynamics) and imitation learning which is compared to evolutionary algorithms (in Brenner 1997a it is shown that some crucial difference between both dynamics exist).

Thus, it seems to be justified to use the replicator dynamics (see Hofbauer & Sigmund 1984 for a detailed description) and the concept of ESSs to describe reinforcement learning while in the case of social learning (including imitation and selection of behaviours according to the individuals' experience) genetic algorithms should at least be modified before they are used to describe learning processes.

To sum up, the use of concepts adopted from biological evolution to describe learning processes is not adequate in all cases. Whether evolutionary algorithms or the replicator dynamics are adequate depends on the features of the learning process. The literature suggests that reinforcement learning can be adequately described by the replicator dynamics. In the case of social learning, based on imitation and the gathering of information, instead, evolutionary algorithms fail to capture all relevant aspects. This shortcoming may be eliminated by a redefinition of genetic algorithms with respect to the features of social learning.

5 Conclusion

Preferences are the fundamental tool to describe behaviour and decisions of individuals in the economics literature. Subsequently, the question about the origin of preferences and their changes in time seems to be of crucial importance. Nevertheless, economists generally neglect this question. They assume preference to be constant. Only recently the question of how preferences evolve has been approached (cf. e.g. Witt 1991 and Güth & Yaari 1992) and different concepts to analyse the dynamics of preferences have been proposed.

However, the analysis of preferences is still at its beginning. Above I outlined three aspects that are not yet sufficiently understood in the context of preferences. I claim that an approach to preferences has to begin with a clarification of these three aspects. First, preferences have to be redefined. The traditional definition of preferences in the context of economics is based on the assumption that preferences are constant and defines preferences on the level of actions or bundle of goods. Such a definition is inappropriate if the dynamics of preferences is to be explained. In this case preferences have to be defined based on certain aspects of the state of affairs. The identification of these aspects is an important prerequisite for the study of the dynamics of preferences. Second, the processes responsible for the change of preferences have to be identified. Several theories are supposed in the literature. However, a discussion of their empirical evidence is missing. Third, if the first two questions are solved, the final question how to model the evolution and change of preferences can be addressed. Different learning models as well as evolutionary algorithms or the replicator dynamics may be adequate tools. However, this is the last question to be answered.

It is important to understand changes in preferences if we intend to understand economic change. Therefore, a study of preferences is worthwhile. However, there is much to be clarified before we really are able to model the evolution of preferences.

References

Barash, D. P. (1982): *Sociobiology and Behavior;* London: Hodder & Stoughton.

Börgers, T. and Sarin, R. (1993): Learning Through Reinforcement and Replicator Dynamics; Discussion Papers in Economics 93-19, London: University College.

Brenner, T. (1997a): Can Evolutionary Algorithms Describe Learning Processes ?; Jena: mimeo.

Brenner, T. (1997b): Learning - An Economic Perspective; PhD thesis, Jena.

Brenner, T. and Witt, U. (1997): Frequency-Dependent Pay-offs, Replicator Dynamics, and Learning Under the Matching Law; Jena: mimeo.

Dawid, H. (1996a): Learning of Cycles and Sunspot Equilibria by Genetic Algorithms; *Journal of Evolutionary Economics*, 6, 361-373.

Dawid, H. (1996b): *Adaptive Learning by Genetic Algorithms*, Lecture Notes in Economics and Mathematical Systems 441, Berlin: Springer.

Dekel, E. and Scotchmer, S. (1992): On the Evolution of Optimizing Behavior; *Journal of Economic Theory*, 57, 392-406.

Gale, J., Binmore, K. G. and Samuelson, L. (1995): Learning To Be Imperfect: The Ultimatum Game; *Games and Economic Behavior*, 8, 56-90.

Güth, W. and Yaari, M. E. (1992): Explaining Reciprocal Behavior in Simple Strategic Games: An Evolutionary Approach; in U. Witt (ed.), *Explaining Process and Change*, Ann Arbor: University of Michigan Press.

Harbach, H. (1992): *Altruismus und Moral*, Opladen: Westdeutscher Verlag.

Hofbauer, J. and Sigmund, K. (1984): *Evolutionstheorie und dynamische Systeme*, Berlin: Paul Parey.

Liebrand, W. B. G. (1986): The Ubiquity of Social Values in Social Dilemmas; in: H. A. M. Wilke, D. M. Messick, and C. G. Rutte (eds.), *Experimental Social Dilemmas*, Frankfurt am Main: Peter Lang.

Symons, D. (1992): On the Use and Misuse of Darwinism in the Study of Human Behavior; in: J. H. Barkow, L. Cosmides, and J. Tooby (eds.): *The Adapted Mind*, New York: Oxford University Press.

Witt, U. (1987): *Individualistische Grundlagen der Evolutorischen Ökonomik*, Tübingen: J. C. B. Mohr.

Witt, U. (1991): Economics, Sociobiology, and Behavioral Psychology on Preferences; *Journal of Economic Psychology*, 12, 557-573.

Wuketits, F. M. (1990): *Gene, Kultur und Moral*; Darmstadt: Wissenschaftliche Buchgesellschaft.

PART II

Cognition and Rationality

Rent Leaving

Bruno S. Frey and Iris Bohnet[*]

Economic rents are the driving force of market economies. Resource owners constantly look for opportunities to create and exploit economic rents which, however, in the dynamics of the market process dissipate as new entrants try to appropriate the profits. In equilibrium, economic rents are eliminated. Not so in different institutional settings. While rents in the market endogenously come and go, they are artificially created and sustained in political and bureaucratic decision-making. In analogy to individuals' behaviour in the market, it is assumed that politicians, bureaucrats, pressure groups, voters and taxpayers strive for political rents. Rent seeking in the political arena may also increase an individual's income but in contrast to the market, is not socially beneficial. "The term rent seeking is designed to describe behavior in institutional settings where individual efforts to maximize value generate social waste rather than social surplus" (Buchanan1980, 4).

We argue that institutional settings are not only apt to *rent seeking* but allow for *rent leaving* as well. While the market mechanism induces the profit seeking butcher and baker to produce collectively beneficial results, in non-market decision-making, individual profit maximization has to be traded off against socially productive investments. We speak of rent leaving when subjects do not invest in something that is unproductive for others but that would increase their own income. Rent leaving thus encompasses all forms of other-regarding behaviour such as charitable giving or contributions to public goods, independent of whether prosocial behaviour is Pareto-improving in pay-offs as the pie gets bigger. For the purpose of this paper, we do not need to differentiate between altruism in the form of purely helping others and cooperative behaviour in the form of helping others and oneself. In both cases, individuals have to decide whether they want to maximize their personal income - which is the dominant strategy - or whether they prefer to take into account somebody else's well-being, i.e. to leave rents.

Rent leaving exists as long as individuals derive intrinsic benefits from other-regarding behaviour. Such behaviour need not to be irrational. The formation of

---

[*] The authors are grateful to Heiko Geue, Marcel Kucher, Andreas Ortmann, and the participants of the conference on "Cognition, Rationality and Institutions" for their helpful comments. We acknowledge the financial support provided by the Schweizerischer Nationalfonds (Grant No. 12-42 480.94).

such preferences may be the result of selfish parents trying to rig their children's preferences toward pro-social behaviour (Becker 1992). Individuals then raise their utility by living up to their moral obligation to leave rents. This moral obligation, however, can be crowded out. A group of cognitive social psychologists[1] has analyzed the phenomenon that external rewards undermine intrinsically motivated moral obligations. Extrinsic incentives deprive individuals of the possibility of indulging in pro-social feelings. After all, no one can pretend to act out of intrinsic motivation if extrinsic incentives offset the disutility generated by a certain act. Thus, by destroying the possibility of showing one's intrinsic motivation, extrinsic incentives can negatively affect the motivation itself.

Building on 'the hidden cost of reward', Frey (1997a) formulates a generalized *Crowding Effect:* Extrinsic incentives and intrinsic motivational forces are regarded as scarce factors guiding human behaviour. In the case of both motivators being active, individuals reduce the scarce motivator that is under their control, namely intrinsic motivation. In this paper, we investigate the extent to which intrinsic motivation is crowded in if extrinsic incentives are insufficient to produce socially efficient outcomes. Which institutional setting is able to activate intrinsic motivational forces?

The concept of intrinsic motivation is developed in the next section 1. Private donations are often intrinsically motivated. Empirical evidence shows that they may not easily be substituted by public contributions. This non-substitutability, however, only holds as long as individuals' capacity to derive intrinsic value from the act of voluntary giving, i.e. from rent leaving, is not destroyed. Section 2 argues that a specific institutional framework is required to allow for intrinsic motivation to be active. *Motivation Compatible Mechanisms (MCM)* enable individuals to live up to their intrinsic motivation. To qualify as MCM, an institution must fulfil two requirements: It must allow individuals to send (i) and to receive (ii) messages on the motivational basis of an action:

1. The sender of a message must be able to credibly demonstrate that his behaviour results from intrinsic and not from extrinsic motivation. MCM must allow for *motivational self-determination.*
2. The recipient of a message must be able to credibly demonstrate that she acknowledges intrinsic motivation. MCM must allow for *motivational acknowledgement.*

What rent leaving means in the most prominent social dilemma, the prisoner's dilemma, is analyzed in section 3. It is argued that communication allows for rent leaving. Section 4 discusses the empirical relevance of rent leaving in politics. Intrinsic motivation is of major importance for the relationship between the citi-

---

[1] The work is summarized in Deci and Ryan (1985) and Deci with Flaste (1995). A recent survey is given in Lane (1991, especially chapter 19). Extensive meta-analyses are presented by Wiersma (1992), Cameron and Pierce (1994), and Eisenberger and Cameron (1996).

zens and the state. It contributes to solving difficult problems such as NIMBYs (Not In My Backyard), and to better understanding why people pay their taxes. Section V offers concluding remarks.

1 Intrinsic Motivation

Intrinsic preferences relate to activities one undertakes for one's own sake. "One is said to be intrinsically motivated to perform an activity when one receives no apparent reward except the activity itself" (Deci 1971,105). Many different conceptualisations of intrinsic preferences exist (see, e.g. Deci and Ryan 1985), but the phenomenon corresponds well with many everyday observations, including scholars who do research simply because of their curiosity about life and nature. The distinction between intrinsic and extrinsic preferences has been made not only because of the different reactions to external interventions but also because it might lead to different modes of behaviour. Extrinsically motivated behaviour invites, or is at least associated with, calculativeness and marginal comparisons (opportunity cost), but also with discipline and professionality (see Hirschman 1982). Intrinsically motivated behaviour, on the other hand, leads to playfulness and idiosyncrasy, convictedness and amateurish actions, as well as to more innovativeness. Psychological research has associated intrinsic motivation with spontaneity (Koestner et al. 1984) and creativity (Amabile 1983).

While intergenerational altruism towards one's kin is not considered to be intrinsically motivated rent leaving, anonymous gifts to support unrelated strangers or worthy causes meet the criteria: Individuals are prepared to give up part of their income - well beneath opportunity cost earnings - for the common good. In the United States, donations to "organizations organized for charitable or mutual benefit purposes" amounted to $122.6 billion in 1990. Of the total, 90 percent was personal giving. In addition, people contribute to good causes by voluntarily working for free. The value of volunteer labour in the United States provided to charitable organizations was estimated to be $182.3 billion in 1993. While part of the donations are tax deductible for donors, this decrease of tax bills cannot account for the quite substantive amount of rent leaving (Rose-Ackerman 1996).

In 1993, total monetary contributions to charities were $646 or 1.7 percent of household income in the United States (Hodgkinson and Weitzman 1994). In Switzerland, 0.46 percent, in Germany, 0.18 percent and in France, 0.13 percent of personal income was donated in 1990. Charitable contributions in the United States drop to an annual average of 0.57 percent when giving to religious groups is excluded. In most countries, personal giving is less than 1 percent of personal income (Salamon and Anheimer 1994). Even though the share of income donated seems quite low, it clearly indicates that individuals do not act as free riders or rent seekers all the time. Rather, human beings seem to be intrinsically motivated to leave rents. That individuals derive personal satisfaction from the act of giving is corroborated by empirical evidence. Several studies have demonstrated that the standard public good model which assumes that charity is motivated by "a desire to improve the general well-being of recipients" (Becker 1974) cannot explain the data in a satisfactory way. In this case, individuals should not care whether the contribution is in the form of a voluntary private gift or an involuntary tax transfer. Contributions by the government and private giving are taken to be perfect substitutes. Field studies of charitable giving, however, have found that substitution is imperfect. An increase in government spending on charitable contributions only leads to very small decreases in private giving, ranging from 5 to 28 percent (e.g. Clothfelter 1985; Kingma 1989; Khanna, Posnett and Sandler 1995).

The study by Kingma (1989) is especially illuminating as it is the first one which controls for the type of public good which is voluntarily financed. All other studies compare aggregate private contributions with aggregate government funds to charity and are thus unable to check whether individuals voluntarily give to organizations or good causes to supplement government funding of other organizations. Kingma (1989) finds that for private and public contributions to public radio, a $10'000 increase in public funds only results in a $0.15 decrease in an agent's private contribution. This significant but tiny effect indicates that public and private funding are far from being perfect substitutes. Individuals do not only derive benefits from the overall level of contributions but also from their personal giving. This benefit of giving, the 'warm glow' (Andreoni 1990), is not related to the amount contributed by others but directly depends on the act of giving[2].

People are 'committed' (Sen 1977) or intrinsically motivated to leave rents. An involuntary, and thus extrinsically motivated, transfer does not provide the same satisfaction as voluntary, intrinsically motivated giving. It is intrinsically motivated rent leaving which induces individuals to refrain from income maximizing and to invest in the common good.

2 Motivation Compatible Mechanisms

Economic theory suggests to build human interaction on incentive compatible mechanisms. Individuals' opportunity sets are altered so as to make rent leaving the rational response. This focus on the relative performance of different contractual arrangements has been a successful research strategy. The standard relative price effect, e.g., applies to rent leaving as well as to all other human actions (North 1990). Individuals are less other-regarding, the higher the cost is. They systematically reduce the extent to which they conform to environmental norms the more expensive compliance becomes (Diekmann 1996). In experiments, a

---

[2] For experimental and empirical evidence, see Bohnet (1997a). Intrinsic motivation leads to constant giving independent of the number of beneficiaries in dictator games and in contingent valuation studies.

relative price effect may almost always be produced. Subjects in the laboratory are less other-regarding in dictator games the higher the price of fairness is (Eichenberger and Oberholzer-Gee 1997) and contribute less to public goods, the more attractive private investments are (Smith and Walker 1993).

Rule-guided behaviour, however, makes it impossible for the observer - be it a scientist or another actor in the game - to learn about individuals' underlying motivations. Within an incentive compatible regime, individuals never know whether their counterparts would have been intrinsically motivated to leave rents absent of any external restrictions. Indeed, if all behaviour could be governed by imposing constraints - costlessly -, mankind should not care about intrinsic motivation. Motivational dispositions to leave rents would become superfluous, no investments would be undertaken to nourish one's capability to be intrinsically motivated.

The price of incentive compatibility is the loss of intrinsic motivation. This becomes the more regrettable, the costlier it is to secure productive interaction by relying on economic incentives alone. While incentive compatible devices improve technical and allocative efficiency, social efficiency, i.e. the production of the public good, seems much harder to achieve. Compliance with the law, e.g., has been shown to hardly depend on deterrence (Tyler 1997). Research on all types of law-related behaviour such as tax cheating, shoplifting or drug use indicates that the probabilities of being caught and punished would have to be extremely high for deterrence to influence behaviour. In the United States, the objective risk of being caught and imprisoned for assault, burglary, larceny and motor vehicle theft is only 1 percent, for robbery it is 4 percent and for rape it amounts to 12 percent. However, for a deterrence based strategy to be effective, the risk would have to be as high as 45 percent - which is the probability that offenders in case of homicide are caught and punished (Robinson and Darley 1995).

While theoretically, it would be possible to create an 'incentive compatible equilibrium' by raising probabilities to very high levels, most societies are not prepared to carry the monetary and social cost accompanying such a policy. Big brother would be watching extremely closely over everybody's shoulders. A second equilibrium can evolve if institutions are not 'incentive compatible' but rather 'motivation compatible'. *Motivation compatible mechanisms* do not restrict individual actions but allow intrinsic motivations to govern behaviour. Thus, only an unrestricted opportunity set allows individuals to act according to their motivations and to learn about others' underlying motivations. Imagine a person A who wishes to cooperate with B. A can either take all possible precautions by making sure that defection would be very costly for B, or she can test B's intrinsic motivation by purposely not doing so. B, on the other hand, knows that only in the latter case, he is able to exhibit his intrinsically motivated willingness to cooperate.

This kind of voluntary rent leaving is thus only possible if A gives B the chance to show his motivation and if B knows that A is in a position to acknowledge his motivation. Self-determination and acknowledgement are crucial for A's and B's willingness to voluntarily leave rents:

(a) *Self-Determination:* When individuals perceive an external intervention to reduce their self-determination, they substitute intrinsic motivation by extrinsic control. Following Rotter (1966), the locus of control has shifted from the inside to the outside of the person affected. Individuals who are forced to behave in a specific way by outside intervention feel overjustified if they maintained their intrinsic motivation ('Overjustification Effect').

(b) *Acknowledgement:* When an intervention from outside or other people's reactions carry the notion that the actor's motivation is not acknowledged, intrinsic motivation is rejected. The person affected feels that his involvement is not appreciated which debases the value of being intrinsically motivated.

A motivation compatible mechanism must provide both, for B to be self-determined and for A to acknowledge B's self-determined choice. This is not possible if A and B decide in an abstract setting, isolated from one another. In perfect competition or in the pure price system, the relationship between the individuals is solely guided by the price, and there is anonymity between the partners. Hence, there is no chance for intrinsic motivation to evolve. As soon as one moves outside the pure price system, to hierarchical or democratic decision-making and to bargaining, personal interactions become important. The degree of 'social embeddedness' (Granovetter 1985) or 'cojointness' (Coleman 1990) among two actors systematically influences crowding. Personal relationships may be created in the laboratory by permitting the subjects to communicate with each other. This face-to-face interaction allows for intrinsic motivation to play a role in influencing individual decisions.

3 Communication

The dilemma between private income maximization and social efficiency may be best demonstrated by referring to the prisoner's dilemma. Free-riding is individually rational but produces collectively sub-optimal results. An individual is worse off if everybody defects compared to a situation where everybody contributes to the public good. Consider the pay-off matrix depicted in table 1.

Table 1 shows that the marginal opportunity cost of cooperation is constant in all situations. Choosing X instead of Y costs a subject Sfr. 6.50. Rent seeking implies aspiring the highest absolute rent. Everybody should try to convince everybody else to contribute to the public good but choose the defective solution. Earning Sfr. 9.-- should thus be the goal of all players. Opportunistic utility maximization relies on all weapons available, such as cheating and lying, as long as they do not have any negative consequences for the individual.

Rent leaving, on the other hand, means not taking advantage of a situation where the individual may produce the socially optimal outcome by forgoing individual benefits. It is equally active as rent seeking. Conditions are created which give people the chance to leave rents. Communication transforms anonymous others into specific human beings and creates personal relationships crowding in intrinsic motivation. As no binding contracts can be closed, pre-play communication - in a formal sense - does not provide any extrinsic incentives to leave rents. Non-binding pre-play communication is labelled 'cheap talk' by game theory and is not expected to exhibit any influence on individual behaviour in public good type settings (Farrell and Rabin 1996). Thus, communication is a motivation compatible mechanism as it does not externally restrict individuals' opportunity sets. Subjects are *self-determined*.

Table 1: The Four-Person Prisoner's Dilemma Game

Number of persons choosing X	outcome for X (SFr.)	number of persons choosing Y	outcome for Y (SFr.)
4	2.50	0	--
3	- 0.50	1	9.00
2	- 3.50	2	6.00
1	- 6.50	3	3.00
0	--	4	0

We suppose, however, that subjects are able to learn about others' likelihood of cooperation. In typical public goods games, subjects do not know what others do but have expectations about others' behaviour. Expectations, it is often argued, may only be specified by experience, by a joint history. In repeated and 'serial interaction' games, individuals learn about others' likelihood of cooperation (Andreoni 1988; Macy 1991). In one-shot games, on the other hand, no such specification seems possible - unless individuals are able to talk to each other before taking a decision. Communication thus helps subjects in learning to what extent others *acknowledge* their intrinsic motivation to leave rents, thereby decreasing the fear of being exploited by others.

While communication informally provides for acknowledgement of intrinsic motivation, a formal institution also has been experimentally explored. Those who are not intrinsically motivated to leave rents can be forced to acknowledge cooperators' intrinsic motivation by extrinsic incentives. As the defectors are not intrinsically motivated in the first place, crowding out is not a problem. The cooperators' fear of being suckered is accounted for by guaranteeing that all beneficiaries of the public good will have to pay their share if a minimally needed part of the public good is provided. If in a 'minimal contributing set game' or a 'step level public goods game', the previously specified number of people chooses cooperation, everybody else will be forced to contribute, too. Using the 'enforced contribution mechanism' significantly increases cooperation (Isaac et al. 1989).

Such a formal mechanism, however, is absent in most real life rent leaving situations while communication is much more prevalent (Ostrom, Gardner and Walker 1994). By now, a wealth of experimental evidence exists showing that communication strongly and significantly raises cooperation. In our four-person prisoner's dilemma experiment at the University of Zurich, non-binding pre-play communication for ten minutes induced subjects to cooperate significantly more often than under anonymous conditions. While in anonymity, 12 percent of the subjects (N=172) decided for cooperation, after communication, 78 percent of the participants (N=100) chose the cooperative solution (Frey and Bohnet 1995). These results were corroborated by other experiments with one-shot communication and decisions. A meta-analysis (Sally 1995) comparing over 100 studies in the principal (English language) journals of political science, social psychology, economics and sociology strongly supports the cooperation-increasing effect of communication. 130 different treatment conditions are included, one third of which involve communication among the participants. In a multiple analysis, the author finds that the presence of discussion in one-shot games is highly significant, and on average raises the cooperation rate by more than 45 percentage points.

None of these studies investigated rent leaving. In order to understand to what extent individuals are ready to leave rents, we need to know whether participants are able to determine to what extent their intrinsic motivation is acknowledged by talking to other people. Frank (1988, 140) reports that subjects are able to predict others' behaviour quite accurately in a Prisoner's Dilemma. After having talked to one another, 75 percent of the participants correctly predicted whether others would cooperate or defect in the following Prisoner's Dilemma game. In our experiment, we did not ask subjects to predict others' likelihood of cooperation. Looking at the individual data, however, reveals to what extent participants took advantage of a situation where they were decisive for the provision of the public good. Only 7 out of 100 subjects took advantage of a situation where everybody else in their group cooperated (and had to pay Sfr. 0.50) while they defected and earned Sfr. 9.- (Bohnet 1997).

An experiment by Braver and Wilson (1986) further stresses the power of communication. Groups consisting of nine members were confronted with two institutional settings: Half of the groups had to decide anonymously whether they wanted to cooperate or to defect. All other groups were split into three sub-groups so that only three persons could talk to each other. As the minimal contributing set consisted of five persons, no sub-group could provide the public good unilaterally. Subjects had clear ideas about the effect of communication: They expected other communicating persons to cooperate with the probability of 88 percent when the others were included in their group and with 65 percent when others were part of another group. Only 48 percent of the anonymous participants were expected to cooperate. Interestingly, participants also predicted higher cooperation rates for communicating persons with whom they had never interacted. Their predictions were quite accurate again. Compared to the anonymous treatment condition, subgroup communication increased cooperation from 48 percent to 75 percent on average. This contradicts the much discussed 'in-group effect' in psychology (Turner 1987; Caporael et al. 1989). Partial (sub-group) communication substantially increases cooperation in this public good framework. Subjects were prepared to contribute to the public good because they believed in the cooperation-increasing effect of communication.

The experiment suggests that communication does not only work through the information exchanged. Rather, individuals take communication to contribute to changing behaviour. That expectations about people's impending behaviour are shaped by procedures alone, is a hypothesis which we advance here without being able to fully support it by empirical evidence, yet. Surveys indicate that people have clear and stable ideas about which processes they like and which ones they don't like. A consistent result seems to be that individuals are reluctant to rely on the price mechanism in exactly those circumstances where economics suggests its use. Canadians opposed the price system in an excess demand situation when they were asked whether they would find it acceptable for a hardware store to raise the price of snow shovels the morning after a large snowstorm. 82 percent of the participants (N=107) considered the price increase to be unacceptable (Kahneman, Knetsch and Thaler 1986). A replication of the survey got almost identical reactions in Switzerland and Germany. 83 percent of the respondents (N=155) were against raising the price (Frey and Pommerehne 1993).

The results are corroborated by a survey on the siting of noxious facilities in Switzerland. Respondents did not consider the price mechanism to be an acceptable allocation procedure for the siting of nuclear waste facilities. Rules based on pricing rank last in a questionnaire comparing the acceptability of different decision mechanisms. 79.6 percent of the subjects (N=500) were against compensations offered by the national government for communities willing to accept the repository. Individuals had clear ideas about how such a procedure would affect behaviour. They did not expect the price mechanism to induce experts to care about safety. Neither did they predict that compensations would lead to fair outcomes. When asked how this decision rule fared in terms of local influence of the citizens living in the prospective host community, however, compensations were judged superior to other mechanisms, such as a foreign expert decision or a lottery (Oberholzer-Gee, Bohnet and Frey 1996). As a result of the extensive survey, we concluded that people clearly understand the implications of various institutional procedures. Psychological research on the relevance of procedures supports this conclusion (Tyler 1990; Kramer and Tyler 1996).

4 Rent Leaving in Politics

The resistance to the siting of locally unwanted projects (the so-called 'Not In My Backyard' or NIMBY-syndrome) also reflects a Crowding Effect. Crowding theory suggests that when personal relations prevail between the citizens, the compensation offer reduces the intrinsic motivation to leave rents, i.e. to support the noxious facility (see Frey, Oberholzer-Gee and Eichenberger 1996). In Wolfenschiessen, the later designated host community, more than half of the respondents (50.8%) agreed to have the repository built in their community though a large majority of the respondents (80%) were well aware of the risks involved (N=305). To test the effect of a monetary reward offered, we repeated the same question, but added that the Swiss government had decided to compensate all residents of the host community. The amount offered varied between CHF 2,500 per individual and year (N=117), to CHF 5,000 (N=102), and CHF 7,500 (N=86) which is substantial in view of a median household income of our respondents of CHF 63,000 per year. While 50.8% of the respondents agreed to accept the nuclear waste repository without compensation, acceptance in Wolfenschiessen *drops* to 24.6% when compensation is offered. This (surprising) result is consistent with the hypotheses about crowding out intrinsic motivation also found in other research. Thus, increased tax rebates did not elicit an increased willingness to accept a nuclear waste facility in Nevada, and the suspicion that the rebates offered were simply too small is explicitly rejected (Kunreuther and Easterling 1990).

Crowding theory also helps to explain how constitutional and other legal rules affect the individual citizens. Intrinsic motivation in the form of civic virtue is bolstered if the public laws convey the notion that citizens are self-determined and that their intrinsic motivation is acknowledged. Such self-determination is reflected in extensive democratic participation possibilities. Citizens are given the freedom to express themselves, to be heard by the politicians and public officials, and to carry out discussions with them. The basic notion enshrined in the constitution that citizens are on average, and in general, reasonable human beings thus crowds in civic virtue. In contrast to such self-determination stands a constitution which curtails political participation rights because the 'classe politique' feels that citizens are unable to take reasoned political decisions.

Being determined by others also manifests itself in a constitution which gives the government great power to intervene in the economy and society, thus leaving little room for the individuals to act on their own. Controls by bureaucracy and police are extensive, and no citizen is taken to be intrinsically motivated. Without possibilities for self-determination and acknowledgement, citizens are not prepared to leave rents and take full advantage of all opportunities by breaking the law whenever they expect to do so at low cost. They become rent seekers.

Attempts to measure the effect of different constitutional conditions on citizens' intrinsic motivation to leave rents are faced with obvious difficulties. Most promising is an indirect approach looking at revealed behaviour in equilibrium. It is applied here to rent leaving in the form of tax morale (see more fully Frey 1997b). As has been well-established, tax paying behaviour cannot be explained in a satisfactory way without taking tax morale into account. Thus, based on the American Internal Revenue Service's Taxpayer Compliance Maintenance Program, Graetz, Reinganum and Wilde (1986) attribute the falling tax compliance in the United States to the erosion of tax morale (see also Slemrod 1992). To what extent tax morale can be crowded in depends on the type of constitution. Switzerland presents a suitable test case because the various cantons have different degrees of political participation possibilities (see more fully, Pommerehne, Hart and Frey 1994). The more extended are political participation possibilities in the form of citizens' meetings, obligatory and optional referenda and initiatives, the more rent leaving is expected. An econometric cross-section/time series analysis (relating to 26 cantons and three years) reveals that in cantons with a high degree of direct political control, tax morale is (cet. par.) higher. In contrast, in cantons with a low degree of direct political control, tax morale is (cet. par.) lower.

5 Conclusions

People don't exploit all opportunities available to them - not because they lack information or intelligence but because they conceive themselves as human beings who want to live up to their intrinsic motivation. We investigate the extent to which institutional arrangements crowd in intrinsic motivation to produce socially efficient outcomes. Intrinsically motivated pro-social behaviour is called rent leaving. It may only emerge absent of extrinsic incentives as they deprive individuals of the possibility of indulging in pro-social feelings. Only an unrestricted opportunity set allows individuals to act according to their motivations and to learn about others' underlying motivations.

Motivation compatible mechanisms (MCM) - in contrast to incentive compatible mechanisms - do not restrict individual actions but allow intrinsic motivations to govern behaviour. Individuals are prepared to voluntarily leave rents if they are self-determined and if their intrinsic motivation is acknowledged. Empirical evidence, including econometric research and experimental studies, strongly suggests that institutions providing possibilities for self-determination and acknowledgement crowd in rent leaving in the form of civic virtue, voluntary tax compliance, work moral and environmental ethics. Experimentally, it was shown for a Prisoner's Dilemma that personal relations enabled by face-to-face communication strongly increase individuals' willingness to leave rents. Field data, comparing different forms of democratic governance, further suggest that institutions fostering self-determination induce the citizens to leave rents. Rent leaving in the form of voluntary tax compliance is more broadly observed in direct democracies than in representative democracies.

References

Amabile, T. (1983): *The Social Psychology of Creativity,* New York: Springer.
Andreoni, J. (1988): Why Free Ride? Strategies and Learning in Public Goods Experiments; in: *Journal of Public Economics,* 37, 291-304.
Andreoni, J. (1990): Impure Altruism and Donations to Public Goods: A Theory of Warm Glow Giving; in: *The Economic Journal,* 100, 464-477.
Becker, G. S. (1974): A Theory of Social Interactions; in: *Journal of Political Economy,* 82, 1063-1093.
Becker, G. S. (1992): Habits, Addictions, and Traditions; in: *Kyklos,* 45, 327-345.
Bohnet, I. (1997a): Identifikation als institutionelle Bedingung individueller Kooperation: Theorie und Experimente, in: D. Aufderheide and M. Dabrowski (eds.), *Wirtschaftsethik und Moralökonomik: Beiträge zur Umsetzung ordnungsethischer Erkenntnisse,* forthcoming.
Bohnet, I. (1997b): *Kooperation und Kommunikation. Eine ökonomische Analyse individueller Entscheidungen,* Mohr (Siebeck): Tübingen.
Braver, S. L. and L.A. Wilson (1986): Choices in Social Dilemmas: Effects of Communication within Subgroups; in: *Journal of Conflict Resolution,* 30, 51-62.
Buchanan, J. M. (1980): Reform in the Rent-Seeking Society; in: J. M. Buchanan, R. D. Tollison and G. Tullock (eds.), *Toward a Theory of the Rent-Seeking Society,* Texas A&M University Press: College Station.
Cameron, J. and W. D. Pierce (1994): Reinforcement, Reward, and Intrinsic Motivation: A Meta-Analysis; *Review of Educational Research,* 64 (Fall), 363-423.
Caporael, L. R., R. M. Dawes, J. M. Orbell and A. J.C. van de Kragt (1989): Selfishness Examined: Cooperation in the Absence of Egoistic Incentives; in: *Behavioral and Brain Sciences,* 12, 683-739.
Clothfelter, C. T. (1985): *Federal Tax Policy and Charitable Giving,* Chicago: University of Chicago Press.
Coleman, J. S. (1990): *Foundations of Social Theory,* Cambridge, MA: Harvard University Press.
Deci, E. L. (1971): Effects of Externally Mediated Rewards on Intrinsic Motivation; in: *Journal of Personality and Social Psychology,* 18(1), 105-15.
Deci, E. L. with R. Flaste (1995): *Why We Do What We Do. The Dynamics of Personal Autonomy;* New York: Putnam.
Deci, E. L. and R. M. Ryan (1985): *Intrinsic Motivation and Self-Determination in Human Behaviour,* New York: Plenum Press.
Diekmann, A. (1996): Homo Ökonomicus. Anwendungen und Probleme der Theorie rationalen Handelns im Umweltbereich, *Kölner Zeitschrift für Soziologie und Sozialpsychologie,* 36 (Sonderheft); also published in: A. Diekmann and C. C. Jaeger (eds.), *Umweltsoziologie,* Opladen: Westdeutscher Verlag, 1996, 89-118.
Eichenberger, R. and F. Oberholzer-Gee (1997): Rational Moralists: The Role of Fairness in Democratic Economic Politics; *Mimeo,* University of Zurich.

Eisenberger, R. and J. Cameron (1996): Detrimental Effects of Reward. Reality or Myth? in: *American Psychologist,* 51(Nov), 1153-1166.

Farrell, J. and M. Rabin (1996): Cheap Talk; in: *Journal of Economic Perspectives,* 10 (summer), 103-118.

Frank, R. H. (1988): *Passions Within Reason,* New York: W.W. Norton.

Frey, B. S. (1997a): *Not Just for the Money. An Economic Theory of Personal Motivation;* Edward Elgar, Cheltenham, U.K. and Brookfield, USA.

Frey, B. S. (1997b): A Constitution for Knaves Crowds Out Civic Virtues; in: *Economic Journal,* forthcoming.

Frey, B. S. and I. Bohnet (1995): Institutions Affect Fairness: Experimental Investigations; in: *Journal of Institutional and Theoretical Economics,* 151(June), 286-303.

Frey, B. S. and W. W. Pommerehne (1993): On the Fairness of Pricing - An Empirical Survey among the General Population; in: *Journal of Economic Behavior and Organization,* 20, 295-307.

Frey, B. S., F. Oberholzer-Gee and R. Eichenberger (1996): The Old Lady Visits Your Backyard: A Tale of Morals and Markets; in: *Journal of Political Economy,* 104 (6), 193-209.

Graetz, M., J. F. Reinganum and L. L. Wilde (1986): The Tax Compliance Game: Toward an Interactive Theory of Law Enforcement; in: *Journal of Law, Economics and Organization,* 39, 1-32.

Granovetter, M. (1985): Economic Action and Social Structure: The Problem of Imbeddedness; in: *American Journal of Sociology,* 91, 481-510.

Hirschman, A. O. (1982): Rival Interpretations of Market Society: Civilizing, Destructive, or Feeble?; in: *Journal of Economic Literature,* 20(Dec), 1463-1484.

Hodgkinson, V. A. and M. S. Weitzman (1994): *Giving and Volunteering in the United States,* Washington: Independent Sector.

Isaac, R.M., D. Schmitz and J. M. Walker (1986): The Assurance Problem in a Laboratory Market; in: *Public Choice,* 62, 217-236.

Kahneman, D., J. Knetsch and R. Thaler (1986): Fairness and the Assumption of Economics; in: *Journal of Business,* 59, 285-300.

Khanna, J., J. Posnett and T. Sandler (1995): Charity Donations in the UK: New Evidence based on Panel Data; in: *Journal of Public Economics,* 56, 257-272.

Kingma, B. R. (1989): An Accurate Measurement of the Crowd-out Effect, Income Effect, and Price Effect for Charitable Contributions; in: *Journal of Political Economy,* 97, 1197-1207.

Koestner, R., R. M. Ryan, F. Bernieri and K. Holt (1984): Setting Limits on Children's Behavior: The Differential Effects of Controlling vs. Informational Styles on Intrinsic Motivation and Creativity; in: *Journal of Personality,* 52(3) (September), 233-248.

Kramer, R. M. and T. R. Tyler (eds.) (1996): *Trust in Organizations,* Sage: Thousand Oaks.

Kunreuther, H. and D. Easterling (1990): Are Risk Benefit Tradeoffs Possible in Siting Hazardous Facilities?; *American Economic Review,* 80 (May), 252-56.

Lane, R. E. (1991): *The Market Experience,* Cambridge: Cambridge University Press.

Ledyard, J. (1995): Public Goods; in: J. Kagel and A. E. Roth (eds.), *Handbook of Experimental Economics,* Princeton: Princeton University Press, pp. 111-194.

Macy, M. W. (1991): Chains of Cooperation: Threshold Effects in Collective Action; *American Sociological Review,* 56, 730-747.

North, D. C. (1990): *Institutions, Institutional Change, and Economic Performance,* Cambridge: Cambridge University Press.

Oberholzer-Gee, F., I. Bohnet and B. S. Frey (1996): Fairness and Competence in Democratic Decisions; in: *Public Choice,* 91, 89-105.

Ostrom, E., R. Gardner and J. Walker (1994): *Rules, Games, and Common-Pool Resources,* University of Michigan Press: Ann Arbor.

Pommerehne, W.W., A. Hart and B. S. Frey (1994): Tax Morale, Tax Evasion and the Choice of Policy Instruments in Different Political Systems; in: *Public Finance,* 49, 52-69.

Robinson, P.H. and J.M. Darley (1995): The utility of desert; Working paper, Northwestern University School of Law.

Rose-Ackerman, S. (1996): Altruism, Nonprofits and Economic Theory; in: *Journal of Economic Literature,* 34, 701-728.

Rotter, J. B. (1966): Generalized Expectancies for Internal versus External Control of Reinforcement; in: *Psychological Monographs,* 80 (1, Whole No. 609).

Salamon, L. and H. K. Anheimer (1994): *The Emerging Sector: The Nonprofit Sector in Comparative Perspective - An Overview;* John Hopkins University Institute for Policy Studies, Baltimore.

Sally, D. (1995): Conversation and Cooperation in Social Dilemmas; in: *Rationality and Society,* 7, 58-92.

Sen, A. K. (1967): Isolation, Assurance and the Social Rate of Discount; in: *Quarterly Journal of Economics,* 81, 112-124.

Sen, A. K. (1977): Rational Fools: A Critique of the Behavioral Foundations of Economic Theory; in: *Philosophy and Public Affairs,* 6, 317-44.

Shapiro, C. and J. E. Stiglitz (1984): Equilibrium Unemployment as a Worker Discipline Device; in: *American Economic Review,* 74(June), 433-44.

Slemrod, J. (ed.) (1992): *Why People Pay Taxes. Tax Compliance and Enforcement,* University of Michigan Press, Ann Arbor.

Smith, V. L. and J. M. Walker (1993): Monetary Rewards and Decision Cost in Experimental Economics; in: *Economic Inquiry,* 31, 245-261.

Turner, J. C. (1987): *Rediscovering the Social Group,* Oxford: Oxford University Press.

Tyler, T. R. (1990): *Why People Obey the Law,* New Haven and London: Yale University Press.

Tyler, T.R. (1997): Procedural fairness and compliance with the law; in:" *Swiss Journal for Economics and Statistics,* forthcoming.

Comment on Bruno S. Frey and Iris Bohnet

Heiko Geue

Institutional Controls of Human Behaviour

In modern New Institutional Theory of Economics the concept of the "homo oeconomicus" is recognized as bounded rational and opportunistic. Bounded rationality leads to high costs for individuals who try to be completely informed. In particular, informational asymmetries in transaction processes and the resulting possibilities for opportunistic behaviour are taken into consideration. If the participants are not fully informed and the costs of acquiring a supply of all relevant information are too high, then room for discretion in exchange relationships exists. Better informed participants can shrewdly take advantage of "rent seeking". Thus the assumption that the rational, egoistic "homo oeconomicus" pursues rent seeking in institutional realms, seems to be a logical continuation of the profit maximization assumption in market relations.

But is their any conceivable society in which individuals just maximize profits and seek rents?

According to Frey and Bohnet, there is not. They choose another approach, opposite to that of the New Institutional Economics: Based on the premise that humans are in principle intrinsically motivated, Frey and Bohnet question why humans don't always choose to "leave rents".

In this context they define intrinsically motivated "rent leaving" as follows: If the possibility of rent seeking exists, but the individual consciously abstains from seeking rents, this may be referred to as "rent leaving". From this point of view the contrasting approach to the New Institutional Economics is clear.

Altogether Frey and Bohnet's analysis has two points of emphasis. First, they examine the reasons for rent leaving. They identify the importance of personal relations, participation (in political decision-making processes: mechanisms of direct democracy), communication and criticalness of individual investments for producing and financing public goods. Second, they question the reasons for crowding out intrinsically motivated morale in modern societies. The choice to opt-out in particular situations can be explained by extrinsic motivations such as monetary rewards or strict instructions in political or economic relationships which undermine intrinsic motivation. Such monetary measures, based on the price system, can lead to an "overjustification effect". In this case the intrinsic motivation is suppressed and substituted by extrinsic control. And the additional "motivational transfer effect" could cause this negative effect to be transferred to other realms of one's life. In addition these are *"The Hidden Costs of Reward"*.

According to Frey and Bohnet especially the following institutional arrangements cause the "crowding effect": the type of intervention (strict commands are more harmful than monetary rewards/communist societies are more harmful than market economies); the dependence on rewards for performance; anonymity instead of personal relationships; and finally inadequate participation in important decision-making processes.

Therefore Frey and Bohnet come to the following thesis:

Anonymous control mechanisms of human behaviour crowd out intrinsically motivated morale and first then cause the problem of "rent seeking".

Hence follow two main areas of examination. First, it is necessary to explore whether anonymous mechanisms of control - and here above all the price system - always crowd out intrinsically motivated morale or if they could be complementary to the intrinsically motivated control of human conduct. In this regard, it's a matter of whether the differentiation between intrinsically and extrinsically motivated behaviour is feasible, and also to consider if complex interdependencies exist that may be problematic.

Second, it must be verified, which controls are necessary in modern, open societies, simply due to the size of the society and the correspondingly unavoidable anonymity of relationships. Anonymous controls in form of competition (due to uncertainty) are important for decreasing private and public fulfilment of power when personal relationships are seldom, because of the number of individuals in society and the therewith connected complexity of the division of labour and knowledge. In that respect, the principle of subsidiarity as a guide for building socially justified societies must also be considered.

Now the aspects of moral behaviour no longer play a significant role in the Neoclassical theory, which wasn't always so in the field of economics. Previously the economic classics and the Scottish moral-philosophers examined the role of morale in controlling human conduct. Especially Adam Smith analysed in his "Theory of Moral Sentiments" which (institutional) controls of human behaviour are necessary in order for societies to work. Therefore Smith's theory of human conduct under different institutional arrangements will be discussed in the next section. This provides the background information necessary to discuss Frey and Bohnet's examination of the conditions that allow "rent leaving" in modern societies.

1 Adam Smith's Theory of Controls of Human Behaviour

In his "Theory of Moral Sentiments" Smith discusses societal problems which could derive from uncontrolled individual egoism. Following the traditional ideas of Humanism and the Enlightenment, Smith looks for controls of human behaviour which prevent naturally self-interested individuals from acting egoistically, e.g. opportunistically, or uninterested in the performance principle or careless conduct.

Both manners of behaviour, egoism and irresponsibility, are rejected (Recktenwald 1984, 51-55; Recktenwald 1990, LXXVII). Smith indicates sympathy,[3] moral rules, legal rules and competition as controls of human conduct. These controls promote the natural self-interest of human beings which is necessary for assuming responsibility. Without these controls individual responsibility is only otherwise derived from the conscience - in Smith's terminology the "impartial spectator". All of these controls are necessary for transforming selfish conduct of individuals into behaviour which promotes common weal - or in modern terms which limits opportunistic behaviour owing to egoism (Geue 1997; Meyer 1976, 18 f.; Samuels 1964I, 3) (see figure 1 by which Recktenwald expresses the core of Smith's social theory).[4]

According to the studies done by Frey and Bohnet the (institutional) controls of human behaviour can be differentiated between intrinsic and extrinsic motivation that promotes the common weal. The "impartial spectator" (the conscience), based on sympathy and ethical rules is intrinsically effective while legal rules and competition are extrinsic controls.

As mentioned previously Frey and Bohnet's main thesis is that these controls of human behaviour are mutually exclusive, i. e. extrinsic controls (law and competition) crowd out intrinsic ones (conscience, based on sympathy, and ethics). In this context it has to be pointed out that transitions between both groups of motivation flow freely and complex interdependencies or rather problems of transfer exist (Rüttinger et al. 1974, 84). What Frey and Bohnet don't explain however, is the primary phenomenon, i.e. the existence of intrinsically motivated morale. Another thing to consider is that human beings are capable of learning. If they have learned to reward and punish themselves the ability of self-determination increases. It is quite possible that in the learning history of individuals, intrinsic motivation originally results from extrinsic reward before the individuals had learned to motivate themselves (Wiswede 1991, 217f.).

---

[3] Here it should be noticed that Smith's definition of "sympathy" is unusually broad. According to him, sympathy denotes the fellow-feeling with any passion whatsoever. Without this feeling no orderly society could exist at all (Smith 1759/1985, 1ff.). Smith's definition of "sympathy" must not be confused with the modern meaning (Elsner 1989, 199f.; Eckstein 1985, LXIV-LXVI; Recktenwald 1990, XXXVI; Coase 1976, 529f.).

[4] Even now it should be evident that the ever reoccurring idea, that Smith would defend egoistic behaviour as being socially necessary, is wrong (Hayek 1952, 24-28; Hayek 1978, 268). On the contrary controls of human behaviour are necessary to transform the actions of egoistic individuals into self-interested and at the same time responsible behaviour. Only then is the development of a desirable order possible. This should also be sufficient to show that the controversial so-called "Adam Smith-Problem", i.e. the theoretical discrepancy between an alleged "egoism-ideal" in the "Wealth of Nations" and an alleged "altruism-ideal" in the "Theory of Moral Sentiments", is a pseudo-problem (Coase 1976, 541; Eckstein 1985, LVIIIf.; Geue 1997).

Figure 1: (Institutional) Controls of Human Behaviour

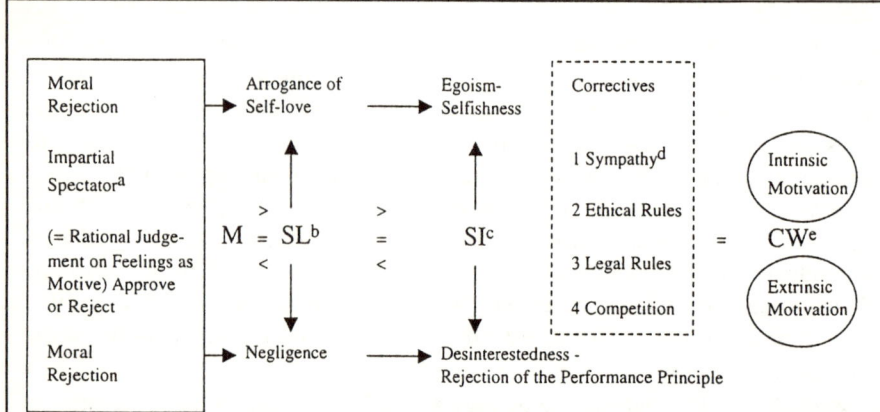

a   "Spectator" is a principle of rational judgement, which determines moral standards (M); the "spectator-principle" is neither Kant's "transcendental conscience" nor does it have an aristotelian meaning. ">" and "<" express divergent conduct from harmony (=) or equalisation between self-interest (SI) and common weal (CW), bonum commune.

b   Self-love (= motive for individual actions) is a natural feeling, "which comes to us from womb and never leaves us till we go into the grave".

c   Self-interest in all possible expressions (e.g. pursuit of profit) as a form of virtue and as a form of vice; as an endeavour to improve our life it is a relative goal - relative to space, time and information.

d   This is not the same as charity or altruism (= beneficence as opposed to benevolence); without sympathy reason is inhumane and powerless, without reasonable judgement sympathy remains empty. An order based on it or on charity isn't really stable.

e   Common Weal or bonum commune or public interest.

Source: Own translation of Recktenwald 1985, 23; Geue 1997.

The complexity of interaction between the not clearly differentiable groups of motivation therefore reminds one to be careful with deductions of theorems from the premise of the principal existence of intrinsic motivation - thus, the informational content of the premises cannot be enlarged by deduction. Hence, if the truth value of the premise is problematic the same problem exists for the deducted theorems (Engelhard, Fehl, Geue 1996, 272).

Going back to Smith's theory. According to Smith intrinsic motivation isn't enough to control human behaviour. Especially in large and open societies, relationships between the members of the society are characterised by their anonymity. Therefore ethical rules are typically weakened. Different people with different experiences have different ideas about ethical rules. If people can't communicate because of the sheer largeness of society, extrinsic motivations are a necessity. According to Smith competition under legal rules is the mechanism which ensures economic welfare and social justice (Recktenwald 1984,54; Recktenwald 1985,24; Recktenwald 1987, 523).

From Smith's ideas it is possible to derive a hierarchy of institutions which shows the position of institutions from the perspective of the acting individual.

Figure 2: Hierarchy of Institutions in Smith's Social Theory

↑ Power, Government, State, Law
Transaction and Competition
Norms, Ethical and Moral Rules
Values, Socialisation

Source: Geue 1997.

Figure 2 must be read from bottom to top and shows the different levels of corrective of self-interest human behaviour. The differentiation of levels is derived from the degree of institutional anonymity, i.e. the "social distance" between the individual and the institution. In developed economies most economic relationships are characterised by anonymity. Controls of human behaviour in form of ethical rules, values and socialisation are not enough to guarantee a "system of natural order and freedom" as Smith would say. Further levels of institutions are necessary in form of rules of competition and legal rules (Krüsselberg 1991, 29-32; Meyer 1976, 18).

The question remains: Do these controls of human behaviour crowd out intrinsical motivation - as Frey and Bohnet suspect - or are they complementary - as Smith expects? To solve the problem whether the price system crowds out intrinsically motivated morale or not, it is necessary to examine the effects of competition and the kinds of critical state activities more closely.

2 Competition as a means of control

Smith emphasises the importance of competition as a non-authoritarian control of human conduct. Hayek and other economists are convinced that this form of control is important for the development of orders (Krüsselberg 1984, 190-193; Samuels 1964II, 99). Hayek adopted Smith's approach to solve the problems of coordination which derive from dispersed knowledge of concrete circumstances:

> "The recognition that a man's efforts will benefit more people, and on the whole satisfy greater needs, when he lets himself be guided by the abstract signals of prices rather than by perceived needs, and that by this method we can best overcome our constitutional ignorance of most of the particular facts, and can make the fullest use of the knowledge of concrete circumstances widely dispersed among

millions of individuals, is the great achievement of Adam Smith" (Hayek 1978, 269).

If transactions between human beings are voluntary, i.e. if competition works, this is a sign of freedom and peacefulness of social relationships. The coordination of individual plans by means of competition for the best position in the market process increases wealth more than the wisest bureaucrat's plan could ever achieve. According to Hayek it is possible to use more knowledge in market economies than in any other order of society (Hayek 1978, 268f.; Hayek 1988, 14). This is an achievement of the price system which is implicitly recognized by Frey and Bohnet.

Yet another important achievement lies in the effect that in societies, which are characterized by the division of labor and knowledge, competition as a means of control prevents that people are subject to the intrinsic motivation of their transaction partners. In Smith's own words:

> "It is not from the benevolence of the butcher, the brewer, or the baker, that we expect our dinner, but from their regard to their own interest. We address ourselves, not to their humanity but to their self-love, and never talk to them of our own necessities but of their advantages. Nobody (...) chooses to depend chiefly upon the benevolence of his fellow-citizens." (Smith 1776/1990, 17).

Competition as a means of control and (in Hayek's terminology) of discovery guides human behaviour and leads to coordination through voluntary - perhaps intrinsically, but by all means extrinsically motivated - cooperation. Individual freedom will be protected from the degeneration of human behaviour in form of egoism or irresponsibility. An immanent dualism of Freedom and social control exists (Geue 1997; Samuels 1964I, 4 f.). Competition between a sufficiently number of competitors limits their possibilities of conduct and increases the degree of liberty on the demand side. Competition is not only necessary to establish "consumer sovereignty" - or better "individual sovereignty - but is also a means of external control to prevent that behaviour of just intrinsically motivated individuals degenerates. This is essential because *ex ante* intrinsical motivation isn't the same as morally correct conduct, as Frey and Bohnet themselves emphasize.

Hence, the possibilities of behaving opportunistically are to a certain extent diminished by competition, which is dependent on the knowledge problem. But are the possibilities to act intrinsically motivated in the form of "rent leaving" also limited? In order for competition to work in the described manner, rules for the order of competition are necessary. These rules must in addition to other accomplishments reduce the possibilities to act opportunistically. Precisely this perspective is criticized by Frey and Bohnet as inadequate. The rules of the order of competition must be regarded as fair, so as to preserve the intrinsically motivated morale of the citizens instead of crowding them out. This becomes a task for "Ordnungspolitik".

With this we are following one of Frey and Bohnet's main points of emphasis. They analyse how extrinsical motivation in the form of monetary rewards or direct directives crowd out intrinsical motivation by means of the "overjustification-effect". Now, this effect is not really to be expected in situations in which an individual acts under the condition of competition. If intrinsical motivation is a precondition to fulfill economic tasks efficiently the individual can't afford to lose his intrinsic motivation since he will be punished by negative extrinsic incentives - i.e. workers are threatened to lose their jobs and entrepreneurs are threatened to lose their market shares.

Monetary rewards under competition prevent that intrinsic motivation gets lost, if the reward of performance is considered as justified. But this requires establishment and guarantee of a functioning order of competition.

Frey and Bohnet have come up with criteria which are relevant to solve this task of "Ordnungspolitik": participation and communication are important to create criticalness. However these criteria are not complete until participation is emphasised by liability and the principle of subsidiarity. Only if participation is connected with liability the process of communication in firms and also in political decision-making situations secure that all participants take on responsibility. Intrinsic motivation will not be crowded out by the price system. The principle of subsidiarity ensures that the possibilities in a society to participate and to decide are utilised. In most modern societies mechanisms of direct political control can only be restrictedly brought into action. Therefore the principle of subsidiarity is a leitmotif for the building of societies in which citizens ensure through communication that their contribution will become critical. Common (intrinsic) values will be protected in such a society, in contrast to an order with strict hierarchies - a point which is stressed by Frey and Bohnet. For example they expect that in communist countries and in totalitarian systems citizens will become rent seekers because their intrinsic motivation is crowded out.

On a whole Smith's hypothesis, which is compatible with the approach of Frey and Bohnet, is as follows: different mechanisms of control of human behaviour must be combined in a consistent way. The formulation of the "pattern prediction" is: if only one level of institutional control drops out the system will not become a system of "natural liberty" - as Smith would call it. According to him the important motive of human action - i.e. self-interest, *not* egoism - creates the desired results only than, if all mechanisms of control work (Geue 1997).

Finally the outcome is that the transformation of individual actions into behaviour that promotes into common weal does not work automatically. There is always the danger that intrinsically motivated morale will be crowded out. But the event of this opportunity is only probable if extrinsic incentives are regarded as unfair. In economies in which neither private nor public power intentionally hinder individual elbow-room these controls will be considered as fair. Participation which is supported by liability in form of communication in enterprises and in the political process ensures that responsibility of all citizens is acquired. In those societies intrinsically motivated morale will lead to "rent leaving". The development of an order of competition which enables people to leave rents is the main task of "Ordnungspolitik" which is orientated by the principle of subsidiarity. Finally, it has to be remembered that this task is very complicated if the problem of avoiding "constructivism" is taken seriously.

References

Coase, R. H. (1976): Adam Smith's View of Man; in: *The Journal of Law and Economics*, 19, 529-546.

Eckstein, W. (1985): Einleitung des Herausgebers; in: A. Smith, *Theorie der ethischen Gefühle*, Hamburg: Felix Meiner, XI-LXXI.

Elsner, W. (1989): Adam Smith's Model of the Origins and Emergence of Institutions: The Modern Findings of the Classical Approach; in: *Journal of Economic Issues*, 23(1), 189-213.

Engelhard, P., U. Fehl and H. Geue (1996): Praxeology as a 'Quasi-Formal' Science; in: *Cultural Dynamics*, 8(3), 271-293.

Geue, H. (1997): *Evolutionäre Insititutionenökonomik - Ein Beitrag aus der Sicht der österreichischen Schule*, Diss., forthcoming.

Hayek, F. A. von (1952): Wahrer und falscher Individualismus; in: F.A. von Hayek, *Individualismus und wirtschaftliche Ordnung*, Erlenbach-Zürich: Eugen Rentsch, 9-48.

Hayek, F. A. von (1978): Adam Smith's Message in Today's Language; in: F.A. von Hayek, *New Studies in Philosophy, Politics, Economics and the History of Ideas*, London-Henley: Routledge & Kegan Paul, 267-269.

Hayek, F. A. von (1988): The Fatal Conceit. The Errors of Socialism, London: Routledge.

Krüsselberg, H.-G. (1984): Wohlfahrt und Institutionen: Betrachtungen zur Systemkonzeption im Werk von Adam Smith; in: F.-X. Kaufmann and H.-G. Krüsselberg (eds.), *Markt, Staat und Solidarität bei Adam Smith*, Frankfurt-New York, pp. 185-216.

Krüsselberg, H.-G. (1991): Adam Smith und die Deutschen: Gedanken zu den Ethischen Grundlagen von Wirtschaftssystemen; in: Forschungsstelle zum Vergleich wirtschaftlicher Lenkungssysteme (ed.), *Zur Transformation von Wirtschaftssystemen: Von der sozialistischen Planwirtschaft zur sozialen Marktwirtschaft*, Marburg: 2. überarbeitete und erweiterte Auflage, 15, 27-43.

Meyer, W. (1976): Das Vermächtnis des Adam Smith; *Rheinischer Merkur*, Nr. 11, 18-19.

Recktenwald, H. C. (1984): Die Klassik der ökonomischen Wissenschaft; in: O. Issing (ed.), *Geschichte der Nationalökonomie*, München:Vahlen, 49-71.

Recktenwald, H. C. (1985): *Ordnungstheorie und ökonomische Wissenschaft*, Erlanger Forschungen, Reihe A, Geisteswissenschaften, Band 36, Universitätsbund Erlangen-Nürnberg: Erlangen.

Recktenwald, H. C. (1987): Über das Selbstinteresse, Ein (auch) ethisches Prinzip moderner Ordnungstheorie; in: M. Borchert, U. Fehl and P. Oberender (eds.), *Markt und Wettbewerb*, Festschrift für Ernst Heuß zum 65. Geburtstag, Bern-Stuttgart: Haupt, 513-530.

Recktenwald, H. C. (1990): Würdigung des Werkes; in: A. Smith, *Der Wohlstand der Nationen. Eine Untersuchung seiner Natur und seiner Ursachen*, 5. Auflage, München: dtv klassik, XV-LXXIX.

Rüttinger, B., L. von Rosenstiel and W. Molt (1974): *Motivation des wirtschaftlichen Verhaltens*, W. Kohlhammer: Stuttgart-Berlin-Köln-Mainz.

Samuels, W. J. (1964I und II): The Classical Theory of Economic Policy: Non-Legal Social Control, Part I und Part II; in: *The Southern Economic Journal*, 31(1), 1-20 (I) and 31(2), 87-100 (II).

Smith, A. (1776/1990): *Der Wohlstand der Nationen. Eine Untersuchung seiner Natur und seiner Ursachen*; 5. Auflage, München: dtv klassik.

Smith, A. (1759/1985): *Theorie der ethischen Gefühle;* Felix Meiner, Hamburg.

Wiswede, G. (1991): *Einführung in die Wirtschaftspsychologie*; E. Reinhardt, München-Basel.

Comment on Bruno S. Frey and Iris Bohnet

Andreas Ortmann

An old problem, a new solution?

Frey and Bohnet (F&B from here on) address an old problem of economic modeling. Do people give without receiving some reward in return? Do they leave rents? In other words, are people altruistic? If so, why? The answers one gives to these questions have important consequences for the design of a wide array of institutions, from voluntary contribution and contingent valuation mechanisms, to civic governance, educational settings, other human services (child care, elder care, health), and activities involving adjustable effort and quality.[5]

The authors suggest that rent leaving, in contrast to extrinsically motivated moral behavior (Binmore 1994, 1997), is the result of intrinsic motivation. Whether intrinsic motivation exists at all is thus the first important issue. The second issue is to what extent it is negatively influenced by external intervention. F&B suggest that it is: "Intrinsic motivation is systematically influenced by external intervention. A group of cognitive social psychologists has identified particular conditions under which monetary (external) rewards undermine intrinsic motivation. The promise of rewards for undertaking an activity thus has indirect negative consequences. ... Many laboratory experiments support this motivational effect." In footnote 1, F&B identify Deci and collaborators as key contributors to

---

[5] Appealing to the authority of Arrow (1970), F&B throw the net even further. They claim that the price system would not work because "huge costs arise when people renege on contracts. As it is infeasible to draft every contract in complete detail, morale helps in supporting efficient exchange. Indeed ... an effort to draft contracts in greater detail worsens efficiency. It tends to crowd out the intrinsically motivated morale to observe the essence of the contract, and opens the path to opportunistic exploitation. For that reason, only fools would try to write a detailed marriage contract, or even a complete work contract." (2) As Klein and Leffler (1981) and many others thereafter (for example, Holmstroem and Tirole (1989); Kreps (1990) showed, reputational enforcement is a highly viable, and arguably more reliable way to prevent opportunistic exploitation, even in situations of adjustable effort and quality. A fool is the person who relies on the intrinsic motivation of those that sell car repair services, organic fruit, or health, child, and elder care. Given present and predicted divorce rates, a fool is also one who commits to marriage without writing a clear-cut prenuptial agreement (marriage contract). (Frey and Eichenberger1996; Sullivan 1997)

the relevant literature; the authors suggest that surveys and meta-analyses by Lane (1991, especially chapter 19), Wiersma (1992), Cameron and Pierce (1994), and Eisenberger and Cameron (1996) also support their assertion that rewards drive out intrinsic motivation.

Do monetary rewards really undermine intrinsic motivation: Debunking a myth

The analysis by Eisenberger and Cameron (1996) (which draws on the extensive meta-analysis by Cameron and Pierce (1994)) is the most recent and it is worth recalling its message: "We argue here that claimed negative effects of reward on task interest and creativity have attained the status of myth, taken for granted despite considerable evidence that the conditions producing these effects are limited and easily remedied. Our examination of the research literature revealed that (a) detrimental effects of reward occur under highly restricted, easily avoidable conditions; (b) mechanisms of instrumental and classical conditioning are basic for understanding incremental and decremental effects of reward on task motivation; and (c) positive effects of reward on generalized creativity are easily attainable using procedures derived from behavior theory." (1154)[6]

Specifically, Eisenberger and Cameron discuss Deci and Ryan (1985) who argued that rewards offered for taking part in an activity, completing a task, or solving a problem, reduce intrinsic interest by lessening self-determination. Eisenberger and Cameron, on theoretical and empirical grounds, refine Deci and Ryan's reinforcement classification of *task-contingent* into *performance-independent* and *completion-dependent* rewards (1155). They find "that the sole reliable decremental effect (on intrinsic motivation, AO) involves the time spent carrying out the activity following performance-independent reward." (1158) Interestingly, such measures as task interest, enjoyment, or satisfaction are not affected by performance-independent rewards. The same is true for completion-dependent rewards, and *quality-dependent rewards* -- rewards that are a function of "the quality of one's performance relative to some normative information or standard" (Deci and Ryan 1985, 74). Of course, it is these two latter reinforcement situations that are mostly relevant for economic interaction, especially situations of adjustable effort and quality, etc.

Eisenberger and Cameron remind us furthermore that the definition and measurement of (the crowding-out of) intrinsic motivation typically involves a group of experimental participants which is given a task for which they receive

---

[6] Eisenberger and Cameron trace the genesis of this myth to basic beliefs about human nature -- namely the widespread acceptance in Western civilization of the primacy of the individual -- as well as biases in the publication process (1157).

some reward. A control group performs the same activity without reward. Both groups then are observed during a nonreward period in which they can choose between continuation of the old activity or a new one. Intrinsic motivation is measured in this nonreward period. Clearly, this poses all kinds of interesting questions. For example, if motivation is intrinsic, why does intrinsic motivation not resort to the old level in the nonreward period? Also, the seeming detriments to intrinsic motivation were found in one-shot implementations of these experimental conditions; they have not been found under conditions of repeated reward presentations (Eisenberger and Cameron 1996, 1159/60). That is bothersome since most interactions, in particular those regarding principal-agent interaction as described by F&B are of the repeated-game variety.

Findings on (the crowding-out of) intrinsic motivation, furthermore, are nearly exclusively of the laboratory variety; it strikes me as a dubious leap of faith to assert that the intrinsic motivation that people may display when they take part in a typical laboratory activity, constitutes evidence that similar motivations drive people's actions in field settings. Last but not least, as I shall argue presently, findings from the field such as those regarding donations and the siting of locally unwanted projects come afflicted with serious methodological problems.

Eisenberger and Cameron's debunking of the myth that rewards drive out intrinsic motivation cannot come as a surprise to those who have followed some of the recent developments in experimental economics. Since altruism is often linked to (intrinsically motivated) morale, (laboratory) public good settings are a good point of departure for an understanding of the degree to which intrinsic motivation exists in such experiments and what recent developments in experimental economics teach us. I shall turn to these issues next.

Recent methodological advances in experimental economics

Recent experimental work has clarified the conditions under which in the past, deviations from game-theoretic predictions (=anomalies) have been generated. Of particular interest here are methodological issues regarding laboratory studies of voluntary contribution mechanisms and contingent valuation. As regards the former, until recently it seemed a well-established fact that subjects in laboratory voluntary contribution experiments overcontributed to a significant extent (Davis and Holt 1993; Ledyard 1995), typically between 30 to 70 % of their endowment.[7]

Recent advances in experimental economics, however, suggest strongly that these earlier results were artifacts of experimental design. Hoffman, McCabe, and

---

[7] Ledyard (1995) is often mentioned as an article documenting the numerous violations of game-theoretic predictions in public good experiments. My reading of his article is different. Ledyard is disconcerted by the failure of the free-rider hypothesis to be fully supported or fully rejected, and his very explicit admonition to those doing experiments is to better understand what happens in the laboratory.

Smith (1996) convincingly demonstrated for dictator games that the larger the social distance between experimenter and participants, the more subjects' choice behaviour corresponds to game-theoretic predictions. Andreoni followed up his earlier 'warm-glow' experiments cited by F&B and demonstrated both the impact of framing effects (Andreoni 1995a) and the importance of subject confusion (Andreoni 1995b); according to him, subject confusion explains roughly half of the warm-glow that he found in his earlier experiments. Similarly, Palfrey and Prisbey find that "overcontribution" is driven by "a combination of random variation in behavior and a few altruistic players." (1996, 409); they also find in about equal proportions altruistic and spiteful subjects although the intensity of altruism and spite seems small (1996, 422).

The preceding experiments all have corner-point Nash equilibria. This crucial aspect of the design makes confusion or random variation in behaviour appear to be altruism (intrinsic motivation) when it is not. To address this problem Keser (1996) recently presented the results of an ingenious experimental design in which she explored the suggestion that over-contribution is due to the corner-point solution design. In her experiment the dominant strategy for the constituent game requires partial contribution to the public good, thus creating an interior Nash equilibrium. She reports that her subjects still over-contribute, with the initial rate being 33 % -- roughly in line with results from corner-point solution experiments. Using Keser's parameterisation, Ortmann, Hansberry, and Fitzgerald (1997) modified three problematic aspects of her experimental design. First, following the lead of Hoffman and her colleagues, we implemented a double-blind design to eliminate confounding participant-experimenter effects. Second, in contrast to Keser's partners treatment, we used a strangers treatment (Andreoni 1983; Croson 1996; Keser and Van Winden 1996). Third, in contrast to Keser's 25 rounds of play we used 8. Our results yield an average contribution roughly in line with the game-theoretic prediction for repeated finite voluntary contribution games under complete information.

The above results and similar results by McKelvey and Palfrey (1992) for centipede games and Kagel, Kim, and Moser (1996) for ultimatum games, suggest that if altruism and intrinsic motivation are wide-spread, they are nevertheless unimportant if experimental conditions control appropriately for important design parameters.

As regards contingent valuation studies, Cummings and Harrison (1995) and Harrison (1996) have summarised masterfully the sorry state of affairs of experimental research in that area concentrating on such issues as the extent to which people actually pay the amounts they say they would in a contingent valuation study (No, they don't by a wide margin!), whether there is evidence that such studies can reliably elicit real economic commitments (No, again.), and whether there is evidence that subjects in contingent valuation studies generally will not free-ride (No, once again.)

On section IV: F&B's discussion of public good provision experiments

F&B discuss public good provision experiments. In support of their thesis that communication will advance willingness to give, they refer to Sally's (1995) meta-analysis of over 100 studies. Unfortunately, that study did not take into account the advances in experimental economics documented above. F&B also present studies from their own laboratory that seem to support their claim. Unfortunately, the results reported in their paper draw on experiments that were conducted during lecture time with economics students (Frey and Bohnet 1995), inviting experimenter-participant effects and -- because there was a chance that the participants would have interactions with each other in the future -- transforming the nature of the experiment to that of a repeated game. In this context, communication acted as additional confound. Interestingly, F&B get in their (one-shot) anonymity treatment wide-spread defection roughly in line with the results discussed in the previous section.

On sections II and III: Private donations

Frey and Bohnet claim that "private donations (to charity) are often intrinsically motivated." Based on my personal experience with the non-profit and voluntary sector in the USA, I doubt very much that private donations reflect lots of intrinsically motivated giving behavior. As a matter of fact, private donations more likely reflect aggressive fund raising techniques and people's attempt not to have their reputations impugned, or attempts to build reputations as charitable human beings -- reputations that can then be milked.

Take, for example, the extremely sophisticated fund driving techniques of the United Way which not only pit firms against each other via publicly announced participation rates, but do so within firms by pitting one department against the other. As Harbaugh (1996) has demonstrated, the United Way strategists also understand well donors' tastes for having their donations made public in order to gain prestige, and how to maximize their revenue by using categories including those that reflect tithing. Just in case potential donors are not sufficiently motivated by these strategies, the United Way employs drive coordinators at the department level that do not hesitate to remind you that surely you have forgotten to contribute to the common good.

Whatever the degree to which private donations are voluntary, the assumption that those who work professionally in the non-profit and voluntary sector are altruistic has been disastrous for the functioning of the sector. Not only is there disturbing evidence that questions the widespread perception that non-profits are in the business of providing for those in need (Clotfelter 1992), there is also disturbing evidence that non-profit organizations are riddled with systematic failures

On section V: Did monetary rewards drive out intrinsic motivation in Wolfenschiessen?

F&B claim that "the resistance to the siting of locally unwanted projects (the so-called 'Not In My Backyard' or NIMBY-syndrome) also reflects a Crowding-Out Effect." Drawing on Frey, Oberholzer-Gee and Eichenberger (1996) they suggest that in Wolfenschiessen more than half of the respondents to a survey initially agreed to have the repository built. To test the crowding-out of intrinsic motivation, the authors "repeated the exact same question, asking our respondents whether they were willing to accept the construction of a nuclear waste repository if the Swiss parliament decided to compensate all residents of the host community." (Frey, Oberholzer-Gee and Eichenberger 1996, 1306) The authors report that support for the facility in response to this hypothetical question dropped by more than half, to less than 25 percent of the respondents. F&B suggest that this result reflects the crowding-out of intrinsic motivation; I propose that the interview situation (and the hypothetical nature of the question) produced good-subject behavior or apprehension (Rosenthal & Rosnow 1991)^8. It is interesting to note, and F&B don't mention it in their paper, that one year after the survey the community of Wolfenschiessen accepted a formally offered compensation package. (Frey, Oberholzer-Gee and Eichenberger 1996, 1308) Talk was cheap after all.

Conclusion

My conclusions then are very different from those reached by Frey & Bohnet:
1) While the applicability of the price system is -- without doubt -- restricted in important respects, there is little evidence that rent leaving can be explained by way of intrinsic motivation. Better not to do it then.
2) The (laboratory and field) evidence that the application of external interventions affects intrinsically motivated morale is questionable at best. Surely, it is a shaky foundation to build the design of incentive compatible institutions on.
3) Since intrinsically motivated morale does not seem exist to any appreciable extent, economics as a science wanting to be politically relevant, instead of

---

[8] As Frey, Oberholzer-Gee and Eichenberger (1996, 1302) makes clear the survey was a one-hour personal interview. At the time of the interview Wolfenschiessen was one of four sites under consideration.

wasting resources on how to create and increase it, ought to allocate its resources to create institutions that take the scheming nature of homo oeconomicus as point of departure and try to prevent severe misalignments of incentives.

My conclusions imply a very different research strategy. Instead of building new economic theories on the shaky assumption of intrinsically motivated morale, I propose that we spend more resources on understanding the way laboratory data and certain field data are being generated. It is not that the kind of questions that F&B ask are not important: their results on the impact of communication are intriguing and surely deserve further investigation. However, before we try to reinvent economics through "empirical assumption making" (Rabin 1996, 57) of the kind that we also see practised in the paper discussed here, we ought to make sure that alleged patterns of behavior identified by psychological research are indeed a robust phenomenon and apply to the domain we claim it applies to. I'm not at all convinced that this is true for the case of intrinsically motivated morale.

In light of this, it strikes me as a dangerous enterprise to throw the child (game-theoretic, economic predictions) out of the bathtub because the water is a bit dirty. Rather, I am all in favor of better understanding methodological issues provoked by the way (experimental) economists and psychologists produce (laboratory) data. As recent developments have demonstrated, our understanding of the social psychology of the psychological and economic experiment and the reliability of our empirical knowledge base is rather poor. In light of recent methodological advances in experimental economics, much of the laboratory evidence on voluntary contribution and contingent valuation ought to be dismissed. I am convinced that the question of what it is that we elicit in the laboratory is the major issue that both (experimental) economists and (experimental) psychologists have to address.

References

Arrow, K.J. (1970): The Organization of Economic Activity: Issues Pertinent to the Choice of Market Versus Non-Market Allocation; in: R.H. Haveman and J. Margolis (eds.), *Public Expenditure and Policy Analysis*, Chicago: Rand McNally,67 - 81.

Andreoni, J. (1983): Why free ride? Strategies and Learning in Public Goods Experiments; *Journal of Public Economics*, 37, 291 - 304.

Andreoni, J. (1995a): Warm-Glow Versus Cold Prickle: The Effects of Positive and Negative Framing on Cooperation Experiments; *The Quarterly Journal of Economics*, 100, 1 - 21.

Andreoni, J. (1995b): Cooperation in Public Goods Experiments: Kindness or Confusion?; *The American Economic Review* 85, 891 - 904.

Ben-Ner, A. (1994): Who Benefits from the nonprofit sector? Reforming law and public policy towards nonprofit organizations; *Yale Law Journal* 104, 731 - 762.

Binmore, K. (1994): *Game Theory and the Social Contract, Volume 1: Playing Fair;* Cambrige, MA:The MIT Press.

Binmore, K. (1997): *Game Theory and the Social Contract, Volume 2: Just Playing;* Cambridge, MA: The MIT Press.

Cameron, J. and W.D. Pierce (1994): Reinforcement, Reward, and Intrinsic Motivation: A Meta-Analysis; *Review of Edcuational Research*, 64, 363 - 423.

Clotfelter, C.T. (ed.) (1992): *Who Benefits From the Nonprofit Sector?* Chicago: University of Chicago Press:.

Croson, R. (1996): Partners and Strangers Revisited; *Economics Letters,* 53, 25 - 32.

Cummings, R.G. and G. Harrison (1995): Was the Ohio Court Well Informed in its Assessment of the Accuracy of the Contingent Valuation Method?; *Natural Resources Journal*, 34, 1 - 36.

Davis, D.D. and C.A. Holt (1993): *Experimental Economics,* Princeton: Princeton University Press.

Deci, E.L. and R.M. Ryan (1985): *Intrinsic Motivation and Self-Determination in Human Behaviour*, New York :Plenum Press.

Eisenberger, R. and J. Cameron (1996): Detrimental Effects of Reward. Reality or Myth?; *American Psychologist*, 51, 1153 - 1166.

Frey, B.S. and I. Bohnet (1995): Institutions Affect Fairness: Experimental Investigations; *Journal of Institutional and Theoretical Economics*, 151, 286 - 303.

Frey and Eichenberger (1994): Economic Incentives Transform Psychological Anomalies; *Journal of Economic Behavior and Organization*, 23, 215 - 234.

Frey, B.S. and R. Eichenberger (1996): Marriage Paradoxes; *Rationality and Society*, 8, 187 - 206.

Frey, B.S., F. Oberholzer-Gee, and R. Eichenberger (1996): The Old Lady Visits the Backyard: A Tale of Morals and Markets; *Journal of Political Economy*, 104, 1297 - 1313.

Harbaugh, W.T. (1996): What Do Donations Buy? A Model of Philanthropy and Tithing Based on Prestige and Warm Glow.; Working paper (See http://harbaugh.uoregon.edu/).

Harrison, G. (1996): Experimental Economics and Contingent Valuation; Working paper (See http://theweb.badm.sc.edu/glenn/eecv.html).

Hoffman, E., K. McCabe and V. Smith (1996): Social Distance and Other Regarding Behavior in Dictator Games; *American Economic Review*, 86, 653 - 659.

Holmstroem, B. and J. Tirole (1989): The Theory of the Firm; in: R. Schmalensee and R.D. Willig (eds.), *Handbook of Industrial Organization*, Amsterdam-New York-Oxford-Tokyo: Vol. 1, North Holland, 61 - 133.

Kagel, J.H., C. Kim, and D. Moser (1996): Fairness in Ultimatum Games with Asymmetric Information and Asymmetric Payoffs; *Games and Economic Behavior*, 13, 100 - 110.

Keser, C. (1996): Voluntary contributions to a public good when partial contribution is a dominant strategy; *Economics Letters*, 50, 359 - 366.

Keser, C. and F. Van Winden (1996): Partners Contribute More to Public Goods Than Strangers: Conditional Cooperation; Working paper.

Klein, B. and K. Leffler (1981): The Role of Market Forces in Assuring Contractual Compliance; *Journal of Political Economy*, 91, 615 - 640.

Kreps, D.M. (1990): Corporate Culture and Economic Theory; in: J. Alt and K. Shepsle (eds.), *Perspectives Positive Political Economy*, Cambridge, UK: Cambridge University Press, 90 - 143.

Lane, R.E. (1991): *The Market Experience*, Cambridge: Cambridge University Press.

Ledyard, J. (1995): Public Goods; in: J. Kagel and A.E. Roth (eds.), *Handbook of Experimental Economics*, Princeton: Princeton University Press, 111 - 194.

McKelvey, R. and T. Palfrey (1992): An Experimental Study of the Centipede Game; *Econometrica*, 60, 803 - 836.

Ortmann, A. (1996): Modern Economic Theory and the Study of Nonprofit Organizations: Why the Twain Shall Meet.; *Nonprofit and Voluntary Sector Quarterly*, 25, 470 - 484.

Ortmann, A., K. Hansberry, and J. Fitzgerald (1996); Voluntary Contributions to a Public Good When Partial Contribution is a Dominant Strategy: A Re-examination; Working paper.

Palfrey, T.R. and J.E. Prisbey (1996): Altruism, Reputation and Noise in linear public goods experiments; *Journal of Public Economics*, 61, 409 - 27.

Rabin, M. (1996): Psychology and Economics; Manuscript.

Rosenthal, R. and R. Rosnow (1991): *Essentials of Behavioral Research: Methods and Data Analysis (Second Edition,* McGraw-Hill, New York.

Sally, D. (1995): Conversation and Cooperation in Social Dilemmas; *Rationality and Society*, 7, 58 - 92.

Sullivan, A. (1997): Kiss Me and Sign Here, Darling. Demand for Prenuptial Agreements Is on the Rise. International Herald Tribune, February 8-9, 1997.

Wiersma, U.J. (1992): The Effects of Extrinsic Rewards in Intrinsic Motivation: A Meta-Analysis; *Journal of Occupational and Organizational Psychology*, 65, 101 - 114.

Reasoning in Economics and Psychology: Why Social Context Matters

Andreas Ortmann and Gerd Gigerenzer

Introduction

Both psychology and economics have been shaped by two sets of competing programs. Roughly, traditional programs in both disciplines have postulated the existence of norms of optimal reasoning and/or behavior. In both disciplines these programs have been challenged by competing ones that, while maintaining the traditional norms of sound reasoning and/or behavior, have argued that human beings fail miserably at both.

This article is organized as follows: We first discuss traditional programs of thinking about reasoning in psychology and their problems. Next we identify a set of parallel programs and problems in economics. In the third section we present new models of thinking about reasoning in psychology. In the last section, we discuss the implications of these new models for experimental economics.

1 Traditional Models of Reasoning in Psychology

Two programs. Research on human reasoning, judgement, and decision making has been shaped by two major programs. The first assumed that the laws of logic and probability theory represent the laws of rational reasoning, and that humans actually follow these laws. This view is captured in Pierre Laplace's famous phrase that probability theory is "only common sense reduced to a calculus." Variants of this view, which traces its origin to the Enlightenment, can be found from Jean Piaget's formal operations to Bayesian models of cognitive processes. The first program thus emphasizes human rationality. The second program emphasizes human irrationality. Like the Enlightenment program, it assumes that rational judgement and behavior can be reduced to the laws of logic and probability, but claims that human cognition systematically deviates from these norms. Examples of the second program are the heuristics-and-biases research of Daniel Kahneman and Amos Tversky, confirmation bias research, and research on the Wason selection task.

Two problems. The problem with these two programs is that (a) rationality is reduced to mere syntactical relations, to the exclusion of the semantic, pragmatic, ecological, and social[1], and (b) for any real-world situation of some complexity, the human mind is assumed to be a supercomputer like a Laplacean demon, with almost unlimited knowledge, time, and computational capacity. To use Simon's intriguing metaphor, both of these competitors ignore that rationality is "a scissors whose two blades are the structure of task environments and the computational capabilities of the actor" (Simon 1990, 7).

An outstanding example: Wason selection task. Wason (1966, 1968) designed what has become "the most intensively researched single problem in the history of the psychology of reasoning" (Evans, Newstead, and Byrne 1993, 99). The Wason selection task has arguably raised more doubts about human reasoning than any other toy problem with which psychologists play. In the Wason selection task, an experimenter presents subjects with a conditional claim of the form *If p, then q.* One such conditional claim is the following letters-and-numbers rule, *If there is an "A" on one side (p), then there is a "2" on the other side (q).* Subjects are shown four cards, each with a number on one side and a letter on the other. The cards are face down, and the top sides show A, K, 2, and 7. Subjects are then asked to select those cards, and only those, that allow them to determine whether the rule is violated. See Table 1.

Table 1

Letters-and-numbers rule:
If there is an "A" on one side (p), then there is a "2" on the other side (q).
Each of the following cards has a letter on one side and a number on the other. Indicate only the card(s) you definitely need to turn over to see if the rule has been violated.
[A]   [K]   [2]   [7]

The Wason selection task has been interpreted as a laboratory version of Popper's falsificationist strategy of testing hypotheses. This strategy is based on the insight that verification and falsification of general laws are asymmetric.[2] For

---

[1] "Pragmatic" relates the semantic (i.e., the meaning of a proposition) to the goals of an individual, "ecological" describes decision theoretic situations (games against Nature), and "social" describes game theoretic situations (games against other players). See Gigerenzer (1995, 1996, 1996a), Gigerenzer and Hoffrage (1995), Gigerenzer and Hug (1992), Gigerenzer and Murray (1987), Hertwig, Gigerenzer, and Hoffrage (1996), Hertwig and Gigerenzer (1997) for publications that belabor this point; see Kahneman and Tversky (1996) for a contrary view.

[2] Obviously, this is true only for the deterministic case. The argument does not apply for the probabilistic case, and hence situations of risk and uncertainty. We will not discuss the implications of this important case distinction. Some interesting recent developments take the probabilistic case as point of departure arguing the selection task ought to be understood as decision-making rather than a deductive reasoning task. Oaksford and Chater (1994, 1996) and Green and Over (1996) are three recent examples of this rapidly expanding research area.

example, assume you were asked to test the claim, "All flamingos are pink." It takes one counterexample to falsify the claim. In contrast, even if one observed thousand flamingos and found them to be all pink, one would not be able to ultimately verify the claim. Popper thus suggested that the optimal strategy is a falsificatonist one: Find that one maroon flamingo that refutes the claim and you're home free. In terms of the Wason selection task, the only way to falsify the conditional claim *If p, then q* is to look for cards with *p* on one side and *not-q* on the other. Following Popper's logic, subjects should hence choose to turn over the *p*-card and the *not-q*-card. For the letter-and-numbers example of Table 1, subjects should choose to turn over the A-card and the 7-card.

Experimental tests of the Wason selection task. Wason found that only about 10 percent of the subjects made this selection in his toy problem. This result lead to an avalanche of studies that confirmed Wason's result under numerous slight changes in the protocol. Specifically, it was found that most people select the *p*-card and the *q*-card, or only the *p*-card. Manktelow and Evans (1979), Pollard (1982), Cosmides (1989), and Gigerenzer and Hug (1992) soon found, however, that the selections were highly dependent on the content of the conditional statement. These results -- a low overall proportion of *p & not-q* answers and the content effect -- contradicted the model of human reasoning provided by propositional logic. Human reasoning was blamed as irrational.

2   Traditional Models of Reasoning in Economics

Two programs. Research on human rationality in economics has likewise been shaped by two major programs. The first program is the neo-classical paradigm. Going back to Adam Smith, it assumes that people are self-interested[3], and has found its modern expression in the eductive (deductive) approach to non-cooperative game theory[4] of which the neo-classical paradigm has become a special case (Barro 1990; Kreps 1990). The eductive approach to game theory is based on strong rationality and knowledge assumptions. The second program emphasizes human irrationality by identifying ever new anomalies, or systematic deviations from predictions of standard economic (game-theoretic) models. Like the eductive

---

[3]   "It is not from the benevolence of the butcher, the brewer, or the baker, that we expect our dinner, but from their regard to their own interest." (Smith 1776, 26/27)

[4]   Binmore explains "There are two types of influence, not necessarily independent, which could well be relevant to an explanation of why *homo oeconomicus* might be a useful approximation to *homo sapiens* in a given context. The first is the influence of *education* and the second of *evolution*." (Binmore 1990, 15). "The word *eductive* will be used to describe a dynamic process by means of which equilibrium is achieved through careful reasoning on the part of the players. ... The word *evolutive* will be used to describe a dynamic process by means of which equilibrium is achieved through evolutionary mechanisms. ... adjustment takes place as a result of *iterated* play by *myopic* players." (Binmore 1990, 155)

approach to game theory, it assumes that rational decision making and behavior can be reduced to norms of reasoning such as avoidance of dominated strategies, use of backward induction, etc., but claims that human decision making and behavior deviates from these norms. This program, now becoming known as behavioral economics (Camerer, 1997; Rabin 1996) draws heavily on the heuristics-and-biases research of Kahneman and Tversky.

Two problems. The problem with these two programs is that they, like their counterparts in psychology, ignore the semantic, pragmatic, ecological, and social -- this being most dramatically illustrated by the abstract settings which experimental economists use as testbeds. Furthermore, for any real-world situation of some complexity, the normative models assume that the human mind is a supercomputer like a Laplacean demon, with almost unlimited knowledge, time, and computational capacity. In other words, these programs do not account for the complexity of task environments and the computational capabilities of actors (Simon 1990, 7).

An outstanding example: Principal-agent games. Principal-agent games are arguably the most important class of toy problems in economics. They draw their importance from their role as building blocks in the analysis of the internal organization of for-profit and non-profit firms (Kreps 1990a, Ortmann 1996, 1999), Tirole (1988, 1994), markets involving adjustable quality (Klein and Leffler 1981), acquisition of self-command (Meardon and Ortmann 1996, 1996a), and so on.

Assume that you are about to start working for a small company, and are told that the company has the following day-off rule, *If an employee works on the weekend, then he gets a day off during the week.* You understand that the employer faces a moral hazard problem: Why give you a day off during the week if you have worked on the weekend? You also understand that the answer to the question depends on whether the situation is a repeated game, and how well information travels within the company. Will you trust what you have been told about the day-off rule? A typical parameterization of the normal form of this principal-agent game is shown in Figure 1.[5]

---

[5] Each pair of numbers represents the payoffs of the employer and the prospective employee. The first number denotes the payoff of the employer, the second denotes the payoff of the prospective employee. For a more detailed justification of the payoffs chosen here, see Ortmann and Colander (1997).

Figure 1

		Prospecctive employee	
		Trust	*Do not*
Employer	*Adhere to rule*	(1, 1)	(0, 0)
	Do not	(2, -1)	(0, 0)

If this game were a one-shot game, then the game-theoretic prediction (and implicit norm of reasoning) would be for the prospective employee to reason through the employer's incentives and, upon realizing that the employer has a (weakly) dominant strategy, not to trust the employer.[6] The prospective employee is thus assumed to "solve" this game by putting himself in the employer's shoes, meaning he is assumed to compare the employer's payoffs under the different scenarios, to anticipate the likely choices of the employer, and then to make the decision whether the employer can be trusted or not. The resulting outcome (don't, don't) would be socially suboptimal. The mode of reasoning employed by the prospective employee -- analyzing the smallest subgames at the end of the decision tree first, and thus "folding" the tree back to the initial node -- represents the essence of backward induction and can be illustrated in one of the extensive forms associated with the normal form. See Figure 2.

Figure 2

	Trust	Employer	Adhere to rule	1, 1
			Do not	2,-1
Prospective employee				
	Do not	Employer	Adhere to rule	0, 0
			Do not	0, 0

Do people backward induct? Experimental evidence. The evidence is rather mixed. In part that is a function of how one evaluates the behavior of subjects in experiments that involve backward induction. For example, in a centipede game it makes perfect sense not to defect in early stages if one has reason to believe that the relevant population contains (even a small fraction of) altruists. (Reny 1992 offers an excellent discussion of this argument in the context of a three dollar

---

[6] In other words, (weak) dominance and common knowledge induce a Nash equilibrium.

Take-Or-Leave-It game.) It is an open question whether this assumption is justified.[7]

The experimental results of the guessing game discussed in Nagel (1995), Stahl (1996), Stahl (1997), or the alternating offer games discussed in Camerer, Johnson, Sen, and Rymon (1993) and Johnson, Camerer, Sen, and Rymon (1996) confirm the earlier assessment that "despite the theoretical elegance of backward-induction rationality, it often fails to predict the behavior of subjects." (Davis and Holt 1993, 109) However, it is noteworthy that people can be taught to apply backward induction and find the equilibrium for the alternating offer game studied in Camerer et al. (1993) (see Johnson et al. 1996).

3 New Models of Reasoning in Psychology[8]

The role of content and context in reasoning. In the wake of Wason's result, content was added to experimental tasks. The traditional letters-and-numbers selection tasks were put into thematic garb. Subjects would now be tested on thematic rules such as, *If a person goes into Boston, then he takes the subway.* Or, they would be given the day-off rule, *If an employee works on the weekend, then that person gets a day off during the week.* See Tables 2 and 3.

It turned out that the number of "logical" answers increased dramatically. About 30 % to 40 % of subjects typically chose the *p* and *not-q*-cards in the transportation problem (Cosmides 1989), while 75 % did so in the day-off problem (Gigerenzer and Hug 1992). These results -- a low overall proportion of *p* and *not-q* answers and the content effect -- contradicted the model of human reasoning provided by propositional logic. While propositional logic was subsequently abandoned as a *descriptive* model, many researchers retained it as the *normative* model of reasoning.

---

[7] Recent evidence from centipede (McKelvey and Palfrey 1992), ultimatum (Kagel, Kim, and Moser 1996), voluntary contribution (Palfrey and Prisbey 1996), and prisoners' dilemma (Cooper, Dejong, Forsythe, and Ross 1996) experiments suggest strongly that if altruism is wide-spread, it is nevertheless unimportant. These recent results suggest that the self-interest model works reasonably well, especially if one takes into account that, among other things, the social distance between experimenter and participants was not controlled for in any of these experiments. The importance of social distance was recently driven home by Hoffman, McCabe, and Smith (1996). Their results indicate that increasing the social distance between experimenter and subjects moves experimental results even closer to the standard game-theoretic predictions for games under complete information, at least for certain games (dictator games). While the impact of social distance for other games is disputed, the results by Hoffman and her colleagues pose serious enough questions about the validity of past experimental results. (See the literature on the social psychology of the psychological experiment (Rosenzweig 1933, Rosenthal and Rosnow 1991 for similar insights.)

[8] This section draws heavily on Gigerenzer (1996b).

Table 2

Transportation rule:
If a person goes into Boston, then he takes the subway.   The cards below have information about four Cambridge residents. Each card represents one person. One side of the card tells where the person went and the other side tells how the person got there. Indicate only the card(s) you definitely need to turn over to see if the rule has been violated.   [Subway]   [Arlington]   [Cab]   [Boston]

Table 3

Day-off rule:
If an employee works on the weekend, then that person gets a day off during the week.   The cards below have information about four employees. Each card represents one person. One side of the card tells whether the person worked on the weekend, and the other side tells whether the person got a day off during the week. Indicate only the card(s) you definitely need to turn over to see if the rule has been violated.   [worked on the weekend]   [did get a day off]   [did not work on the weekend]   [did not get a day off]

In the mid-1980s a few researchers in the psychology of reasoning freed themselves of the straitjacket of propositional logic, and looked at dimensions of reasoning beyond entailment and contradiction. Cheng and Holyoak (1985), Cosmides (1989), and Cosmides and Tooby (1992), Gigerenzer and Hug (1992), among others, dared to introduce the content of the p's and q's into their theories, and thus to start with the *content* of a conditional statement rather than with propositional logic. The terra incognita of content thus became a legitimate topic of study.

While Cheng and her collaborators postulated a set of pragmatic reasoning schemas such as permission and obligation, Cosmides and Tooby connected information search with pragmatic goals such as cheater detection, with cost-benefit analyses, and the broader evolutionary theory of reciprocal altruism. Cosmides and Tooby's central point is that humans are one of the very few species that practice cooperation between unrelated conspecifics ("reciprocal altruism"), and that selective cooperation demands the ability to detect cheaters. This ability presupposes several others, including that of distinguishing different individuals, recognizing when a social contract is offered, and computing the costs and benefits. An important point is that selective cooperation would not work without a cognitive program for detecting cheaters - or, more precisely, a program for directing an organism's attention to information that could reveal that it (or its group) is being cheated: whether this happens automatically through some module specifically designed for social contracts, or as the domain-general reasoning process modeled by game theory, is at the heart of the debate over domain specificity.

An aside on domain specificity. The basic idea is that human actors invoke different cognitive modules for different adaptive problems. This idea of modular intelligence builds on Simon's notion of bounded rationality; however, it goes beyond his notion by postulating that through evolutionary pressures the mind has developed mental models or algorithms that apply to specific problems (domains) such as distinguishing safe from poisonous foods, choosing a mate, and detecting cheaters in social exchanges (Cosmides 1989, Cosmides and Tooby 1992, 1994, 1996, Gigerenzer and Hug 1992, Gigerenzer 1996a, Wang 1996).

The results regarding thematic selection tasks -- presently to be discussed -- have been interpreted as evidence for the existence of "domain-specific, content-dependent rules of inference that are adaptively appropriate only to that task." (Cosmides and Tooby 1994, 62/63). Whether this is indeed so, is an issue on which the present authors disagree. This difference in opinion seems to reflect a general difference of opinion concerning the issue of modularity and plasticity of the brain. The key issue is whether the same convincing evidence that exists for example for the separation of primary cortices into cortices dedicated to visual, auditory, and gustatory/olfactory cortices, or the further subdivision of the visual system into the dorsal and ventral streams (McClelland 1996) can be mustered for the sphere of social interaction.

Cosmides' and Gigerenzer's thesis is that some "cheating detection mechanism" (which alternatively may be interpreted as a convenient descriptor for a, possibly quick-and-dirty, game-theoretic analysis) guides reasoning in the following selection task:

> If the conditional statement is coded as a social contract, and the subject is cued in to the perspective of one party in the contract, then attention is directed to information that can reveal being cheated.

Being cheated in a social contract means that someone takes the benefit, but does not pay the cost.[9] In other words, a subject should select those cards that correspond to "benefit taken" and "cost not paid," whatever the cards' logical status is. For the day-off rule (Table 3), the employer takes the benefit of the employee working on the weekend, without paying the cost of giving the employee the promised day off.

Experimental results. Cosmides has shown that her results as well as earlier studies corroborated her thesis. If the conditional statement expressed a social contract, then the percentage of "benefit taken" *and* "cost not paid" selections was very high. For instance, in the day-off problem and similar social contract situations typically 70 - 90 % of subjects make these choices (Gigerenzer and Hug 1992). Since these results are consistent with three competing accounts that do not

---

[9] Cosmides and Tooby (1992) make it clear that this idea was informed by simple game-theoretic toy games of the (one- and two-sided) prisoners' dilemma variety.

relate to cheating detection, researchers also looked at tests that differentiate between them.

Availability or cheater detection? The major accounts of the content effects in the 1970s and 1980s were variously called "familiarity" and "availability" (Manktelow and Evans 1979, Pollard 1982). The basic idea is that familiarity with a situation makes violations more "available" in memory; selection may thus reflect availability. If familiarity were indeed the guiding cognitive principle, then *unfamiliar* social contracts should not elicit the same results. However, Cosmides (1989), Gigerenzer and Hug (1992), and Platt and Griggs (1993) showed that social contracts with unfamiliar propositions elicit the same high percentages of "benefit taken" and "cost not paid" selections.

Are people simply good at reasoning about social contracts? Another, closely related conjecture claims that people are, for some reason, better at reasoning about social contracts than about letters-and numbers problems. Social contracts may be more "interesting" or "motivating," or people may have some "mental model" for social contracts that affords "clear" thinking. Although this alternative is nebulous, it needs to be taken into account; in her tests, Cosmides (1989) did not distinguish between social contracts and cheating detection. Gigerenzer and Hug (1992) disentangled social contracts from cheating detection. They used social contracts, but varied whether the search for violations constituted looking for cheaters or not. For instance, consider the following social contract: "If someone stays overnight in the cabin, then that person must bring along a bundle of wood from the valley." This was presented in one of two context stories.

The "cheating" version explained that a cabin high in the Swiss Alps serves as an overnight shelter for hikers. Since it is cold and firewood is not otherwise available, the Swiss Alpine Club has made the rule that each hiker who stays overnight in the cabin must bring along a bundle of firewood from the valley. The subjects were cued to the perspective of a guard who checks whether any of four hikers has violated the rule. The four hikers were represented by four cards that read "stays overnight in the cabin," "does not stay overnight," "carried wood," and "carried no wood." The instruction was to indicate only the card(s) you definitely need to turn over to see if any of these hikers have violated the rule.

In the "no-cheating" version, the subjects were cued to the perspective of a member of the German Alpine Association, visiting the same cabin in the Swiss Alps to find out how it is managed by the local Alpine Club. He observes people carrying firewood into the cabin, and a friend accompanying him suggests that the Swiss may have the same overnight rule as the Germans, namely, "If someone stays overnight in the cabin, then that person must bring along a bundle of wood from the valley." That this is also the Swiss Alpine Club's rule is not the only possible explanation; alternatively, its members (who do not stay overnight in the cabin), and not the hikers, might bring firewood. The subjects were now in the position of an observer who checks information to find out whether the social contract suggested by his friend actually holds. This observer does not represent a party in a social contract. The subjects' instruction was the same as in the cheating version.

Thus, in the cheating scenario, the observation "benefit taken and cost not paid" means that the party represented by the guard is being cheated; in the no-cheating scenario, the corresponding observation suggests only that the Swiss Alpine Club never made the supposed rule in the first place.

Gigerenzer and Hug (1992) found that in the overnight problem 89 % of the subjects selected "benefit taken" and "cost not paid" when cheating was at stake, compared with 53 % percent in the no-cheating version. Similarly, the averages across all four test problems used were 83 % and 45 %, respectively.

Do social contracts simply facilitate logical reasoning?

In most of Cosmides' tests, the predicted "benefit taken" and "cost not paid" selections corresponded to the truth conditions of conditionals in propositional logic. Thus, a third conjecture would be that social contracts may somehow facilitate logical reasoning. Gigerenzer and Hug (1992) tested this conjecture by deducing predictions from the cheating-detection hypothesis that contradicted propositional logic. The key to these tests is that cheating detection is pragmatic and perspectival, whereas logic is aperspectival. For example, in the day-off problem subjects were originally cued to the perspective of an employee, in which case cheating detection and propositional logic indeed predict the same cards. Gigerenzer and Hug (1992) switched the perspective from employee to employer but held everything else constant (the conditional statement, the four cards, and the instructions). For the employer, being cheated meant that the employee "did not work on the weekend and did get a day off"; that is, in this perspective subjects should select the "did not work on the weekend" and the "did not get a day off" cards, which correspond to the not-p and q cards. (Note that "*not-p & q*" selections have rarely been observed in selection tasks.) Thus, perspective change can play cheating detection against propositional logic. The two competing predictions are: If the cognitive system attempts to detect instances of "benefit taken and cost not paid" in the other party's behavior, then a perspective switch implies switching card selections; if the cognitive system reasons according to propositional logic, however, pragmatic perspectives are irrelevant, people should reason "logically", and there should be no switch in card selections.

The results showed that when the perspective was changed, the cards selected also changed in the predicted direction. The effects were strong and robust across problems. For instance, in the employee perspective of the day-off problem, 75 % of the subjects had selected "worked on the weekend" and "did not get a day off," but only 2 % had selected the other pair of cards. In the employer perspective, this 2 % (who had selected "did not work on the weekend" and "did get a day off") rose to 61 % (Gigerenzer and Hug 1992). The result is consistent with the thesis that attention is directed toward information that could reveal oneself (or one's group) as being cheated in a social contract, but is inconsistent with the claim that reasoning is directed by a logic independent of content.

Thus, social contracts do not simply facilitate logical reasoning. We believe that the program of reducing context, merely to an instrument for "facilitating" logical reasoning, is misguided. Reasoning consistent with propositional logic is entailed by some perspectives (e.g., the employee's), but is not entailed by other perspectives (e.g., the employer's).

4 New Models of Reasoning in Economics?

Gigerenzer and Hug's discovery of perspective effects -- "one of the most interesting findings in the recent literature on the selection task" (Girotto 1995, 333) -- has ambiguous implications especially for experimental economics -- the main provider of the anomalies on which behavioral economics is built.

On the one hand, Gigerenzer and Hug's results are a ringing endorsement of experimental economists' practice of not only cueing subjects in, but letting them enact the roles of employees and employers, agents and principals. On the other hand, their results erect important warning signs regarding experimental economists' practice of putting their subjects into settings that are as abstract (content-free) as possible. We believe that this practice, in light of the content effects documented above, warrants re-examination. To extrapolate from the new models of reasoning in psychology, and the experimental support in their favor, there is abundant evidence that people do not fail as miserably in their decision-making and judgement abilities, as has been suggested by the heuristics-and-biases program or behavioral economics. Rather, people seem to bring a sound social intelligence into the laboratory that often seems to serve them well in their "natural" environment, though it may fail them in the artificial world of the laboratory. When experimental economists elicit subjects' responses in the laboratory, and try to do this in a context-free way, it is not always clear how subjects' social intelligence affects the results.

As regards the day-off rule and the associated principal-agent game, subjects might interpret the situation with which they are confronted as that of an indefinitely repeated game that makes backward induction indeed unnecessary. That subjects (who seem to act as intuitive statisticians) do not apply backward induction is thus not indicative of their inability to reason properly, but the experimenter's failure to create the laboratory situation that he or she allegedly investigates.

We believe that there are two important avenues to pursue (that at first sight may be contradictory): First, exploration of experimental practices in economics as reflected in the important work of Harrison (1992) and Hoffman, McCabe, and Smith (1996). Second, an exploration of the impact of content in economics experiments. That such content effects matter has been recently suggested by

Camerer (1997), Dyer and Kagel (1996) and Harrison (1996).[10] However, experimental economics has a way to go toward an understanding of issues of content and context.

It is not without irony that Adam Smith had figured things out more than two hundred years ago. The quotation with which we kicked off this article documents his deep skepticism of the utility of logic exercises devoid of content -- "an artificial method of reasoning," as his biographer called it. For Smith the powers of the human mind had to be gauged by an examination of the social context in which communication and persuasion happened. Two hundred years later, economists still ought to heed Smith's advice.

References

Barro, R. (1990): *Macroeconomic Policy;* Cambridge, MA: Harvard University Press.

Binmore, K. (1990): *Essays on the Foundations of Game Theory;* Cambridge, MA : Basil Blackwell.

Camerer, C. (1997): Progress in Behavioral Game Theory; *Journal of Economic Perspectives*, 11, 167-188.

Camerer, C., E.J. Johnson, S. Sen, and T. Rymon (1993): Cognition and Framing in Sequential Bargaining for Gains and Losses; in: K. Binmore, A. Kirman and P. Tani (eds), *Frontiers of Game Theory*, Cambridge, MA: MIT Press.

Cheng, P.W. and K.J. Holyoak (1985): Pragmatic Reasoning Schemes; *Cognitive Psychology*, 17, 391 - 416.

Cohen et.al. (1995): Routines and Other Recurrent Practices; Working paper, Santa Fe Institute.

---

[10] Dyer and Kagel (1996) address the issue why "sophisticated bidders" -- executives drawn from the commercial construction industry suffer, like other subjects, from winner's curse in common value auctions. Simple survivorship arguments suggest that that should not be so. The authors identify a number of differences between theoretical and experimental treatments of one-shot common value auctions and practices in the commercial construction industry. One of the important differences is that there are repeated play elements to the commercial contracting game. For example, there are certain ways out -- "arithmetic errors" -- that often allow low bidders to withdraw bids without penalty. The results then suggest that experimenters may not have managed to cue their sophisticated subjects successfully into what they mean the experimental situation to represent. Harrison (1996) addresses a similar problem in the context of contingent valuation and suggests that more attention be paid to explicit linguistic representations in experiments. He identifies the avoidance of ambiguity as a key problem and proposes "to regain control over the linguistic representations that subjects might entertain by use of a 'little language' that is specific to the experiments." (48)

Cooper, R., D.V. Dejong, R. Forsythe, and T.W. Ross (1996): Cooperation without Reputation: Experimental Evidence from Prisoner's Dilemma Games; *Games and Economic Behavior*, 12, 187 - 218.

Cosmides, L. (1989): The Logic of Social Exchange: Has Natural Selection Shaped How Humans Reason? Studies with the Wason Selection Task; *Cognition*, 31, 187 - 276.

Cosmides, L. and J. Tooby (1992): Cognitive Adaptations for Social Exchange; in: J.H. Barkow, L. Cosmides and J. Tooby (eds.), *The Adapted Mind: Evolutionary Psychology and the Generation of Culture*, Oxford: Oxford University Press, 163 - 228.

Cosmides, L. and J. Tooby (1994): Beyond Intuition and Instinct Blindness: Toward an Evolutionarily Rigorous Cognitive Science; *Cognition*, 50, 41 - 77.

Cosmides, L. and J. Tooby (1996): Are Humans Good Intuitive Statisticians After All? Rethinking Some Conclusions From the Literature on Judgement Under Uncertainty; *Cognition*, 58, 1 - 73.

Davis, D.D. and C.A. Holt (1993): *Experimental Economics*, Princeton: Princeton University Press.

Dyer, D. and J.H. Kagel (1996): Bidding in Common Value Auctions: How the Commercial Construction Industry Corrects for the Winner's Curse; *Management Science*, 42, 1463 - 75.

Evans, J.St.B.T., S.E.Newstead and R.M.J.Byrne (1993): *Human Reasoning: The Psychology Of Deduction*, Erlbaum, Hillsdale, N.J.

Gigerenzer, G. (1991): How To Make Cognitive Illusions Disappear: Beyond Heuristics and Biases; in: W. Strobe and M. Hewstone (eds.), *European Review of Social Psychology*, 2, Chichester, England: Wiley, 83 - 115.

Gigerenzer, G. (1995): The Taming Of Content: Some Thoughts About Domains And Modules; *Thinking & Reasoning*, 1, 324 - 333.

Gigerenzer, G. (1996): On Narrow Norms and Vague Heuristics: A Reply to Kahneman and Tversky (1996); *Psychological Review*, 103, 592 - 96.

Gigerenzer, G. (1996a): The Modularity of Social Intelligence; in: A. Whiten and R.M. Byrne (eds.), *Machiavellian Intelligence II*, Cambridge: Cambridge University Press.

Gigerenzer, G. (1996b): Rationality: Why Social Context Matters; in: P.B. Baltes and U.M. Staudinger (eds.), *Interactive Minds. Life-span Perspectives on the Social Foundation of Cognition*, Cambridge: Cambridge University Press, 319 - 346.

Gigerenzer, G. and U. Hoffrage (1995): How To Improve Bayesian Reasoning Without Instruction: Frequency formats; *Psychological Review*, 102, 684 - 704.

Gigerenzer, G. and K. Hug (1992): Reasoning About Social Contracts: Cheating and Perspective Change; *Cognition*, 43, 127 - 171.

Gigerenzer, G. and D.J. Murray (1987): *Cognition as Intuitive Statistics*. Erlbaum, Hillsdale, NJ.

Girotto, V. (1995): Contextual Factors in Deontic Reasoning; *Thinking and Reasoning*, 1, 333 - 339.

Green, D.W. and D.E. Over (1996): Causal Inference, Contingency Tables and the Selection Task.; Working paper, University College, London.

Harrison, G. (1992): Theory and Misbehavior of First-Price Auctions; *American Economic Review*, 82, 1426 - 43.

Harrison, G. (1996): Experimental Economics and Contingent Valuation; Working paper (See http://theweb.badm.sc.edu/glenn/eecv.html).

Hertwig, R. and G. Gigerenzer (1997): The 'Conjunction Fallacy' Revisited: How Intelligent Inferences Look Like Reasoning Errors.; Working paper, Max-Planck-Institute, Muenchen.

Hertwig, R., G. Gigerenzer and U. Hoffrage (1996): The Reiteration Effect in Hindsight Bias; *Psychological Review*, 104, 194 - 202.

Hoffman, E., K. McCabe and V. Smith (1996): Social Distance and Other Regarding Behavior in Dictator Games; *American Economic Review*, 86, 653 - 659.

Johnson, E.J., C. Camerer, S. Sen and T. Rymon (1996): Limited Computation and Fairness in Sequential Bargaining Experiments; Working paper, Wharton School, University of Pennsylvania.

Kagel, J.H., C. Kim and D. Moser (1996): Fairness in Ultimatum Games with Asymmetric Information and Asymmetric Payoffs; *Games and Economic Behavior*, 13, 100 - 110.

Kahneman, D. and A. Tversky (1996): On the reality of cognitive illusions; *Psychological Review*, 101, 582 - 591.

Klein, B. and K. Leffler (1981): The Role of Market Forces in Assuring Contractual Compliance; *Journal of Political Economy*, 91, 615 - 640.

Kreps, D.M. (1990): *Microeconomic Theory*; Princeton: Princeton University Press.

Manktelow, K.I. and J.S.B.T. Evans (1979): Facilitation of Reasoning by Realism: Effect or Noneffect?; *British Journal of Psychology*, 70, 477 - 488.

McClelland, J.L. (1996): The Basis of Organization in Interactive Processing Systems; Cognitive Science Conference Proceedings 1996, 41.

McKelvey, R. and T. Palfrey (1992): An Experimental Study of the Centipede Game; *Econometrica*, 60, 803 - 836.

Meardon, S.J. and A. Ortmann (1996): Self-Command in Adam Smith's Theory of Moral Sentiments. A game-theoretic re-interpretation; *Rationality and Society*, 8, 57 - 80.

Meardon, S.J. and A. Ortmann (1996a): Yes, Adam Smith Was an Economist (A Very Modern One Indeed): A Reply; *Rationality and Society*, 8, 348 - 52.

Nagel, R. (1995): Unraveling in Guessing Games: An Experimental Study; *American Economic Review*, 85, 1313 - 1326.

Oaksford, M. and N. Chater (1994): A Rational Analysis of The Selection Task As Optimal Data Selection; *Psychological Review*, 101, 608 - 31.

Oaksford, M. and N. Chater (1996): Rational Explanation of The Selection Task; *Psychological Review*, 103, 381 - 91.

Ortmann, A. (1996): Modern Economic Theory and the Study of Nonprofit Organizations: Why the Twain Shall Meet; *Nonprofit and Voluntary Sector Quarterly*, 25, 470 - 484.

Ortmann, A. (1999): "The Nature and Causes of Corporate Negligence, Sham Lectures, and Ecclesiastical Indolence: Adam Smith on Joint-Stock Companies, Teachers, and Preachers," *History of Political Economy*, 297-315.

Ortmann, A. and D. Colander (1997): A Simple Principal-agent Game for the classroom; *Economic Inquiry*, 35, 443 - 450.

Palfrey, T.R. and J.E. Prisbey (1996): Altruism, Reputation and Noise in linear public goods experiments; *Journal of Public Economics*, 61, 409 - 27.

Platt, R. and R. Griggs (1993): Darwinian Algorithms and the Wason Selection Task: A Factorial Analysis of Social Contract Selection Task Problems; *Cognition*, 48, 163 - 192.

Pollard, P. (1982): *Human Reasoning: Some Possible Effects of Availability*, *Cognition*, 36, 1 - 16.

Rabin, M. (1996): Psychology and Economics; Manuscript.

Reny, P.J. (1992): Rationality in Extensive-Form Games; *Journal of Economic Perspectives*, 36, 103 - 118.

Rosenthal, R. and R. Rosnow (1991): *Essentials of Behavioral Research: Methods and Data Analysis (Second Edition,* New York: McGraw-Hill:.

Rosenzweig, S. (1933): The Experimental Situation As A Psychological Problem; *Psychological Review*, 40, 337 - 54.

Simon, H.A. (1990): Invariants of Human Behavior; *Annual Review of Psychology*, 41, 1 - 19.

Smith, A. (1776): *The Wealth of Nations*. Modern Library edition (1937).

Stahl, D. (1996): Boundedly Rational Rule Learning in a Guessing Game; *Games and Economic Behavior*, 16, 303-330.

Stahl, D. (1997): Is Step-j Thinking an Arbitrary Modelling Restriction or a Fact of Human Nature?; Working paper, University of Texas, Austin.

Stewart, D. (1982): Account of the Life and Writings of Adam Smith; in: A. Smith (1982), *Essays on Philosophical Subjects*, Oxford: Oxford University Press, 269 - 351.

Tirole, J. (1988): *The Theory of Industrial Organization*. Cambridge, MA: The MIT Press:.

Tirole, J. (1994): The Internal Organization of Government; *Oxford Economic Papers*, 46, 1 - 29.

Wang, X.T. (1996): Domain-specific Rationality in Human Choices: Violations of Utility Axioms and Social Contexts; *Cognition*, 60, 31 - 63.

Wason, P.C. (1966): Reasoning; in: B. Foss (ed.), *New Horizons in Psychology*, Middlesex, England: Penguin, Harmonsworth, 135 - 151.

Wason, P.C. (1968): Reasoning About A Rule; *Quarterly Journal of Experimental Psychology*, 20, 273 - 281.

Comment on Andreas Ortmann and Gerd Gigerenzer

Markus Pasche

On the main empirical results

In their contribution, Ortmann and Gigerenzer summarize shortly two main research paradigms on reasoning and decision making which seem to be the same in psychology and economics. Let us call them shortly the *rational* and the *behavioral* approach. The former focuses on the formal laws of reasoning, statistical inference, and rational decision making, the latter emphasizes observed systematic deviations from the rational approach and prefers descriptive models of routine or heuristic guided behavior. Such empirical violations of economic standard assumptions are well investigated by psychology and experimental economics (Davis and Holt 1993, Hogarth and Reeder 1987, Kagel and Roth 1995, Kahneman, Slovic and Tversky 1982). The interesting point is that Ortmann and Gigerenzer among others show, that (a) the presence of a social context, (b) the content of the situation, and (c) the perspective of the decision maker in this context significantly determines the reasoning and (therefore) decision behavior. These results could be interpreted as special cases of framing effects which are empirically well known (Conlisk 1996). But in contrast to the heuristics-and-biases research which overemphasizes the deviations from rational decisionmaking, Ortmann and Gigerenzer argue, that a clear experimental design could also reduce these biases. They criticize that experimental economics did not sufficiently take care about the impact of experimental design on the results, thus often producing artifacts. Of course the results even from context-free experiments show that hypotheses of behavior following an abstract calculus do not fit the data. Moreover the "design" of real-world situations is also imprecise and often unknown. But any theory explaining the conditions and the extent of (non-) rational reasoning and decision making requires a clear design to detect the determinants mentioned above. Later on, it will be argued that the suggestion to take context and content of a problem into consideration should also be addressed to theoretical economics as well.

The main experimental results are drawn from the illustrative day-off problem. The rational choice of the agents *(Don't trust, Don't give a day off)* is not due to the elimination of weakly dominated strategies, which is *generally* neither necessary nor sufficient to establish a Nash solution. The claim that weak dominance induce a Nash solution is true only *in this special case*. Since the payoff structure is Common Knowledge the monitoring of employer's behavior by solving the Wason selection task makes sense only in repeated games where Pareto-optimal Non-Nash behavior could be established. The results show that embedding agents in a social context could direct their reasoning and decision making closer to the rational norm. Thus, the skepticism of many authors about rational modeling comes from their specific experimental design. Nevertheless the empirical results and their explanation by social context dependent reasoning is related to the behavioral research paradigm.

On the evolutionary explanation of empirical results

At the present state the notion of bounded rationality only seems to be a semantic bridge between both research programs which express that the rationality concept of standard economic analysis is too narrow (Simon 1986). In fact the optimization approach as the kernel of the rational paradigm is often rejected as not appropriate for explaining boundedly rational behavior (Selten 1990, in contrast see Simon 1991 and Lipman 1995). From an evolutionary point of view it seems to be questionable if rational and behavioral explanations are such oppositional. Firstly it has to be stated that limited cognitive facilities or computational constraints are not necessarily the same as a lack of rationality (Langlois 1990, Heiner 1988). The observed deviations from rational behavior need not to be a consequence of "irrationality". As Heiner (1988) argues, observed behavioral regularities could be interpreted as a reasonable control of errors which necessarily occur when agents have a limited competence, compared to the complexity of the problem. The notion of *imperfection* should be preferred in favor of bounded rationality.

Secondly the presence of adaptive heuristics, routines, and framing effects requires an economic explanation. Following Ortmann and Gigerenzer, the evolutionary selection process is such an explanation device, at least in domains which are relevant for surviving (see also Cosmides 1989, Cosmides and Tooby 1994, Langlois and Csontos 1993). Especially in situations where agents could be cheated and therefore have comparative disadvantages, the evolutionary pressure is higher than in other situations. Hence, cheating detection mechanisms are relatively sophisticated. The authors refer to Gigerenzer and Hug (1992) who have shown, that a change of perspective from the eventually cheated to the non-cheated person in the *same* social context matters. Since being cheated bears a high incentive not to loose relative fitness, the observations confirm results from experimental economics that incentives could improve decision quality (Smith and Walker 1993). It has to be remarked that a change of perspective also changes the incentives for a *strategic handling of information* which is an implication of rationality. This strategic incentive may be invoked by taking a certain perspective, even if the experiment is not designed as a strategic interaction and the participants have no choice whether to cheat or not. It seems not to be clear how it could be argued with cheating detection, dependent on the agent's perspective, *and* eliminating any strategic aspect of the Wason selection task. Therefore a high rate of "wrong" selections could indicate a rational strategic behavior and it implies nothing about the abilities of logically reasoning. Anyhow the important conclusion of Gigerenzer and Hug that the possibility of being cheated directs attention, and that reasoning behavior does not follow a context-free general-purpose logic is confirmed by many other experiments.

Combining these two aspects, regular behavior patterns (such like cheating detection mechanisms) could be interpreted as a consequence of an evolutionary process which optimizes cognitive and behavioral procedures *under the condition of limited cognitive abilities and limited memory*, or shortly: under the condition of imperfectness. The high performance of a behavioral strategy, by means of objectively expected outcome or fitness, is an explanation for observing such patterns in reality. Due to vague knowledge, information processing and decision errors the performance is also a *robustness property* of a cognitive or behavioral rule. Of course the impact of imperfectness on the expected fitness is related to the social context and content of a situation where the rules are applied to.

The first crucial point of this argument is that approximating rational reasoning and decision making will *not* necessarily improve the performance. This is because of its enormous claims to computational power and its lack of robustness against errors. The "as if" justification of rational models do not generally hold in the context of imperfect agents. As Blume and Easley (1992), Barnerjee and Weibull (1995) show theoretically, rational behavior is *not* the only surviving strategy mutant in an evolutionary process (see also Conlisk 1996, pp.683, Sethi 1996). Only in situations of low complexity or high losses in case of non-optimizing rational behavior has a comparative advantage since the impact of imperfectness is negligible or compensated by strong incentives (Wilcox 1993). The second crucial point of the argument is that agents could not maximize the behavioral performance ex ante, since the objectively expected outcome and the distribution of the information processing errors are not known. Hence, invoking an evolutionary optimization argument does not imply that individual behavior is conducted by some calculus.

New models of reasoning and decision making in economics

Investigation of behavioral rules which are evolutionarily optimized under the condition of imperfection and in the context of social interaction seems to be the avenue of new economic models of reasoning and decision making, Ortmann and Gigerenzer ask for. Psychology and experimental economics, especially their new research directions, lead to a valuable insight into reasoning and decision making under imperfection. But further work has to be done to make a step from description to economic explanation. The traditional models of rational behavior like expected and non-expected utility approaches are not only of normative interest.

They could also serve as a benchmark for measuring the relative performance of simple heuristics and therefore as an explanation why some behavioral regularities are more often observed in specific situations than others. At the present state a lot of work is done on generalizing and modifying rational choice models, like non-expected utility approaches (Machina 1989, Fishburn 1994) and models of limited trust into knowledge (Modica 1995), combining rational models with heuristics (Rubinstein 1988, Gilboa and Schmeidler 1995), and applying new theoretical tools to rational decision making like fuzzy-sets (Hougaard and Keiding 1996) or finite automata (Kalai and Stanford 1988). But only few effort is put on an economic explanation of empirically confirmed patterns of reasoning and decision making described by psychology and behavioral science. On the other hand, behavioral economics often emphasizes the paradigmatic gap to the rational approach instead of utilizing its explanatory power in the way described above. Psychology is as important for understanding economic behavior by detecting the underlying cognitive and behavioral procedures as theoretical economics is important to understand why such procedures have been evolved in a world of socially interacting imperfect agents. The contribution of Ortmann and Gigerenzer seem to be fruitful for combining both perspectives.

References

Barnerjee, A. and J.W. Weibull (1995): Evolutionary Selection and Rational Behavior; in: A. Kirman and M. Salmon (eds.), *Learning and Rationality in Economics*, Oxford-Cambridge: Blackwell, 343 - 363.

Blume, L. and D. Easley (1992): Evolution and Market Behavior; *Journal of Economic Theory*, 58, 9 - 40.

Conlisk, J. (1996): Why Bounded Rationality?; *Journal of Economic Literature*, 34, 669 - 700.

Cosmides, L. (1989): The Logic of Social Exchange: Has Natural Selection Shaped How Humans Reason? Studies with the Wason Selection Task; *Cognition*, 31, 198 - 276.

Cosmides, L. and J. Tooby (1994): Beyond Intuition and Instinct Blindness: Toward an Evolutionary Rigorous Cognitive Science; *Cognition*, 50, 41 - 77.

Davis, D.D. and C.A. Holt (1993): *Experimental Economics*, Princeton: Princeton University Press.

Fishburn, P.C. (1994): Utility and Subjective Probability; in: R.J. Aumann and S. Hart (eds.), *Handbook of Game Theory*, Vol.2, Amsterdam: North Holland/Elsevier Science, 1397 - 1435.

Gigerenzer, G. and K. Hug (1992): Reasoning About Social Contracts: Cheating and Perspective Change; *Cognition*, 43, 127 - 171.

Gilboa, I. and D. Schmeidler (1995): Case-based Decision Making; *The Quarterly Journal of Economics*, 59, 605 - 640.

Heiner, R. (1988): The necessity of imperfect decisions; *Journal of Economic Behavior and Organisation*, 10, 29 - 55.

Hogarth, R.M. and M.W. Reeder (eds.) (1987): *Rational Choice: The Contrast between Economics and Psychology;* Chicago: Chicago University Press.

Hougaard, J.L. and H. Keiding (1996): Representation of preferences on fuzzy measures by a fuzzy integral; *Mathematical Social Sciences*, 31, 1 - 17.

Kagel, J. and A.E. Roth (eds.) (1995): *Handbook of Experimental Economics*, Princeton: Princeton University Press.

Kahneman, D., P. Slovic and A. Tversky (eds.) (1982): *Judgement under uncertainty: Heuristics and biases;* Cambridge: Cambridge University Press.

Kalai, E. and W. Stanford (1988): Finite Rationality and Interpersonal Complexity in Repeated Games; *Econometrica*, 56, 397 - 410.

Langlois, R.N. (1990): Bounded Rationality and Behavioralism: A Clarification and Critique; *Journal of Theoretical and Institutional Economics*, 146, 691 - 695.

Langlois, R.N. and L. Csontos (1993): Optimization, rule-following, and the method of situational analysis; in: U. Mäki, B. Gustafsson and C. Knudsen (eds.), *Rationality, Institutions, and Economic Methodology*, London: Routledge, 113 - 132.

Lipman, B.L. (1995): Information processing and bounded rationality: a survey; *Canadian Journal of Economics*, 28(1), 42 - 67.

Machina, M. (1989): Dynamic Consistency and Non-Expected Utility Models of Choice Under Uncertainty; *Journal of Economic Literature*, 27, 1622 - 1668.

Modica, S. (1995): Expected Utility for Decision Making with Subjective Models; Theory and Decision, 39, 157 - 168.

Rubinstein, A. (1988): Similarity and Decision-making under Risk; *Journal of Economic Theory*, 46, 145 - 153.

Selten, R. (1990): Bounded Rationality; *Journal of Theoretical and Institutional Economics*, 146, 649 - 658.

Sethi, R. (1996): Evolutionary stability and social norms; *Journal of Economic Behavior and Organisation*, 29, 113 - 140.

Simon, H.A. (1986): Rationality in Psychology and Economics; *Journal of Business*, 59, 209 - 224.

Simon, H.A. (1991): Bounded Rationality; in: *The New Palgrave. A Dictionary of Economics*, Vol. 1, edited by J. Eatwell, M. Milgate and P. Newman, London-New York-Tokyo: MacMillan Press Limited, 266-267.

Smith, V.L. and J.M. Walker (1993): Monetary Rewards and Decision Cost in Experimental Economics; *Economic Inquiry*, 31, 245 - 261.

Wilcox, N.T. (1993): Lottery Choice: Incentives, Complexity, and Decision Time; *Economic Journal*, 193, 1397 - 1417.

Comment on Andreas Ortmann and Gerd Gigerenzer

Birger P. Priddat

Cognition, Rationality, and Communication

It is an important insight in the development of experimental rational choice, we read in Ortmann/Gigerenzer. Experimental rational choice gives a chance for some reformulations of rational choice theory by content-dependency, context-dependency, and communication.

Let us start with a story. In the 50th Donald Davidson had become a well known experimentator of rational decision behaviour. But he was unable to get valid results of reasonable consistency. In the end of the 50th he stopped his career as an experimental psychologist, and became a philosopher: nowadays one of the famous American analytical philosophers. He had become a famous philosopher, because he tried to solve the unsolvable problems of experimental study in rational behaviour with the help of the so called language philosophy (in the Wittgensteinian tradition, especially in the so called 'Oxford Ordinary Language Philosophy'-approach). In a lecture from 1971 (Davidson 1974) he told his story by giving the following arguments:

- We cannot understand any preference ordering without reference to a coherent mental attitude and belief in the background.
- Insofar we like to interpret any choice-behaviour as a result of a coherent and rational scheme.
- But we do not really know anything about the beliefs of the persons; the detected rationality is a problem of attribution. The problem of attribution is noted as a problem of interpretation, made by the observer. The attribution of rationality assumes the ideas of the same interpretation of words and sentences, used by the experimentalist or observer and the observed person, because there is no experiment on rational behaviour without the use of language.
- Consequently, Davidson postulates the necessity of an additional theory of communication for choice analysis.

I think, Ortmann/Gigerenzer (O/G) just has reached the problem, Donald Davidson had noted in 1971. But they reached this level of analysis by using and developing certain developments of cognitive psychology, Davidson had become critical of before, as a cognitive psychologist. His essay 'psychology as philosophy'

(Davidson 1974) is a philosophical/methodical analysis of some unseen epistemological problems of cognitive psychology.

The theory of communication, Davidson likes to introduce into the analysis of choice-behaviour, is an analytically introduced procedure to get to know something about the beliefs and convictions of the observed person, beyond any attribution by the observer. Both - the observer and the observed - have to become aware of using the same meanings. To be able to understand the language-behaviour, we have to be able to declare, when the speaker himself beliefs of having said a true sentence. All meanings we tend to interpret by a construction of a theory of the belief of the speaker, without really knowing something about that, he really beliefs in.

Ortmann/Gigerenzer's conception

Lets turn back to O/G's conception. O/G use the term 'communication', but do not operate with a theory of communication. They are more interested in the 'content/context'-relationship. Indeed, it is an important step in choice-analysis. The 'thematic selection tasks' (see O/G in this volume) really shows a certain kind of content-dependency of problem-solving. In the first steps (table 2 and 3) there is no context-analysis. The context still is - given by the rule - constant. Context-dependency later on is introduced with the 'cabin/bundle of wood' - experiment. It is again a new step in behaviourial analysis.

Let us take O/G's case of the Swiss-Alpine-Club in the two versions. O/G changed the position of the player of their experiment from an observer of the 1. degree ('the guard') to an observer of the 2. degree ('the German observer'): 'the guard' is more involved than 'the German observer'. To compare two rules - as in the second story - is an other job than detecting possible violations of the rule - as in the first story. In the first story the player has to use the rule by controlling her; in the second story the player has to interpret, which rule may be guilty. Possibly the Swiss people have another interpretation of the rule, which seems to be the same as the German one, but is not the same.

Insofar it is not the same problem: in a syntactical mode both stories uses the same rule. But in semantics there is an ambiguity. 'The German observer' is not able to identify the persons with the bundle of wood as users of the cabin; eventually they are members of the Swiss-Alpine-Club, which are obliged to bring the wood without sleeping in the cabin. The very possibility for another rule changes the observation of defections of the rule.

The content-problem is a problem of the interpretation of the rule. If there is no possibility to communicate, 'the German observer' has his problem of interpretation. But his problem is a very artificial one; observing some people bringing wood, it would be easy for him to ask the Swiss people, which rule they do follow. There is no problem to become irritated by false answers, because the wood-loaden people are evidently those one's, which do follow the rule of the Swiss club. Defectors do not bring wood. Here O/G failed in their intention, to give some pragmatic results. Pragmatically 'the German observer' fails in persisting in his observational standpoint. A small talk would have been solved his problem (besides, because there is no problem of language between the Germans and the Swiss).

Why O/G do not work with a communicational approach? The only communication in the story is the sentence said by the German friend. Communication does matter, but in misguiding sense. At last 'the German observer' in the second story has to trust in his own cognition. In the O/G-context, communication does not solve the problem, it is an element of the problem.

I am not sure, why O/G announced to deal with communication, but deny their intentions in the only example, which is predestinated for dealing with communication. My explanation is: their model of cognition does not really allow to deal with communication. There is a close connection between cognition and context. For different contexts exist different reasoning routines. 'Reasoning routine' is the term used by O/G for cognitive processes or algorithms. O/G prefer to interpret it as 'heuristics, paradigms, or cognitive frameworks'. This model is a mind/world-model, missing any connection to language, the theoretically valid basement for an elaborated communication theory.

Mind/World-Models versus Mind/Language/World-Models

Mind/language/world-models of cognition are able to deal with semantics and content; mind/world-models not. In mind/world-models - as O/G do use it - 'content' is a part of mind, representing a local part of the world. World is annotated as a set of different local parts, also called 'contexts'. 'Content' is the counter-part of 'context' (in this definition), located in that part of mind, which is the representative of the co-relating part of world. In this way, 'content' only formally has to do something with semantics, but is language-independent. Content-dependency without language-dependency allows to deal with semantics without communication, because 'content' is identical with a 'mental model' or 'algorithm'. These 'mental models' are constructed as relatively stabilized and experienced working processes in the mind, without systematically relations to the context of language.

'Content' as a certain kind of representation of world (in the form of a 'context-dependent representation') is closely related to the part of the world, which is represented. O/G give a weak approach of this relatedness, speaking of 'cognitive frameworks'. Within these 'cognitive frameworks' the mind is able to choose, but the general pattern is stable.

In contrary: 'Content' as a part of language and the whole field of semantics within the game of language differs by being able to change the meaning in the context of meaning. The meaning of a word is related to the context of the sentence, of the text, of the story. This is the very meaning of language-dependency.

Without reference to the elaborated literature of language philosophy (Davidson 1984), discourse psychology (Edwards 1997), and philosophy of psychology (O'Donohue/Kitchener 1996), we are able to distinguish between two different meanings of 'content':

- 'content 1' is the term used by O/G, representing a state of world in the mind,
- 'content 2' is a term with reference to a state of world *and* to a field of semantics (a set of meanings). Given this definition, there is no stable relationship, but a process of interpretation. 'Content' in the notion of 'content 2' is no clear relation between 'context' and 'reasonable routine', but includes some contingencies, given by the very process of communication. The possible change of the 'content' of a sentence or a story is leaded by talking about it. Talking or 'discourse' gives dispositions for new interpretations of the same thing. In communication we have to be aware of disturbances of the clear world/mind-relation. In the context of language, meanings are changing by talking about something, if a new interpretation seems more useful than the old one.

The O/G-approach is near to this theme, but has not reached it. They do include 'context', but not language and its very context. If they would include the second context - the context of language -, O/G would have to deal with the problem of interpretation of their experimental problems by the player of their experimental games.

The experimentator's description of the problem to be solved by the players of the experimental game is a form of communication. O/G criticizes the content-free experiments in rational choice; but it is evident, that the experimentators of the content-free experiments also do communicate with their clients. The difference is, that O/G do communicate in every-day-language, the older experimentators did it in an artificial language. Both exprimentators started a discourse with their clients, but the clients are not able to answer in every-day-language. They have to answer in pretended semantics. The semantics of O/G are even more every-day-language-near. But they are also pretended (by using prepared sentences).

These prepared semantics forces the player even more to solve the problem of the experimentator, than his problems. In contrary: Pragmatic solutions of the problems could produce other solutions as the experimentator likes. Real world solutions of choice problems are often really pragmatic and produce unforeseeable results. This is no result of irrationality, but of the possibility of changing semantics in communications (with regard on rational choice processes, we have to deny something like the stability of preferences without any reference to communication or discourse. 'Preference' is - in a communicational setting - a certain kind of consent. Insofar stable preference ordering is a result of a communicational process, but not of mind).

Communication is no added or artificial problem, but the normal condition for all choice problems. Only these choice-situations without any problem of identifying und interpreting the situation can be solved without regard on communication. I do think, most of choice-problems are closely related with communication.

Rational choice and interpretation

But we are not only speaking of interpretations of stories, but of stories, which are told to articulate a choice-problem. Now we come back to the problem of rationality. O/G's analytical work is a very clear demonstration of problems of rational choice-problems, which are formulated in terms of propositional logic. But let us look for the consequences. Looking for the context/content-relation in rational choice analysis, we are confronted with the problem of interpretation of the situation. I do not agree with the idea, to find some reasonable routines, which are related to some contexts. Even if we would be able to find some stable routines, we are always confronted with the problem of interpretation: are the actors able to interpret the concrete situation as a context, which is guilty for starting their reasonable routines?

Or let us have another perspective: why should we be sure of a mechanism of the reasonable routine/context-relation? Using the content/context-relationship, we are not able to guarantee any stability of this relationship. That is why all cognitive processes may be dependent of content/context, but they all are also dependent of language and their changing-field of meanings (in the context of meanings). 'Marketing' - for example - is the economic theory of managing these processes of changing the meaning. Insofar economic theory long ago has recognized this case, but without methodical feed back for the theory of rational choice.

Summing up: I do agree with O/G in their content/context-analysis. But I do not agree with their epistemological basement: their mind/world-model. The 'content-dependency' is able to introduce different content/context relations. The n 'contents' represent relations to n 'contexts'. The empirical research has to find out the relevant relations in any situation.

But 'content' is also language-dependent (to use another term than 'game of language'). Language-dependency introduces some complications, because language implies its own context (the context of meanings). So we have to deal with an autopoetic mode of meaning, which leads us to a constructivistic standpoint. In talk, discourse or communication any people are able to change their interpretation of a situation. But also outside of any communication, persons are members of the game of language and are able to make analogies with other meaning of other contexts, with concrete results for the actual given mind/world-view.

Semantically and pragmatically actors are more flexible in interpreting and performing choice-situations, than the rational choice model in the line of propositional logic is able to model. But also O/G's approach does not allow a really pragmatic interpretation of choice. That is why meaning is a twofold thing: I can agree with others, sharing the relevant meanings of the relevant games of language in the society, and I can disagree with these relevancies by making new interpretations, new meanings. Every innovator is doing so. Having success, all the other people tend to get this meaning. Being unsuccessful, they fall back on the position of the standards of meaning given before.

In a mind/language/world-model the term 'reasonable routines' is no form of standardized answer to the same states of world, but a form of shared meaning on how to behave. 'Shared meanings' are more complicated than 'reasonable routines'. 'Reasonable routines' are individually programmed representations, given by experiences with certain states of the world. 'Shared meanings' are less individualistic, because being a member of social language games, the individual is able to behave without having experiences in a certain state of the world. The supply of meanings gives orientation in behaviour. Many people behave because they are told to behave so. Meaning guides people to behave, without being related to certain states of the world. So communication is able to give new meaning to individuals: mind suddenly is related to another 'world' than before. The 'reason', used in the term 'reasonable routines', is 1. the reason why individuals are using arguments for their actions, and 2., using arguments, is to be able of being changed by communication in using arguments.

Evidently, O/G are right in postulating 'reasonable routines', but they have to be aware of language-dependency of the stableness of these routines. Language is a metaphor for the possibility of floating semantics, forced by forced (and unforced) social communications. Evidently, the stabilization of 'reasonable routines' is a communicational process. Communication not only changes some routines of behaviour, but also stabilizes routines. In the language-independent context of cognitive psychology, routines are something like impressions in the mind. But with this ignorance of communication, it is not possible to detect the very process of producing and reproducing the stable meanings, O/G like to interpret as routines. Routines are a product of communication, not of communication-free impression.

Communication is no process of - reciprocal - information, but a process of conforming and of changing the mind by using meanings. Using meanings is a process being able to interpret the meaning. Insofar is 'using meanings' something other than 'using information'. 'Using meaning' is itself a certain kind of routine, or not, because using a routine of meaning is related to the very process of social communication, which may give other interpretations than the individualistic mind/world-representation-model.

We have do decide, which mode of economics we shall prefer: if we like to prefer a neoclassical mode, we have to ignore the very implications of communication and language-dependency of choices. If we like to prefer Hayekian economics, we are forced to accept the very new interpretations of the innovator, because this innovator causes dynamics to the market-process.

I think, it is time to start an economic theory, based on an model of actor, which is able to communicate and which is aware of the context of language. O/G did the first steps in this direction, not even more.

References

Edwards, Derek (1997): *Discourse and Cognition*, London, Thousand Oaks, New Dehli: SAGE.

Davidson, Donald (1974): Psychology as Philosophy; in: Brown, S.C. (ed.), *Philosophy of Psychology*, London/N.Y.

Davidson, Donald (1984): *Inquiries into Truth and Interpretations*, Oxford: Oxford University Press.

Graesser, Arthur C. and Gernsbacher, Morton A. and Goldman, Susan R. (1997): Cognition; in: Van Dijk and Teun 1997.

O'Donohue, William and Kitchener, Richard E. (eds.) (1996): *The Philosophy of Pschology*, London/Thousand Oaks/New Dehli: SAGE.

Van Dijk and Teun, A. (ed.) (1997): *Discourse as Structure and Process*, London, Thousand Oaks, New Dehli: SAGE.

Decision-Making and Institutionalised Cognition

Gernot Handlbauer

Introduction: Innocent X

In 1953 Francis Bacon[*] painted his "Study after Velasquez's Portrait of Pope Innocent X". According to the original the pope is sitting on a throne, wearing a white gown and a lilac shawl. His forearms are propped up on arm-rest and he is looking at the viewer.

Instead of the serious looking face of Velasquez's portrait, Bacon painted the pope screaming, with a wide opened mouth, even showing his teeth. In the lower part his figure is decomposed: The white gown splits up and fades into the yellow patterns of the melting throne which seems to be placed on a swing. A black haze covers the entire painting and gives the impression of decay. The whole scene reminds one of a dreadful spirit of the dead pope in damnation.

But the painting is more than just a horrible scene: The decomposition of the figure aims at the decomposition of the viewer. The lack of a meaningful back-

---

[*] Irish Painter, 1909-1992.

ground together with the homogeneous structure of the black haze obscures the figure and wipes out the distinction between the background and the subject. Bacon puts fragments of different origin together, without supplying a meaningful frame and without providing the viewer some kind of orientation (Alphen 1992).

The scene seems to be in suspense, it is not embedded into a structure that makes sense. This situation refers also to the visitor: The deep emotion of the picture is caused by the lack of a sensemaking structure. The accumulation of contradictory fragments, the deficit of a background and a meaningful title confront the visitor with the indefinite structure of his own identity. The painting resists the meaningful interaction with the visitor and refers to a basic challenge of human life: The "discursive construction" (Knorr-Cetina 1981, 10) of the individual.

The basic assumption of this paper is, that this discourse happens between the individual and his environment. Throughout a series of (intentional) decisions, actions and perceptions the individual creates identity. This identity is based on a pattern of sensemaking, a meaningful integration of experiences into an existing structure of one's self (Weick 1995, 18).

Sense, Cognitive Maps and Cognition

Decision-making is of major importance throughout this process. The decision-maker tries to elaborate meaningful courses of action and to derive sense and identity from an inherently puzzling environment. Enormous ambiguity is stemming from the diversity of constraints and the multitude of ways that simple elements can be combined and recombined. Coping permanently with such a situation requires a system of representation that provides certain functions (Kaplan and Kaplan 1981, 8):

- Economy of the representation to cope with the continuous flow of vague stimulation stemming from the environment.
- Generality to highlight consequential similarities and to ignore unimportant differences of stimulation. Such a process of selection enables the application of experiences from the past to new situations.
- Connection together with generality allows the transfer of stored representations stemming from a certain situation to a new one. By embedding a perception into the existing pattern of representations we are able to understand what is going on and derive sense.

Cognitive psychologists (Neisser 1976) have introduced the concept of the cognitive map to explain processes such as perception, sensemaking and modification of behaviour. These maps can be described as a relational set of cognitive representations (Weick and Burgon 1986, 106). They provide at least two functions:

- Cognitive maps enable us to be very fast in stressing perceptions that turned out to be important in the past. They represent an anticipation of our envi-

ronment and guide our perceptions as an active structure in search for information. Therefore, most people interested in paintings recognize easily the similarity between Bacons portrait and that of Velasquez since Bacon uses some very popular symbols that are typical for portraits of sovereigns.
— They help us to bring our observations into a meaningful order by creating relations between them. The isolated representation of a certain perception is embedded into a causal and normative pattern of existing knowledge. If we look at the portrait of a pope, we expect him to look sonorous, to sit on a throne, etc. If our observations are contradictory, such as provoked by the painting of Bacon, we suffer from a lack of meaning and are in need of an explanation.

According to the cycle of cognition in Figure 1 the cognitive map represents a scheme of the current environment. It conducts the behaviour of the individual which provokes reactions of the environment. This step refers to Piaget's (1954) idea of exploitative learning by enacting with the environment. The results of these actions in turn modify the cognitive map and lead to an alteration of the selection of information available.

Figure 1: Cycle of Cognition (Neisser 1976, 112)

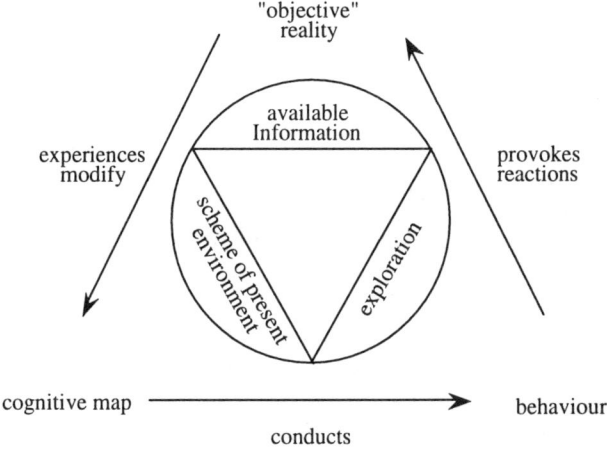

Cognitive maps represent a mentally created painting of the world, built throughout a process of experiences. These experiences are based on the actor's biography or on his observations of others (Bandura 1977). According to our physical abilities, the cognitive system is not able to refer to our environment directly. Perceptions result from a process of construction of stimulations detected by our senses (Roth 1992). "Painting" refers to the fact that the cognitive contents are not identical to the original. It is important to mention that a cognitive representation is a construction based on the already existing representations accumulated in the cognitive map.

Cognitive maps help us to give our thoughts and behaviour a meaningful structure: According to the stored representations and the relations between them we create patterns of cause and effect we call logic. These connections make us think of our environment to be meaningful and predictable. They are even related to our emotional balance: Results of research in cognitive psychology indicate a close relationship between emotions and logical thinking (Damasio 1994).
We use two interrelated concepts to characterise the process of sensemaking:
– Causal maps refer to a cause and effect-structure of representations.
– Hierarchical maps refer to the development of norms and values.

The analysis of the structure of cognition in Figure 1 leads to the result that this cycle indicates a self-referring process of sensemaking: We are creating perceptions based on perceptions that turned out to be meaningful in the past. The present stocks of cognitive contents guide the perception of new stimulations and incorporates their representation into existing relations. Thus the adaptation of the cognitive map is likewise based on what we already know and the present structure of the cognitive map induces the future development. According to Gertrud Stein: A cognition is a cognition is a cognition.

Cognition, Logic and Rationality

We have already mentioned the term logic and described it as a formal sequence of cause and effect. Causal patterns represent also an important part in the structure of related perceptions accumulated in the cognitive map. That means, contents obtained from the stored representations fill the logical form, e.g. the Aristotelian syllogism. We consider such an aggregation of logical structure and individual cognitive contents to be meaningful.

The term logic is closely related to the term rationality: We assume rationality to be the practical application of logic to achieve a given set of preferred outcomes. Rational action means to strive for a desired result by using a logical sequence of cause and effect stored in the cognitive map. Therefore rationality is a meaningful application of cognitive representations to achieve a final result according to the preferences of the actor. In the field of decision-making rationality and rational choice are a matter of broad discussion. Especially uncertainty and bounded rationality (Simon 1967) cause a continuous development of models.

If we connect rationality with the concept of cognitive maps, we can describe rational choice as the decision for a sequence of related representations that apply best to a certain task. We understand bounded rationality as well as uncertainty as weaknesses of a cognitive map: The decision refers to representations and/or connections that are not (yet) integrated in the cognitive structure. The typical behaviour stemming from bounded rationality, e.g. delay of decisions, can be assumed to represent strategies to overcome these weaknesses.

On the one hand the consequence of this assumption is that decision-making will become easier and the perception of uncertainty will decrease if the cognitive map provides a close-knit structure of cause and effect. Therefore we conclude that the self-referring structure of cognition in Figure 1 leads to a cycle of learning by success: If a pattern of cause and effect is applied successfully, the perceived accomplishment will fortify the relations.

Thus the recurring structure of sensemaking can lead to a vicious circle: Due to research based on data from experimental settings, humans "tend to over-exploit 'good' actions that pay off well early thereby inheriting the classic properties of strong self-reinforcement: path dependence, nonpredictability, and possible lock-in to an inferior choice." (Arthur 1994, 152)

On the other hand, the idea of the development of a specific pattern of rationalisation was picked up by several authors to explain strategic success of organisations (Hinterhuber et al. 1996). According to the resource-based view of strategy, intangible resources, especially tacit knowledge stemming from professional experience, build up the cornerstones of competitive advantage (Peteraf 1993). Such a portfolio of specific resources is the result of a particular rationality of decision-makers. Following this approach competition seems to be based on strategic cognition (Handlbauer 1996).

Our conclusion of this discussion is that rationality depends on the contents of the cognitive map. The traditional concept of rational decision-making emphasises the tasks to achieve. Our cognitive view defines rational decisions as an application of an individual pattern of interrelated cognitive representations to reach a certain goal.

Therefore rationality refers not only to the relation between the action and its task. Moreover it is a matter of the constitutional sense of an action: Rational behaviour implies meaningful behaviour according to the structure of the cognitive map. Irrationality (Davidson 1990a) refers to cognitive structures the observer cannot understand. That does not necessarily imply that the actor him- or herself is unable to create a stringent pattern of causal relationships.

Decision-Making

Considering the works of Neisser (1976) and Weick (1979), Prahalad and Bettis (1986) developed a cyclic model of decision-making, the dominant logic. Although the main issue of this model is the relation between managers' assumptions about key success factors stemming from professional experience and preferred management techniques, it applies to all fields of decision-making.

Figure 2: The Dominant Logic

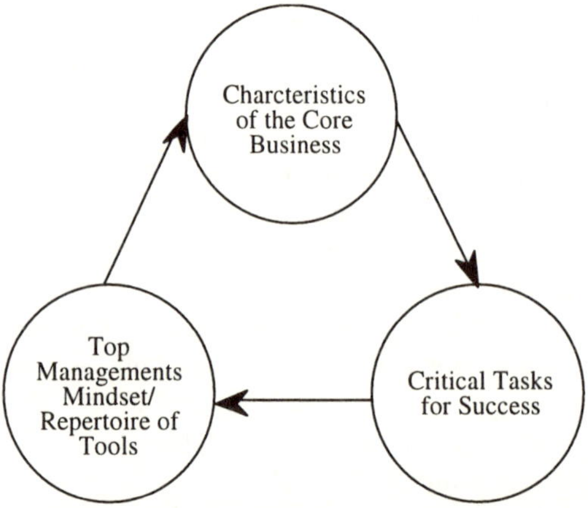

```
         Charcteristics
         of the Core
         Business

Top
Managements
Mindset/            Critical Tasks
Repertoire of        for Success
Tools
```

The structure of this concept is very similar to the cycle of cognition: According to decisions that turned out to be successful in the past, managers develop a concept of key-success-factors in their business that indicates useful tools. Experiences are primarily based on the application of these tools, therefore modifications of key-success-factors are limited to experiences stemming from their application.

To emphasise the self-referring structure of decision-making we adapt the concept: Rational choice is made according to the contents of the cognitive map, where experiences with prior perceptions are accumulated. The consequences of these decisions lead to results, that are perceived according to already known observations. Only this new old piece of information influences the adaptation of the cognitive map. Once again Gertrud Stein: A decision is a decision is a decision.

Figure 3 is based on repeated learning-by-doing loops that lead to a continuous amelioration of decisions. Amelioration means in this context that decisions lead to the desired result. This does not necessarily imply that perceptions fit reality. Sensemaking is much more driven by plausibility rather than accuracy (Weick 1995, 55) and strategies of decision-making are verified by their viability rather than by their fit to some kind of ideal standard of optimality.

The critical step in this process is the observation of consequences. These consequences are in many cases contradictory, their relation to the decision might be fuzzy or they are not noticed at all, e.g. due to their geographical or temporal distance. That means, our perception selects and interprets the ambiguous information, that alters our perception according to (perceived) experiences in the past.

Figure 3: The Self-Referring Structure of Decision-Making

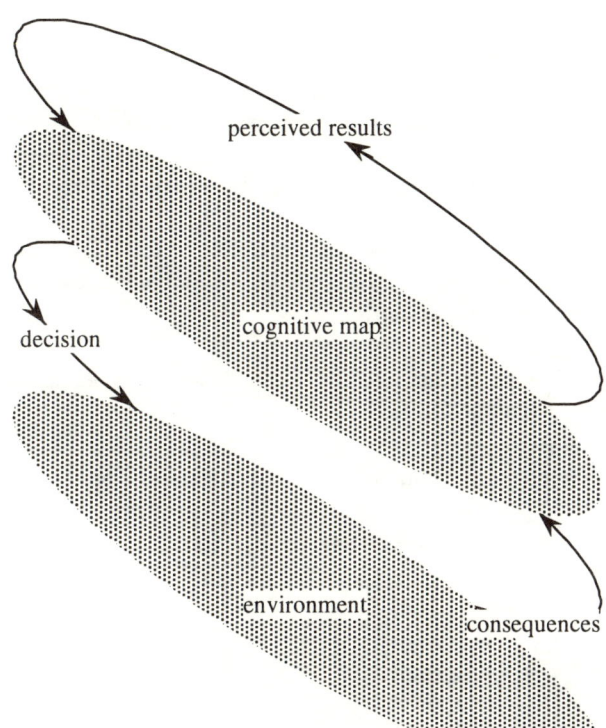

Falsification could interrupt this conservative cycle and prevent us from path-dependence and lock-ins. Regarding management or politics, this would imply a search for senselessness of decisions. According to our basic assumption, the human need for sense, falsification applies only to a small number of exceptional situations, such as therapeutical applications.

The model in Figure 3 refers primarily to individual decision making. Ahead of the introduction of social influences we try to elaborate a cognitive model of decision-making. Since we emphasised the creation of meaning as an important function of cognition, we regard decision-making as sensemaking.

Making Decisions to Create Sense

We have already mentioned that in economics decision making is traditionally seen as an intentional calculation-process (Moser 1990, 2). The basic concept is that the decision-maker has to choose between a set of alternative actions according to his or her preferences. Moreover in most cases risk comes into play: The results of the different alternatives are subject to different degrees of uncertainty.

Usually a lot of (scientific) work is devoted to the development of tools that rationalise this process and affirm rational choice. According to our concept of rationality, rational decision-making refers to the application of the causal structure of the cognitive map to achieve a given task at its best, e.g. in economic terms to maximise profits. Since rationality refers to the individual pattern of sensemaking, it depends on the decision-makers cognitive structures whether a decision is rational or not.

To elaborate our concept and to gain full understanding of social influences, we enlarge the discussion of intentional decision-making by looking at it as a process of sensemaking that consists of three steps:

- Problem-definition
  defining a lack of sense, stemming from a gap between the actual situation and a preferred status in the future
- Search for alternatives
  finding alternative courses of action to handle this gap
- Act of decision-making
  making a choice between alternative courses of action.

The Problem: A Lack of Sense

Decision-making refers to a person that perceives a difference between the actual situation and his or her preferences regarding the future. We are looking at this gap as a lack of sense: A problem occurs if the cognitive structure of cause and effect does not clearly indicate how to reach a desired task. We suffer from a lack of causal knowledge to close the gap meaningfully.

Therefore we look at the problem as a result of the different developments of causal and hierarchical maps: On the one hand the status-quo does not fit important values and norms of the decision-maker indicated by hierarchical patterns of the cognitive map. On the other hand, the causal map does not offer a clear structure of how to reach the desired objective.

The definition of a problem depends on three factors:

- The decision-maker's perception of the actual situation and the ongoing developments, primarily derived from the causal structure of the cognitive map,
- his or her preferences regarding a meaningful development in the future, primarily derived from the hierarchical structure of the cognitive map and

— his or her lack of cognitive competence to reach the desired task, which indicates a deficiency of the causal map.

Obviously this implies that problems are not given objectively. Rather they are created, since our definition of a problem is based on the individual cognitive representation of the situation. Hence the decision-maker's hierarchical and causal maps function as guidelines of the problem-definition. We can call this a definition of the term problem according to constructionism (von Foerster 1984, von Glasersfeld 1984).

Social interaction influences the development of the causal structures of the cognitive map as well as the adoption of norms and values. Therefore, we suppose that the social context influences the construction of a problem through face-to-face interaction as well as through the process of socialisation.

Another important aspect is the dynamic of the definition of a problem: Once it is clearly defined and the shortcoming of the causal map is obvious, awareness is being created. According to the self-referring structure of cognition the definition of the problem can alter the contents of the cognitive map, e.g. sensitivity towards problem-related aspects is being created or these aspects are being repressed.

Solutions: Cognitive Bridges that Create Sense

The second step of decision-making is the search for alternative courses of action to cope with the gap between the actual and the preferred situation. According to our definition of the term "problem", we look at a solution as the attempt to reduce a lack of sense. Obviously there is a close relationship between the definition of the problem and the estimation of the meaningfulness of a certain solution: The individual contents of the cognitive structures and their gaps represent the causal and normative circumstances the solution must fit.

Actually, there are two strategies of problem-solving: Influencing the future situation towards the preferred status or rearranging the preferences. The first Strategy induces the attempt to develop the causal map, the second one refers to an alteration of the hierarchical map. Whether to take action or to rearrange preferences might depend on the perception of the possibility of influence. We suppose the social context to influence the understanding of structures as given or to be flexible. We will refer to this question later on during our discussion of institutional influences on individual decision-making.

The search for solutions as the search for meaningful action means to investigate the causal structure to find the closest-knit pattern that leads to the desired outcome. This individual pattern indicates the most meaningful and rational course of action according to the given task.

Since the contents of the causal patterns are limited to our prior perceived experiences of success and failure, our capacity to find solutions is limited to the past.

Here the self-reinforcing structure of decision-making comes into play: Successfully applied solutions frame our competence to create new solutions especially in complex situations, or: A solution is a solution is a solution.

The Act of Choice

Traditionally, choice is made by a comparison of perceived cost, benefits and uncertainty of the alternatives. To the contrary, according to the cycle of experience, interpretation and decision, the act of choice is embedded into a process of sensemaking. Assuming that this cycle is twofold, an adaptation of the problem-definition and the evaluation of alternative solutions might take place *after* the decision was made.

That means experiences do not only influence problem-definitions and search for alternative solutions in the future, moreover they might also change the perception of what happened in the past. We have to take into consideration that these three steps of decision-making are not chronological. They may be overlapping or the cycle might turn around: Solutions may precede problems and decisions as well as decisions lead to a search for solutions and problems, rationalisation happens ex-post (Figure 4).

Figure 4: Structures of Decision-Making

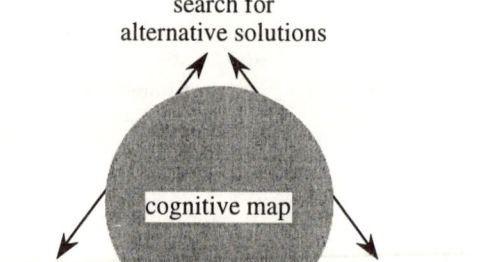

The retrospective structure of sensemaking (Weick 1995, 24) supports to the development of a dominant pattern of decision-making. Subject to uncertainty the re-examination of the problem and possible solutions are necessary to integrate decisions into cognitive patterns.

Such a retrospective integration is especially necessary during the initiation of the individual into already existing social structures: Previously made choices must be integrated meaningfully, problems must be defined ex-post and the search for and the evaluation of alternative solutions must take place retrospectively.

Influences such as organisational culture or social biases on individual cognition and decision-making are hardly to ignore. Dominant patterns of decision-making of individual actors must fit two social levels:
- Such a pattern must fit the frame of the dominant microsocial pattern of sensemaking. Meaningless decisions will hardly be translated into action at lower levels of an organizational hierarchy. Rather we suppose that the individual decision-maker's dominant logic is influenced by and is influencing the microsocial frame.
- According to the intense transactions between individuals, organizations and society, a dominant logic must be at least partially consistent with the institutions of a society. This relationship is twofold: On the one side, "the rational individual is, and must be, an organized and institutionalized individual" (Simon 1967, 102), on the other side, decisions must also be perceived meaningful on the macrosocial level.

In the following sections of the paper we introduce the social context of the individual decision. Social influences on decision-making are divided into three concepts that represent the elaboration of specific situations on a continuous line of social contingencies of decision-making.
- Consequences of individual decisions influence the welfare of other people than the decision-maker. In turn these people will probably change their behaviour that influences the decision-maker's situation. Therefore a reciprocal process of assuming cognitive processes might start.
- Individuals can be forced to agree on one solution. Such a situation of collective decision-making induces a consensus in sensemaking.
- Consequences of individual decisions are influenced by institutions, that are perceived as given circumstances of decision-making.

Decision-Making in a Social Situation

Two points characterize decision-making in a social situation:
- The decision maker perceives the consequences of his or her decision to influence another person's situation.
- The decision maker assumes the other person to respond to his or her decision. These suppositions influence his decision.

A social decision means to apply the causal structure of the cognitive map including assumptions about the map of someone else. The decision maker tries to integrate the process of sensemaking of another person into his or her own cognition. This integration is not only based on the interpretation of the observed (intended or unintended) behaviour. It refers also to assumptions regarding roles and positions of a person within the social network constructed by the decision-maker. Therefore *social* refers not only to the presence of other individuals, it applies to all structures of sensemaking that are based on the social context (Luhmann 1987, 580).

Figure 5: Simple Structure of Individual Decision-Making in a Social Situation

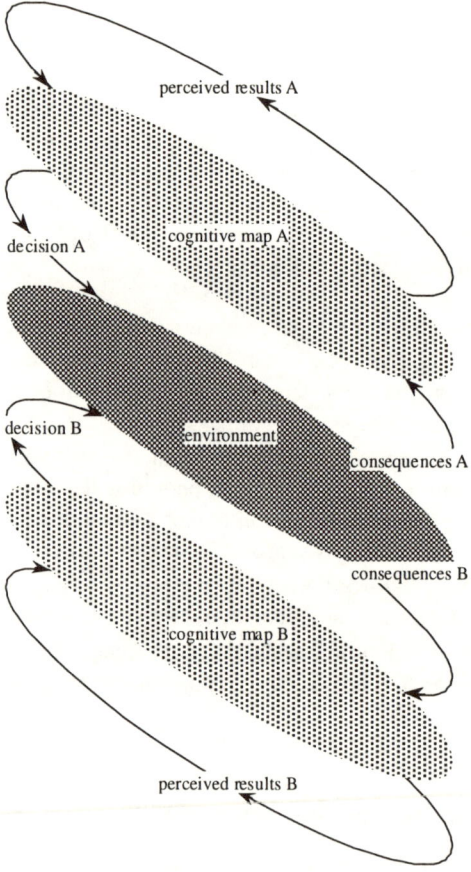

Decision-making in a social situation refers to a process of verbal as well as non-verbal interaction, that represents a translation of really or at least virtually perceived conduct into causal and hierarchical structures according to the cognitive map of the individual. There is neither the possibility of exchanging the contents of the cognitive map nor the chance to communicate perceptions *directly*.

Even language, symbols, behaviour etc. represent only attempts to influence the perceivable environment (Schmidt 1995, 242). Whether these messages are noticed or not and how their reception relates to existing cognitive structures cannot be controlled since the interpretation of verbal and non-verbal notations must be based on the application of one's own causal and normative constructions (Davidson 1990b, 334). We are not able to think the "senseless" structures of someone else, the ability to duplicate another person's sensemaking is limited to someone's own understanding.

Collective Decision-Making

From decision-making in a social situation we move on to situations of collective decision making. Collective decision-making refers to a joint decision of a group of individuals. We assume decision-making in a social situation to be the microstructure of collective decision making: Throughout the process of finding a solution that is accepted by the group, every individual has to decide about his or her behaviour vis-à-vis the other members continuously. Therefore, collective decision-making forces individuals to examine the cognitive structures of other people.

Regarding our emphasis on the creation of sense, decision-making in a social situation refers to individual sensemaking within a social frame whereas collective decision-making means consensual sensemaking. The consensus refers to all steps of the decision-making process. Probably in many cases there is not enough time devoted to the elaboration of the definition of the problem, which might lead to considerable misunderstandings during the search for possible solutions.

Throughout a sequence of repeated individual decision-making within an unchanging group, the perceived consequences of other members' decisions lead to a verification or a falsification of the assumptions regarding their cognitive map. According to the fact that these assumptions must be part of the individual's own cognitive structure and the reinforcement of successfully used cognitive structures, their verifying application will cause their enforcement.

If we take a closer look on reciprocal and repeated social situations of collective decision making, a cycle of mutual reinforcement may arise: The successful projection of cognitive structures leads to their empowerment. Moreover the recognition of individual cognitive structures in the environment might encourage a process of objectivation: The fact, that assumptions about cause and effect as well as norms and values are refound in the environment contributes to their perception as independent structures of human life. Information regarding the falsification of these structures might be replaced, repressed or interpreted according to these structures.

This leads to the question whether or not collective maps or shared cognitions develop. We propose to look at this point from two perspectives:
- Empirical evidence indicates that intensive exchange of information between the members of a group leads to a close relationship of the development of cognitive structures (Janis 1977). On the collective level - according to the process of mutual reinforcement mentioned above - causal and normative

structures develop that are used or at least accepted by all members of the group.
- On the individual level there might happen the adaptation of cognitive structures due to intensive interaction within the group. The recognition of causal and normative structures as well as their successful application reinforces them. But the results of such an adaptation are always due to the self-referring development of an individual cognitive map, because the alteration of the cognitive structure is based on individual prerequisites. That means, that corresponding patterns are embedded into ever specific and autopoetic individual structures.

Therefore shared cognitions represent a twofold fact: Although there is no such thing as a collective section in the individual map, they represent an observable factor of social life.

Decision-Making in an Institutionalized Environment

In this section we move from the microsocial to the macrosocial level and investigate the influence of institutions on individual decision-making. According to Scott (1995, 33) "institutions consist of cognitive, normative and regulative structures and activities that provide stability and meaning to social behaviour." They "are transported by various carriers – cultures, structures, and routines – and they operate at multiple levels of jurisdiction."

Institutional theory originates in economics (Richter 1996) and political science as well as in sociology (e.g. Durkheim 1893/1949, Weber 1947, Berger and Luckmann 1967, Dimaggio and Powell 1991).

Scott (1995, 35) distinguishes three pillars of contemporary institutional theory (Table 1):

Table 1: Three Pillars of Institutions

	Regulative	Normative	Cognitive
Basis of compliance	Expedience	Social obligation	Taken for granted
Mechanisms	Coercive	Normative	Mimetic
Logic	Instrumentality	Appropriateness	Orthodoxy
Indicators	Rules, laws, sanctions	Certification, accreditation	Prevalence, isomorphism
Basis of legitimacy	Legally sanctioned	Morally governed	Culturally supported, conceptually correct

In the broadest sense, all theorists stress that institutions constrain and regularise behaviour (e.g. North 1990, 4). The normative pillar "emphasizes, how values and normative frameworks structure choices" (Scott 1995, 38). Our attention refers to the cognitive approach according to Berger and Luckmann (1967), who relate institutions to the social construction of reality.

Institutions represent a "sedimentation of meanings" (Berger and Kellner 1981, 31) that provides a reliable social frame of individual cognition. They supply causal and hierarchical structures of social life that guide the perception of actual and future situations and prearrange viable strategies to overcome gaps between them. According to our model of decision-making we emphasize three points:

- *Institutions as anchors of sense and problem-definition*
  The experience of ever successful structures of behaviour gives institutions the role of cornerstones of sensemaking. The social notion of institutions provides a basis for a comprehensive definition of individual problems and their social compatible articulation although there might be considerable differences in the specific manifestation of an individual issue.
  Therefore, according to our definition of the term problem, institutions provide the necessary background for the individual cognition to identify a contrariety between causal and hierarchical structures. A lack of sense can only be identified vis-à-vis a meaningful situation. According to our introduction: The meaning of the painting is related to its background.
- *Institutions as frames of viable solutions*
  We have already mentioned that there are two strategies of problem-solving: Influencing the future situation towards the preferred status or rearranging the preferences. Since institutions are perceived as granted structures, they represent important guidelines whether the ability to exert control on causal relationships exists or not.
- *Institutions as patterns of ex-post-sensemaking*
  Institutions arise out of an ex-post rationalisation according to Figure 4: Individuals find themselves in an existing social framework that - according to its collective application - proofs successful. Due to the human need for sense, individuals must find a rational and normative rooting of these already existing structures of their social environment. It is important to mention, that we define *success* as the ability to provide viable structures of social life, but successful institutions do not necessarily lead to the best decision according to the standards of rational choice.

Figure 6 relates to individual decision-making in an institutionalized context. Individual decisions cause consequences on two levels: On the individual level the actor compares his expectations with the perceived outcomes of his behaviour. These consequences are in a predictable way influenced by institutions.

On the collective level societies use mechanisms of public reflection which mirror consequences of individual decisions. These mechanisms can rely on direct reflections, e.g. newspapers, or indirect representations, e.g. arts; they provide information that is accessible to all members of the society. The selection of persons and topics as well as their interpretation and evaluation is based on the institutional background. It is important to notice, that the collective insight into consequences of decisions is limited to communicated tasks, means and results. Therefore, public interpretations and subscriptions to success or failure might differ from those at the individual level.

Figure 6: Decision-making in an Institutionalized Environment

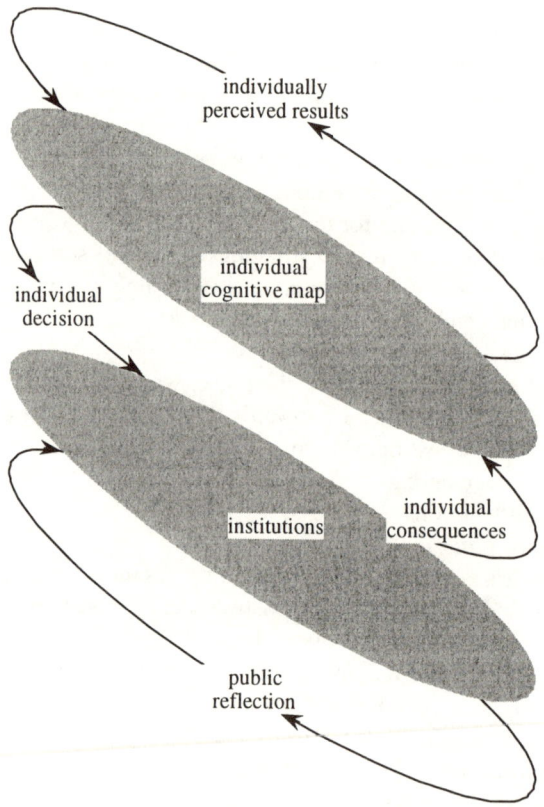

The structure of Figure 6 indicates, that there are two cycles of constructing reality, which relate to each other, but do not necessarily lead to the same results. Consequently, we do not assume an institution to be a part of a individual cognitive map. In fact the perception of individual consequences due to institutionalised influence does not indicate a unification of cognitive structures.

According to the differences in individual perceptions, the impression of institutions can vary between several members of the society, e.g. as advantage or disadvantage. That does not harm their main function: Cognitive stabilisation. As long as they are perceived as fixed part of the environment, as naturally given structure of social life, they enable the individual to make trusty predictions and represent a reliable pattern of cognitive representations that allows for the anticipation of reactions of the social environment.

Finally we conclude from the relation of the two cycles that institutions are products of individual decisions, they do not decide or act themselves (Berger and Luckmann 1967, 75). They live in individual behaviour, based on the assumption of eternal validity. As long as individuals believe in their infinite authority they provide them with structures of sensemaking.

Although the structure of Figure 6 equals the structure of Figure 5 - both contain two related cycles of the social construction of reality - there are at least two important differences between them:

- *Institutions monopolise society*
  Various situations of joint decision-making can usually be compared to each other by the individual decision-maker. To the contrary institutions occupy the whole social space and (most) members of a society lack the experience of different institutionalized environments. Due to their universal authority and the absence of competing or even comparable social structures, that could replace existing institutions, we assume their development to be primarily driven by unconscious ex-post-rationalisation. Within the social context this becomes a self-referring process of reasoning and a cycle of mutual reinforcement: Institutions determine socially viable solutions which imply a definition and articulation of problems in terms of social viability.
- *Institutions as objectivisations of routines in social decision-making*
  Institutions represent - from the perspective of the individual decision-maker - given structures of social life: According to the transfer of habits of social decision-making over social and historical distances, the members of the society abstract from the original problem and disregard all originally possible solutions. Therefore institutions are not perceived as results of interpersonal negotiations and obtain a status of unquestionable legitimacy.

Moreover the repeated experience of a successful reciprocal projection contribute to the objectivisation of institutions and corresponds to unchangeable physical conditions: Institutions become a substantial part of the environment although they represent the product of a social process.

Both points indicate, that the development of institutions underlies a conservative process since they follow a self-referring path of development: The alteration of institutions happens according to those mechanisms of public reflection, that are framed by the institutional context. Once again: An institution is an institution is an institution.

Therefore we finally have to investigate the circumstances of institutional change. We suppose, that fundamental changes of institutional structures occur, if the individual cycle of perception and the public cycle of reflection can no longer be connected meaningfully. In that case, institutions are no longer able to provide reliable structures and a self-referring process of decomposition starts.

Conclusions

According to our introduction we have tried to elaborate a concept of decision-making that is based on the individual need for sensemaking under social influence. At the end of this paper we offer a few thoughts around decision- and sensemaking:

- Regarding the individuality of sensemaking we propose to drop the idea of a homogeneous concept of rationality. Probably the examination of the diversity of rationalities would enrich our insight into decision- and sensemaking. Therefore, it seems interesting to explore behaviour that is traditionally labelled as *irrational*.
- Since decision-making is in most cases a social process it seems important to separate individual from social effects. Collective phenomena such as group dynamics can neither be explained by aggregating individual cognitions nor by subsuming them under a collective frame. Moreover we assume, that *irrational* effects, such as groupthink, must be evaluated on the basis of a heterogeneous concept of rationality and decision-making.
- We suppose to take a closer look at the twofold effects on the collective and the individual level, e.g. the investigation of individually different perceptions of institutions.
- The investigation of mechanisms that are used to reflect the results of individual decisions in public raises critical questions regarding social power: Who selects the reflected persons and topics? How is this done and who has the possibility to express his opinion? Probably a change in the structure of the public articulation of consequences is an important way to change institutions.
- Finally we would like to point out directions for empirical research. First, we urge a processual approach to the concept of problem. Empirical work should be dedicated to the relational development of knowledge and problem-definition not only at the individual level, but also within the micro-and macrosocial context. Second, according to the suggestion to give up the idea of *un-bounded* rationality more empirical attention to so-called irrational behaviour (e.g. Lipshitz 1995) could improve our understanding of decision-making. At last we suggest to investigate the tension between individual, micro- and macrosocial effects on decision-making empirically, e.g. deviations of individual perceptions from public reflections.

References

Alphen, E. V. 8 (1992): *Francis Bacon and the Loss of Self*, London.

Arthur, B. W. (1994): *Increasing Returns and Path Dependence in the Economy*; Ann Arbor: The University of Michigan Press.

Bandura, A. (1977): *Social learning theory*; Prentice-Hall, Englewood Cliffs.

Berger, P. L. and Luckmann, T. (1967): *The Social Construction of Reality*; New York: Doubleday.

Berger, P. L. and Kellner, H. (1981): *Sociology Interpreted: An Essay on Method and Vocation*; Doubleday Anchor, Garden City, NY.

Damasio, A. R. (1994): *Descartes' Error. Emotion, Reason and the Human Brain*; New York: G.P. Putnam's Son.

Davidson, D. (1990a): Paradoxes of irrationality; in: P. K. Moser (ed.), *Rationality in action. Contemporary Approaches*, New York: Cambridge University Press, 449-464.

Davidson, D. (1990b): Psychologie als Philosophie; in: D. Davidson (ed), *Handlung und Ereignis*, Frankfurt/Main: Suhrkamp, 321-335.

Dimaggio, P.J. and Powell, W.W. (1991): *The New Institutionalism in Organizational Analysis*, Chicago: University of Chicago Press.

Durkheim, E. (1839/1949): *The Division of Labour in Society*, Glencoe: Free Press.

Handlbauer, G. (1996): Competing on Cognition?; in: H. H. Hinterhuber, A. Al-Ani and G. Handlbauer (eds.), *Das Neue Strategische Management*, Wiesbaden: Gabler, 61-86.

Hinterhuber, H. H., Friedrich, S., Handlbauer, G. and Stuhec, U. (1996): The Enterprise as a Cognitive System of Core-Competences and Strategic Business Units; *Journal of Strategic Change*, 5(6), 26-54.

Janis, I. L. (1977): Groupthink; in: J. R. Hackmann, E. E. Lawler and L W. Porter (eds.), *Behaviour in Organizations*, New York: 335-342.

Kaplan, S.and Kaplan, R. (1982): *Cognition and Environment*, New York: Praeger.

Knorr-Cetina, K. D. (1981): The microsociological challenge of macro-sociology: Towards a reconstruction of social theory and methodology; in: K. Knorr-Cetina and A V. Cicourel (eds.), *Advances in social theory and methodology*, Boston: Routledge & Kegan Paul, 1-47.

Lipshitz, R. (1995): The Road to Desert Storm; *Organization Studies*, 2(16), 243-263.

Luhmann, N. (1987): *Soziale Systme Grundriß einer allgemeinen Theorie*, Frankfurt: Suhrkamp.

Moser, P. K. (1990): *Rationality in action. Contemporary Approaches*, New York etc: Cambridge University Press.

Neisser, U. (1976): *Cognition and Reality. Principles and Implications of Cognitive Psychology*, San Francisco: Freemen.

North, D. C. (1990): *Institutions, Institutional Change and Economic Performance*, Cambridge, UK: Cambridge University Press.

Peteraf, M. A. (1993): The Cornerstones of Competitive Advantage: A Resource-Based View; *Strategic Management Journal*, 3, 179-191.

Piaget, J. (1954): *The construction of reality in the child*, New York: Basic Books.

Prahalad, C. K. and Bettis, R. A. (1986): The Dominant Logic: a New Linkage Between Diversity and Performance; *Strategic Management Journal*, 7, 485-501.

Richter, R. (1996): Bridging Old and New Institutional Economics: Gustav Schmoller, the Leader of the Younger German Historical School, Seen With Neoinstitutionalists' Eyes; *Journal of Institutional and Theoretical Economics*, 152, 567-592.

Roth, G. (1992): *Das Gehirn und seine Wirklichkeit. Kognitive Neurobiologie und ihre philosophischen Konsequenzen*, Frankfurt/Main: Suhrkamp.

Scheper, W. J. and Faber, J. (1994): Do Cognitive Maps Make Sense?; in: C. Stubbart, J. R. Meindl and J. F. Porac (eds.), *Advances in Managerial Cognition and Organizational Information Processing*, Greenwich-London: Vol. 5 Jai Press, 165-186.

Schmidt, S. J. (1995): Sprache, Kultur und Wirklichkeitskonstruktion(en); in: H.R. Fischer (ed.), *Die Wirklichkeit des Konstruktivismus*, Heidelberg: Carl-Auer-Systeme, 239-252.

Scott, R. W. (1995): *Institutions and Organizations*, Sage: Thousand Oaks.

Simon, H. A. (1967): *Administrative behavior: a study of decision-making process in administrative organization*, 2. ed., New York: Macmillan.

von Foerster, H. (1984): On constructing a reality; in: P. Watzlawick (ed.), *The invented reality*, New York: Norton, 41-61.

von Glasersfeld, E. (1984): An introduction to radical constructivism; in: P. Watzlawick (ed.), *The invented reality*, New York: Norton, 17-40.

Weber, M. (1947): *The Theory of Social and Economic Organization*, New York: Oxford University Press.

Weick, K. E. and Burgon, M. G. (1986): Organizations as cognitive maps: Charting ways to success and failure; in: H. Sims, D. Gioia & ass. (eds.), *The thinking organization*, San Francisco: Jossey-Bass, 102-135.

Weick, K. E. (1979): *The Social Psychology of Organizing*, 2nd ed. Addison-Wesley, Reading.

Weick, K. E. (1995): *Sensemaking in Organisations*, Sage, Thousand Oaks.

Comment on Gernot Handlbauer

Renate Mayntz

Handlbauer's paper practically deals with all of the key concepts of this conference, so in commenting on it I must take up several of the core issues we have been discussing throughout.

The first issue concerns the concept of rationality. By some, rationality is still defined in terms of the theories of rational decision-making and rational choice, which see rationality to rest in the choice of adequate means to reach given ends. This rationality concept has been widely criticized as too narrow, because it sets a standard rarely fulfilled in observable behavior, including behavior that is generally considered as reasonable. Handlbauer is on the side of these critics; without explicitly referring to them, he rather follows the rationality concepts that Alfred Schütz and Raymond Boudon have developed on the basis of Max Weber.

Weber called "rational" not only instrumental behavior, i.e. the calculated choice of means in order to reach a goal (Zweckrationalität), but also behavior in deliberate compliance with given norms or values (Wertrationalität) (Weber 1956, 17). This is roughly reflected in Alfred Schütz' distinction between "Um-zu-Motive" and "Weil-Motive" (Schütz 1960, 93-105). More recently, March and Olsen (1989, 21-26) have taken up the distinction by contrasting the "logic of consequentiality" (or consequential = instrumental behavior) with the "logic of appropriateness" (appropriate = behavior guided by norms). Max Weber, however, supplies us with an important further distinction by differentiating between "objective" and "subjective" rationality: for an action to be called rational it need not be the objectively best means to reach a given goal; an action already qualifies as "rational" if it is based on the actor's best available knowledge (Weber 1968). This is also Boudon's basic point: for him, all <u>reasoned</u> human action can be called rational (Boudon 1995). For Handlbauer similarly all action that is in accordance with an individual's cognitive map can be called rational. Behavior that others would call irrational such as magic practices would thus qualify as rational, since it is rooted in the causal belief that a given practice, for instance a rain dance, serves a collectively appreciated purpose - even if it does not automatically produce rain every time. As Handlbauer puts it, rationality depends on the content of cognitive maps: it is a "meaningful application of cognitive representations" to achieve a certain goal. The cognitive maps in question, incidentally, need not be the result of previous personal experience, but can be based on what other people have told the actor to be true. With his view of rationality, Handlbauer thus stands squarely in a social science tradition of reasoning.

The same is true of a second major point Handlbauer makes. He strongly emphasizes the self-reinforcing effect of successful experience. Though basically referring to a learning mechanism observed by psychologists, the fact that successful past experience may lead to the choice of suboptimal future solutions has also been observed in the social sciences, especially in the analysis of organizational problem-solving and in the reconstruction of technological development. Such truncated learning produces the famous lock-ins. In game theoretic language these are equilibria which it is difficult to get away from in spite of the existence of superior solutions. Again the same effect has been observed in policy studies (see for instance Czada/Windhoff-Heritier 1991); under the de facto dominant strategy of satisficing, any solution to a given policy problem that implies even an incremental improvement over the status quo ante the first time it is applied will be repeatedly chosen thereafter, which means to miss the chance of ulterior improvement.

But policy studies make an important further step. They point out that in many cases of decision-making our capacity to find solutions is not so much limited by successful past experience, as Handlbauer argues, but by the fact that there is no past from which one might infer successful strategies. This is the case whenever we are confronted by a totally new situation. At this conference, such situations of "fundamental uncertainty" have been discussed by Siegenthaler with respect to economic crisis situations, but there are many cases in point beyond the confines of economic policy. A striking recent case has been provided by German unification, which Czada has analyzed in terms of the learning strategies called for in situations of basic uncertainty (Czada 1995). In a more comprehensive treatment of problem-solving, Handlbauer's analysis would have to be extended in this direction.

The concern with problem-solving calls for a brief comment on the concept of "problem". A problem is usually defined as a perceived discrepancy between a given actual state of affairs and a desired (future) state of affairs. To this, Handlbauer adds an additional element: For him, a problem exists if and when the cognitive map lacks causal information that permits to identify the means which would lead to the desired future state. Thus a problem is above all, or at least implies, a <u>cognitive</u> deficiency, though a deficiency with a particular reference, i.e. how to bridge the gap between the actual and the desired future state.

While the emphasis on cognitive deficiencies is important for any analysis of decision-making, I see no need to redefine what a problem is. There are many problems in the conventional sense of the term, i.e. situations which are deficient as measured by our preferences, where we do not lack knowledge of what caused them and how they might be solved, but where we rather lack the capacity to act on such knowledge. To neglect this category of problem situations by virtue of a definition highlighting the cognitive side of problem-solving, much of de facto decision-making would be excluded from analysis.

The lack of knowledge (or at least causal assumptions) about how to improve a presently unsatisfactory situation is a very important, but also a very special kind of cognitive uncertainty. Policy studies have pointed out that there are <u>different kinds</u> of cognitive uncertainty. We may not only lack (subjectively certain) knowledge about the causes of an unsatisfactory situation (a problem) and the way to improve it. Often the very existence of a problem is uncertain. A good case in point is the development of the debate about the dangers to the stratospheric ozone layer caused by CFCs (FCKWs; see Grundmann 1995). For a long time (about 15 years) after the first article appeared that suggested CFCs <u>might</u> damage the ozone layer, available data did not permit to conclude with anything approaching certainty (or the consensus of experts) that an anthropogenic ozone decrease did actually take place. In this situation of cognitive uncertainty, the available data needed to be interpreted - and they were interpreted in different ways by different actors, depending both on their interests and on their principled beliefs. When the experts finally agreed that there was an anthropogenic ozone decrease and that CFCs were a cause of it, there was no uncertainty whatever about the strategy to pursue in order to solve the problem, i.e. by regulating the production and use of CFCs. To concentrate, as Handlbauer does, on the causal structure that leads to a desired outcome, i.e. on the means-end relationships, overlooks a source of cognitive uncertainty that is at least as important in practical action, i.e. uncertainty about the existence or non-existence of a danger.

Having so far focussed on the cognitive aspects of decision-making, we now move, following Handlbauer, to its social aspects. Arguing again like a social scientist (and implicitly following Max Weber here, too), Handlbauer points out that not only interactions among a plurality of individuals should be called "social", but that by virtue of their genesis, "all structures of sensemaking that are based on the social context", and hence also the cognitive maps of individuals, are social in nature. By implication this warns against using "cognitive" and "social" as a dichotomy of mutually exclusive categories, as is often done for instance in the analysis of scientific and technological development, where internal = cognitive and external = social factors are set off against each other. In the sociological theory of action, in contrast, where - following Talcott Parsons (1951) - action orientations are described in terms of their cognitive, evaluative (normative) and cathectic (volitional) dimensions, this false juxtaposition is generally avoided.

If one concentrates on the social aspects of cognition and especially of cognitive maps, the question is bound to arise whether or not it makes sense to speak of collective cognitions. Apparently an adherent of methodological individualism, Handlbauer emphasizes the individual nature of cognitive maps and the impossibility to access directly another person's cognitions. Though he recognizes the existence of shared cognitions, of both causal and normative beliefs that are accepted by a plurality of actors, he avoids an explicitly affirmative answer to the question whether or not, or under what conditions, one might speak of collective cognitive maps. It is evident that other colloquium participants, though using different terms, are less reticent on this issue. To what extent certain beliefs are shared is obviously an empirical question, but that scientific theories, religious dogmas, political ideologies and simple behavioral precepts are often widely shared, and that individual recognition of this shared, "collective" character gives these beliefs a seemingly objective character, has already been pointed out by Emile Durkheim and can be accepted without danger of reverting to some kind of methodological holism. It remains important (a) to distinguish between different kinds of - both individual and "collective" - cognitive contents (e.g. descriptions, causal assumptions, normative beliefs) and (b) to inquire into the mechanisms (e.g. socialization) and the sanctions which underlie the generalization (collectivization) of a specific kind of cognitive content. In this connection it would for instance be instructive to reconstruct the role played by the theory (or ideology) of Marxism-Leninism in the former socialist countries. The individual acceptance of Marxism-Leninism, a theory turned into a dogma, was enforced by manifold social sanctions and clearly affected individual behavior. However, the "collective map" of Marxism-Leninism did not necessarily have to be internalized by the individual and become part of his own cognitive map, as long as he or she conformed to it in his or her observable behavior. The discrepancy between actually shared beliefs and collectively professed beliefs - two different types of "collective map" - can be, as Kuran (1989) among others has shown, the cause of unexpected (and unpredictable) social discontinuities, as for instance exemplified by the break-down of seemly stable socialist regimes.

In Handlbauer's paper, institutions appear as that part of the social context in whose influence on decision-making he is mainly interested. Following Scott (who in fact represents a "culturalist" version of neo-institutionalism), Handlbauer starts with a very wide definition of institutions as including regulative, normative, and cognitive structures, but then decides to emphasize the third of these aspects. Consequently, what he says about the nature and function of institutions has a cognitivistic bias; thus, institutions represent a "sedimentation of meaning" for him, and their function is "cognitive stabilization". Though the complete absence of concrete examples makes it difficult to tell exactly what he has in mind, it seems that for Handlbauer, institutions are basically the same as collective cognitive maps. It follows logically, and is not a theoretical but merely an analytical (tautological) statement that institutions function as "anchors of problem-definitions" and "frames of viable solutions".

In the introductory paper to the Colloquium, a different concept of institution was used, that is in conformity with the mainstream of institutionalist thinking. Along these lines, Fritz Scharpf and I have defined institutions as sets of formal or informal social rules that specify the behavior expected in defined social situations, the relations among the actors involved in these situations, and the resources that specific actors may legitimately claim and use (Mayntz and Scharpf 1995, 43-48) . In this definition, the normative aspect of patterned social behavior is focal, and the function of institutions is the stabilization of behavioral expectations; such expectations can of course be called cognitions, but what is more important is their normative character. This institutionalist perspective permits to ask systematically how institutions (rule systems) affect the motives (or, if you want, preferences) and the cognitions of individual actors, while in Handlbauer's cognitivistic approach, this would be reduced to the (previously formulated) question how collective cognitive maps influence individual cognitive maps.

Handlbauer's view of institutions which emphasizes cognitive aspects may be connected to his emphasis on decision-making, which as an individual choice process is of a basically cognitive nature. However, institutions considered as rule systems do not bear only, and not even primarily, on individual decision-making, but on social behavior generally. As established rule systems, institutions tell people what to do. In behaving accordingly, people largely follow standard operating procedures (or conditional programs) rather than making decisions consciously. In fact, institutions as I define them shape routine behavior much more than they affect decision-making. A deliberate choice of acting in one way rather than in another is called for where institutions do not provide guidance. From a social science perspective, Handlbauer's approach seems too narrow.

Fig. 1: Factors shaping behavior in given situations

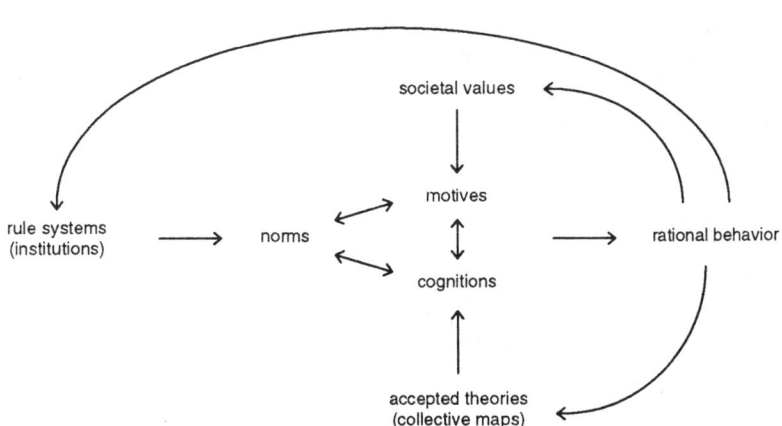

I would like to conclude by trying to sketch an analytical model specifying the relationships among the main concepts we are dealing with at this conference from a social science perspective. Referring back to the briefly mentioned, three-dimensional action frame spelled out by Talcott Parsons that underlies most sociological action theories, I differentiate between norms (institutions), motives (interests, preferences), and cognitions (descriptive/phenomenological and causal beliefs) as proximate determinants of (rational) behavior. The three major determinants are themselves interrelated; thus, acceptable individual motives are normatively shaped, but spontaneous motives can over time change existing, or find expression in new, norms. The proximate determinants of a given unit act are in turn influenced by a set of macro-phenomena that define the action situation: Societal values that affect what individuals strive for, rule systems that define the expected behavior, and accepted theories (collective maps) that influence individual cognitions. This model is rough and highly simplified, but at least it includes motives, which have been rather neglected in Handlbauer's treatment of the colloquium topic, and avoids the conflation of the normative with the cognitive. The model does not, however, go beyond the individual level to include the collective dimension, where unit acts are both related to each other and aggregated to yield a joint effect. To close this so-called micro-macro-gap is the ambition of the social sciences and (at least a large part of) economics as well, but it is definitely beyond the scope of this concluding comment to venture in this direction.

References

Boudon, R. (1995): La rationalité cognitive; in: R. Boudon, *Le juste et le vra*, Paris: Fayard, 97-136.

Czada, R. (1995): Kooperation und institutionelles Lernen in Netzwerken der Vereinigungspolitik; in: R. Mayntz and F. W. Scharpf (eds.), *Gesellschaftliche Selbstregelung und politische Steuerung*. Frankfurt/M.: Campus, 299-326.

Czada, R. and Windhoff-Heritier, A. (eds.), (1991): *Political Choice. Institutions, Rules and the Limits of Rationality.* Frankfurt/M./ Boulder Col: Campus/Westview.

Grundmann, R. (1996): Mending the Ozone Layer: The Role of Transnational Policy Networks, *MPIfG discussion paper* 96/8.

Kuran, T. (1989): Spraks and prairie fires: A theory of unanticipated political revolution; *Public Choice*, 61, 41-74.

March, J. G. and Olsen, J. P. (1989): *Rediscovering Institutions. The Organizational Basis of Politics*, New York: Free Press.

Mayntz, R. and Scharpf, F.W. (1995): Der Ansatz des akteurzentrierten Institutionalismus; in: R. Mayntz. and F.W. Scharpf (eds.), *Gesellschaftliche Selbstregelung und politische Steuerung*, Frankfurt/M.: Campus, 39-72.

Parsons, T. (1951): *The Social System*, Glencoe, Ill.: Free Press.

Schütz, A. (1960) (1932): *Der sinnhafte Aufbau der sozialen Welt*, Wien: Springer.

Weber, M. (1968): *Methodologische Schriften,* S. Fischer Verlag.

___ (1964) (1956): *Wirtschaft und Gesellschaft,* Studienausgabe, Köln: Kiepenheuer & Witsch.

PART III

Rationality and Institutions

Rationally Transparent Social Interactions*

Bruce Chapman

Full Transparency and Cooperation

In his book *Playing Fair*, Ken Binmore (1994, 173) argues that any attempt to rationalise the choice of the cooperative strategy in the one-shot prisoners' dilemma (PD) game is intellectually analogous to attempting to square the circle; it simply cannot be done. Cooperation, of course, is a strongly dominated strategy in the one-shot PD game, and Binmore's point is essentially the tautological one that it is irrational (i.e., part of what irrationality *means*) to choose a dominated strategy.[1]

Nevertheless, having said as much, Binmore is also prepared to concede that there is much to be learned from these arguments for cooperation, wrong though they may be in principle. Binmore argues that such arguments provide the wrong analysis of the wrong game, but, nonetheless, "contain the seeds of an argument that is capable of being the right analysis of the right game in the proper context." (Binmore 1994, 174)

For example, beginning with the PD game, if one could identify the strategy that the other player had adopted before taking action oneself, then it would be rational to cooperate if and only if the other player played the same strategy. Any temptation to defect would, because of the *transparency* of strategy choices that has been assumed, immediately be detected by the opponent, leading the opponent to defect as well. The transparency assumption, therefore, effectively changes the game and helps to provide for a quite different (cooperative) solution from what we see in the more conventional PD game. The deep question, in Binmore's sense, is whether there is any general basis here for thinking that cooperation might be justified as rational in social interactions that, but for the tautology that resists it, we are at least inclined to model as PD games.

---

* This paper was prepared for an international symposium on "Cognition, Rationality, and Institutions", organized by the Max-Planck-Institute for Research into Economic Systems, Jena. I am grateful to the conference participants and to Joe Heath and Hamish Stewart for helpful comments on earlier drafts. Research funding from the Connaught Fund at the University of Toronto is also gratefully acknowledged.

[1] In game theoretic terms a strategy choice x for a player is *dominated* by another strategy choice y if, regardless of the strategy chosen by one's opponent, it results in a payoff for the player that is smaller than what the player would have received with strategy choice y. Strategy choice y is also said to be *dominant* over x.

David Gauthier (1986) probably provides the most influential account of the role that transparency might play in inducing cooperation in a PD game. Gauthier has argued that it is in the interest of a fully rational individual to develop a disposition to cooperate in the PD game, such cooperation being *conditional* on one's opponent in the game being of the same type, and to otherwise defect. Gauthier calls such an individual a *constrained maximizer* (CM). The individual who *always* (unconditionally) plays the dominant non-cooperative strategy, or always defects in the PD game, is said to be a *straightforward maximizer* (SM). As already indicated, dispositions to be one or the other are said to be (fully) public or transparent. Thus, there is no possibility of pretending to be a CM if one is really an SM.

Gauthier's argument for conditional cooperation has attracted a good deal of attention, particularly among philosophers interested in the possibility of grounding the morality of cooperation in the rationality of preference maximization. However, amongst non-philosophers, the transparency assumption has continued to be a sticking point. The economist Karl Warneryd (1997), for example, has argued that Gauthier's analysis, and the sort of transparency that it assumes, fails because it is both logically incoherent and empirically implausible. It also fails, Warneryd suggests, to provide the morality of cooperation with an adequate grounding in rationality, something that can only really be appreciated if one attends adequately to the long run evolutionary success of the CM strategy as compared to other strategies that are less cooperative and, seemingly, less moral.

We shall have reason to look at Warneryd's three criticisms of Gauthier in more detail later in this paper, but for the moment it is sufficient to note that they are offered very much in the spirit of Binmore's above-mentioned concession, namely, that for Warneryd there is the beginning of an argument here, capable of being the right analysis of the right game in the proper context. Specifically, Warneryd's view, like Binmore's, is that cooperation cannot be justified as rational in the one-shot PD game, but can receive some support as part of a larger strategy of conditional cooperation within an extended version of the game. This extended game allows for cooperation to condition on *messages* that the players send to one another, where these messages are a partially transparent reflection of the actual truth about a player's overall strategy.

In this paper I want to suggest that there is something significant to be found in Warneryd's proposal, *even for the one-shot PD game that originally brought Gauthier and Warneryd together.* This will require some adjustment to avoid Binmore's tautology, of course. But the adjustment is not so much to reconfigure the game (viz., the actions and/or the payoffs available to the players), but to rethink the very notion of rational play itself. This more radical rethinking, it will be suggested, is already implicit in Warneryd's use of partially transparent strategies, but because Warneryd does not otherwise range very far from the conventions of game theory he does not provide us with any explicit reason for believing in them. To give transparency some credibility, our analysis will have to borrow from a literature closer to rational cognition (knowledge and understanding) than rational choice (preference maximization). To some extent, and to an extent which is still largely unrecognized in the theory of games, what we can rationally do in any choice situation is conditioned by the strategies that are conceivable to us and, further, by what we can rationally articulate to others under the aspect of concepts, or categories of thought, which we all share. It is this connection between what we can rationally *do* on the one hand, and what we can rationally *say* on the other, and what that connection might imply for the problems of social interaction modeled by the PD game, which is so nicely captured by Warneryd's notion of a conditionally cooperative strategy made partially transparent to another player as a message containing, necessarily, at least some part of the truth.

Cooperation and Rationality

As already indicated above, Warneryd characterises Gauthier's transparent disposition scenario as a "new game", which should not be confused with the original PD game that provided the original motivation for the analysis. And, of course, in an important sense this is true. Given full transparency of one's disposition to cooperate, and given that one only cooperates with others who have a like cooperative disposition, all of the cells in the original PD game except the joint cooperation cell (which, accordingly, provides for the joint cooperation payoffs) reflect the payoffs of joint *non-* cooperation. That is, neither the "free ride" nor the "sucker" payoff in the original PD game are available. Thus, cooperation becomes a weakly dominant strategy for each player in the new game.[2] But in a footnote he goes further, arguing (citing Binmore 1994) that this is something which all attempts at generating cooperation in the PD "must necessarily do", viz., construct a new game which is not, strictly, the same as the original PD. But that is not quite correct, and the difference may be important for where we think Warneryd's project is headed. For consider again the original PD game as laid out in Table 1 below (where c and d stand for the "cooperate" and "defect" strategies respectively):

---

[2] For any player a strategy choice x is *weakly dominant* over another strategy choice y if, regardless of the strategy chosen by one's opponent, x provides for at least as large a payoff as y and, for at least one possible outcome, a strictly larger payoff.

Table 1

		Player 2	
		c	d
Player 1	c	(2, 2)	(0, 3)
	d	(3, 0)	(1, 1)

Instead of reconfiguring the game (i.e., changing the actions and/or the payoffs available to the players), think of a different motivation for their behavior. Suppose merely (and, perhaps, implausibly) that each player in Table 1 chooses to maximize the payoff of her opponent (now, perhaps, not an entirely apposite term).[3] Then, each player would choose to cooperate as a dominant strategy with the consequence that joint cooperation, rather than joint defection, would be the equilibrium outcome of the game.

It will be said immediately that this is an uninteresting quibble. The real interest in the PD game is in the fact that individually rational players, each pursuing their own self-interest (however that is defined, even altruistically[4]) can effect an outcome that is collectively irrational (i.e., Pareto-inferior to another outcome that was available). And that is certainly true. But the point here is only that, on confronting that important claim, a rethinking of the dilemma need not be restricted to reconfiguring the game; it might also take the form of rethinking what is rational behavior *within* the game. In what follows it will be argued that the beginnings of such an approach are to be found in Warneryd's own argument for cooperation

---

[3] The economist as revealed preference theorist will object at this point. She will want to say that if the player is maximizing the payoff of her opponent, then the opponent's payoffs should be modelled as her own and, again, the prisoner's dilemma game in Table 1 simply disappears. But that seems too facile a response. Surely the economist wants to preserve the idea that the description of a given game, with its given payoffs and given strategies, is intelligible apart from the notion of what it is for a player to play that game in some particular way, for example, rationally. Without the game being separately intelligible from the notion of rational play *in* the game, much of the analysis that economists now use in game theory, such as the idea of a trembling hand equilibrium, where a game theoretic equilibrium is required to be robust to the possibility of non-rational play, would be non-sensical.

[4] It is a mistake, of course, to think that the prisoner's dilemma arises only for selfish players and not for altruists. The only situation that cannot give rise to a prisoner's dilemma is one in which each player gives an *exactly* equal weight to the interests of the other player so that each effectively ranks the four jointly determined cells of the game according to the sum total of the payoffs and, therefore, identically to one another. But *any* difference in the player's motivations for ranking the four cells, whether it be motivated by complete (or partial) selfishness or complete (or partial) self-denial in each player, can give rise to a prisoner's dilemma on those preferences. See John Tilley (1996) for further discussion of this sort of confusion.

conditional on the communication of a partially transparent, or semi-public, strategy.

Three Problems for Rational Cooperation

Warneryd identifies three different sorts of problem with Gauthier's argument for CM as a rational disposition. The first is logical. Even if players could observe each others' dispositions or strategies completely, there is still a problem that, in a symmetric normal form game, any non-trivial strategy set, conceived of as conditional on the strategy set of the other player, involves self-reference and, therefore, is not well-defined. Neither player can, without an array of possible strategies already defined for him by the other player, fully define his own strategy set, something that makes it impossible for either to get his strategy "off the ground". Such a mutually conditioned set of strategies is logically incoherent.

The second difficulty, according to Warneryd, is that even if the notion of a full transparency of dispositions, combined with the announcement of conditional strategies, could be made coherent, the idea is not empirically plausible. The hard truth of the matter, suggests Warneryd, is that individuals are not fully transparent to one another.

This suggests, however, that a second more indirect account of conditional cooperation, based on evolutionary selection, might work instead. Perhaps certain physical characteristics of individuals, which *are* observable, can reveal indirectly the relevant dispositions for cooperation and, therefore, can be made to substitute for direct observation. If that is so, then one might expect these physical characteristics, and the dispositions for cooperation they reveal, to be selected for, and prevalent in, the population. After all, CMs seem to be better off than SMs in the long run since they at least secure, from time to time, the gains from cooperating with one another.

But here Warneryd presents the third difficulty with these accounts of conditional cooperation, arguing convincingly that, without actual transparency, there is always room for a mutant (or mimic) to enter the evolutionary game, who has the physical characteristic, but who has no disposition to cooperate, even conditionally. In such circumstances, as Warneryd demonstrates, there is no evolutionarily stable strategy (ESS), and only two neutrally stable strategies (NSS), both of which, however, induce the same inefficient payoffs experienced in the original PD game.[5]

---

[5] In an evolutionary two-person game, where a large population of players are randomly matched in pairs, the ESS criterion requires that if all players play the ESS then, if there is a small invasion of agents (or "mutants") playing some other strategy, those players should do strictly worse than the ESS players. NSS is a slightly weaker criterion than ESS. If all players play the NSS strategy, then the criterion only requires that the mutants not do strictly better than the NSS players, although they could do as well.

Partial Transparency as Solution

The failure of both full strategic transparency (which generates the difficulty of logical coherence) and complete lack of transparency (which leaves open the destabilizing evolutionary effects of mimicry) together suggest that some form of partially transparent strategic interaction might be effective, and it is this possibility which Warneryd explores in the most innovative part of his paper.

Warneryd borrows the general notion of a conditionally cooperative strategy, but avoids the logical problems of self-reference and infinite regress that plague Gauthier's version. In contrast to Gauthier, whose players each try simultaneously (and unsuccessfully) to condition their strategies, and in particular their dispositions to cooperate, on the *strategies* of the other, Warneryd has each of his players condition her cooperation on the other player's communication or message. If strategies condition on the other player's messages, and not on the other player's strategies (themselves so conditioned), then the logical problem of self-reference is avoided.

However, why does conditioning a cooperative choice strategy on messages of cooperation actually work so as to avoid the usual PD result? The answer is that it does so for exactly the same reason that Gauthier suggested it would in his original work; it just pays to be able to induce cooperation in the other player if one can, even if this means one has to cooperate oneself.

Now it is important to recognize that there is still a significant amount of transparency in Warneryd's analysis. Warneryd simply stipulates that the message that a player *can* send (and upon which the other player will conditionally cooperate) has to be some (publicly defined) part of what that player will adopt as an *actual* strategy . Thus, for example, it is not possible for a player whose strategy is always to defect, or to defect regardless of any message received from the other player, to send the message "Cooperate". Thus, as for Gauthier, so for Warneryd, it is not possible for an unconditional defector to induce any cooperation from a conditional cooperator by merely mimicking the message of a conditional cooperator.

The last point simply re-emphasises the *theoretical* advantage of assuming at least some part of Gauthier's transparent dispositions, albeit in a format that now allows for logical coherence. We will have to consider the *practical* possibility of such transparency in a moment. However, before doing so, it is worth emphasising that there is some significant advantage for Warneryd over Gauthier in assuming only partial rather than full transparency, even for what Gauthier himself seeks to accomplish. As others have argued (e.g., Danielson 1991), under full transparency there is a danger that a conditionally cooperating CM will do less well than a so called *reciprocal cooperator* (RC). Within Gauthier's framework of conditional cooperation, RCs are those individuals who cooperate with CMs, but defect on so called *unconditional cooperators* (UCs), that is, those individuals who cooperate regardless of the disposition of the other player. UCs can enter Gauthier's world because, initially at least, they can do as well as CMs. But the presence of UCs allows in turn for the entrance of RCs who, because they secure all the cooperative gains that CMs secure with other CMs and RCs, as well as the additional benefits of occasionally defecting against UCs, actually do better than CMs. This is a problem for Gauthier since not only does it tell against Gauthier's proposed CM as the most successful strategy, but, more to the point of Gauthier's overall project, it tells against CM as the most *rational* strategy, since CM, unlike RC, seems to leave some possible benefits unexploited. However, while RC is perhaps more individually rational than CM, because it calls for opportunistic (although not deceptive, since full transparency is still assumed) defection against UCs, it might be thought to introduce seriously immoral behavior. At a minimum, the gap between the rational and the moral, or the very gap that Gauthier sought to close in his project, seems to grow with the introduction of RCs into the framework.

However, Warneryd's account of conditional cooperation, unlike Gauthier's, avoids the problem because, without *full* transparency, the strategy UC cannot be identified. Under Warneryd's only partially transparent messages, a player P_1 is only told what the other player P_2 will actually do conditional on receiving a message from P_1 that P_1 will cooperate if P_2 sends the message "Cooperate". The *transparency* is what allows P_2 to be sure that he will secure P_1's actual cooperation if P_2 sends the message "Cooperate" and P_1 has himself sent such a message to "Cooperate". But the *partial* nature of that transparency is important as well. For without full transparency or publicity of a player's strategy, P_1 is not told what P_2 will do should P_2 receive any "Defect" message from P_1. Specifically, that P_2 might still cooperate should this particular message be received is not revealed. But this lack of full transparency prevents an RC from identifying and selectively exploiting any UCs. Thus, if the RC strategy is morally unattractive, it is a strategy that is avoided under Warneryd's assumption of partial rather than full strategic transparency.

Thus, in the final analysis, Warneryd's use of partial rather full transparency, achieved because messages are only an incomplete reflection of an individual's full conditional strategy, generates all the benefits of Gauthier's project of conditional cooperation (i) without generating the logical difficulty of self-reference which is implied by mutually conditioned conditional strategies; (ii) without making the empirically implausible claim that an individual's strategies are fully transparent, or completely observable, to others; and, finally, (iii) without allowing entry of the rational but seemingly immoral reciprocal cooperators who take selective advantage of unconditional cooperators.

Nevertheless, despite these theoretical advantages, one might still wonder whether there is any warrant for believing in the *actual* possibility of even *partially* transparent strategies. Certainly full transparency seems implausible and too "convenient" a way to avoid the discouraging implications of the PD game. Yet, there may be some good reason for doubting the assumption on the other extreme as well, namely, the one that assumes that an individual's strategies are completely private or opaque to other players. If that is so, and I shall try to argue now that it is, then Warneryd's more intermediate position of assuming partially transparent strategies does begin to look more promising.

Rational Transparency and the Categorical Identity of Action

It is important to emphasize that the assumption that there can be individual strategies revealed in part by prior communications of the players is a quite radical one within the theory of games. It is radical, first, to assume that some earlier formulated plan of action (whether it is publicly announced or kept private) can genuinely constrain the later choices of a player, particularly if the plan calls for some counter-preferential choice at any point in the plan's overall execution. This is the hurdle which the model of "resolute choice", proposed in McClennen (1990), has always faced and which has made that model so unpalatable to many decision theorists (see, e.g., Binmore 1994, 161-67). Yet something of this is exactly what Warneryd proposes in his paper. Players announce some part of their strategy in a prior message to the other player and are then constrained, because transparency of that partial message is assumed, actually to act on it.

It is also radical to assume, more particularly, that pre-play communication can induce players to act contrary to their own interests. Again, the convention within game theory is to think of all this as merely "cheap talk", which can have no effect on the later actions of the players (except, possibly, to help players in pure co-ordination games where counter-preferential choices are *not* required). Now there is some experimental evidence suggesting a greater propensity for players to co-operate with one another after there has been an opportunity for pre-game interaction and communication (see, e.g., Frey and Bohnet this volume) and in his paper Warneryd also assumes that there is an essential connection between what we say and what we do, albeit not necessarily the same one that is captured in the experimental evidence. Where the evidence suggests that mere "fraternisation" (in which the players, through conversation, come to form informal relationships with one another) might be enough, Warneryd's partial transparency assumption requires that the link between a player's pre-play message and his in-game strategy be more direct and structured: the former must be an accurate if incomplete reflection of the latter, and the latter, as indicated above, once announced, must actually constrain the former. Nevertheless, like the experimental evidence, Warneryd's assumption of partial transparency also challenges the more conventional assumptions in game theory which, typically, deny any substantial connection between what we say and what we do.

Of course, within a quite different tradition of rational decision-making, it should come as no surprise that there might be some connection between what we say and what we do. Within this alternative account, rational *individual* choice is choice based on the self-conscious use of "reasons for acting", the latter being the very notion that Binmore (1994, 180) claims is foreign to the conventions of decision theory, but something which he admits "would need to be explained within a fully articulated theory of rationality". And rational *social* choice is choice explicitly backed up by the sorts of reasons which are capable of public articulation under shared concepts or categories of thought. Thus, within this sort of account, there is an intimate connection between rational "doing" and rational "saying", the latter being measured by the cogency of the reasons, or understandings, being articulated (rational cognition), and the former being judged according to whether it operates under, or is constrained by, the aspect of those reasons so articulated (rational choice).

Warneryd's paper concentrates more on rational choice than rational cognition, that is, more on whether what a player does is consistent with what a player has said or communicated to others, and less on what it is rational to say or think in the first place. This is reasonable enough and, as suggested above, even this more limited agenda already represents a categorical shift away from the conventions of rational choice within game theory. However, had Warneryd considered more what might be implied specifically by the notion of rational cognition or communication (where the latter at a minimum involves shared cognition), then it is at least arguable that the full implications of his account for what Binmore has called a "fully articulated theory of rationality" might have appeared much more radical. More to the point of Warneryd's own project, it might also be that, had he attended more to the disciplining effects of rational cognition, we would have found his assumption of partial strategic transparency to be that much more compelling. The truth is that some things are hard to *do* because they are hard to *think* about, and certainly very hard to *talk* about to others under the aspect of concepts or categories of thought which we all share. This is one way to make the connection between rational cognition and rational choice, and one way to make sense (literally) of Warneryd's assumption of partial transparency. Some strategic interactions are transparent, or at least more transparent than others, simply because they are more rationally comprehensible.

We can illustrate this point with an example taken from the law, an area of rational decision-making that emphasises, very self-consciously, the obligation to give reasons for one's choices (For the following argument in more detail, together with some suggestions for its implications for social choice theory, see Chapman 1998a). Suppose, for example, that there is a panel of three judges considering whether a defendant should pay damages to a plaintiff for breach of contract. Judge A believes that there is a contract, but that the defendant has not breached it in this case. Thus, he would decide in favour of the defendant. Judge B, on the other hand, believes that the defendant's conduct would amount to a breach, but that in this case there is no properly formed contract. Thus she too would find in favour of the defendant. Finally, Judge C believes both that there is a contract and that the defendant's conduct amounts to its breach. Judge C, therefore, would find in favour of the plaintiff. Thus, a majority of the judges, A and B, share the view that the defendant should win the case and, absent an obligation to give reasons, would choose that as their most preferred result.

However, the obligation to provide reasons for their choice should at least induce a moment's hesitation in this majority of the court. There are really only two legal issues in this case, namely, the breach issue and the contract formation issue. One is even tempted to say that a breach of contract action naturally organises itself around these two issues (although the invocation of any notion of a natural rather than, say, a socially constructed ordering will be controversial).

These are the issues that make the legal action rationally comprehensible to us, a proper object of our rational cognition. Yet, on each of these salient issues in the case, the two judges who form the majority have completely opposite views. In such circumstances it seems inaccurate to say that there really is a majority agreement between these two judges on any matter in law. Certainly, it would be a challenge for this majority of judges to articulate any common or coherent legal view.

Now, while we may seem to have left the prisoner's dilemma far behind, there are two points of contact between this example and Warneryd's project that need to be emphasised. One concerns whether this lack of any common or coherent understanding of, or reason for, a shared preference translates into any practical difficulty for this majority actually to act on its preference, that is, whether the failure of rational cognition and/or communication impacts at all on the possibility of rational choice. In a strictly causal sense, of course, there cannot be any such impact. It is always possible to pursue one's preferences without good reasons, and possible for a majority to pursue its preferences without any coherent reason in common across its members. Thus, at first glance there is little in this example that provides any reason for thinking there is some necessary connection between what we can say (together) and what we can do (together). The conventions of rational decision theory seem not to be much affected (although the idea that one can pursue one's preferences without good reasons should surely give a *rational* decision theorist some reason to pause), and Warneryd's claim that public messages can help to pre-commit strategic choice seems to get little support from this legal example.

However, at a second point of contact with Warneryd's work, the legal example does support the idea of a partially transparent strategy. To the extent that the members of this legal majority have no reason in common for their preferred choice, it seems harder for us to think of that choice as rational and harder, perhaps, for us even to know exactly *what it is* the majority is up to. It is as if the choice, without a consistent or coherent rationale for the chooser, lacks any particular *identity*. But this is just another way of saying that the choice of the majority is not rationally transparent to us. Thus, one way to make sense of strategic transparency in another player is to assume that its choices can be organized under the aspect of concepts, or categories of thought, which we share and deem appropriate to the choice at hand. Quite literally, choices that lie outside such an organizing conceptual framework are *inconceivable* to us.

But this brings us back again to the first point of contact with Warneryd's project. If some strategic choice, no matter how much it is preferred, is not transparent to us as players interacting with the chooser, because the choice is quite literally inconceivable, then the chances are that the choice will also be inconceivable to the chooser, at least if the chooser shares the same conceptual framework. But an inconceivable choice, surely, is one which is much harder for the chooser to think about and, ultimately, to make. Thus, the very same conceptual scheme which makes some choices incoherent and, therefore, non-transparent to others as objects of their rational cognition, will also be enough to make these choices largely inaccessible to the player who is actually making the choice. In this respect, therefore, a common conceptual scheme provides the connection, through rational cognition, between strategic transparency and rational choice. Just as we, from the outside, can only see (or comprehend) in another's choice what is rationally transparent to us, so the chooser, from the inside, can only do what is rationally transparent to her.

To say that some strategies are completely "inaccessible" to choosers because they are not conceivable under some rational framework may strike some readers as far too strong a claim, particularly in the context of the prisoner's dilemma. After all, the PD game holds out its intellectual fascination for us precisely because the seeming rationality of choosing the dominant strategy there is all too easy to comprehend, both for the chooser herself and for us as external observers of her choice. But the strong version of this claim is not required to make some sense of Warneryd's notion of partial transparency and the possibility that it might induce some cooperation in the PD game. For example, Michael Bacharach (1997,1998) has suggested that players in the PD might approach the game with "variable frames", that is, with different (not simultaneously available) conceptual representations or understandings of their situation. These variable frames might allow all the players eventual access to all the different issues that a situation might present, although not permit a player, caught at any one moment by a particular frame, to see all these different issues at once. Bacharach thinks of the different conceptual frames as being *psychologically non-integrable*, where any attempt at integration would be a bit like trying simultaneously to see the two figures in the psychologist's familiar rabbit-duck diagram. Where we can see everything that there is to be seen, and may even be able to see these different things at will as we switch back and forth between frames, we cannot see them all at once. This is a much weaker version of the inaccessibility claim.

Bacharach contemplates in particular the idea that in the PD game there might be both an "I/he frame" and a "We frame". These different frames, which pose the quite different questions "What should *I* do?" and "What should *we* do?" call for quite different notions of reasoning.[6] Specifically, the "I/he frame" accommodates

---

[6] Robert Sugden (1993) has argued for something analogous to the We frame under the idea of "team reasoning". He characterises such reasoning (at 86) as follows: "To act as a member of a team is to act as a *component* of the team. It is to act on a concerted plan, doing one's allotted part in that plan without asking whether, taking other's actions as given, one's own action is contributing to the team's objective."

In Chapman (1998b, 474-76) I have also argued that the PD game might be played by those who can see themselves as in being in either an individualistic or collective choice frame, and that the different availability of these different frames might give rise to a defeasible conception of rational choice, that is, a conception that makes one's choice under a rational strategy condition on what the other (otherwise identical and symmetrically placed) player happens to choose. This argument combines features of Sugden's team reasoning and Bacharach's variable frame analysis. For further analysis of the "We frame" outside a game theoretic context, see Tuomela and Miller (1988).

the idea, familiar in game theory, that a player should ask what strategy is best for herself *given* what the other player might do, and allows that player, under common knowledge of such reasoning,[7] to replicate that same sort of thinking in the other player as well. The "We frame", on the other hand, encourages the player to think about what *profile S* of strategies should be adopted by the players as a group, and then identifies the rational strategy for each player as the one that simply (categorically, non-contingently) has that player "doing her part" s_i within that overall profile. Unlike for the "I/he frame", a player who is in the "We frame" does not have to consider whether the other players are themselves doing their parts as components of this profile of strategies in order to justify her strategy choice. Rather, in response to any question about *why* she was doing what she was doing, she would say only "This is simply what *we* do when we do *S* (as best)" or, perhaps, "This is simply what *I* do when *we* do *S* (as best)" or even, most provocatively (because most categorical in tone), "This is simply *what it is* for us, you and me, to do *S* (as best)."

Bacharach (1997) argues not only that these two different frames might be available to each player, but also (Bacharach 1998) that it might be common knowledge that they are so available. And therein is where the advantage lies. Common knowledge of the "We frame" can make it rational for players to achieve certain shared goals, for example, the Pareto-optimal outcome in a co-ordination game, goals which would not be rationally achievable if the players were restricted to (their common knowledge of) the more conventional "I/he frame". Under the "I/he frame" it is only rational for the first player to do "her part" in an attractive co-ordination equilibrium *if* the other player is also doing his part. But that other player (as the first player well knows under the common knowledge assumption) can only rationally do his part *if* the first player does hers. Thus, again (much as for the mutually conditioned strategic dispositions of the CM's in Gauthier's account), under common knowledge of the I/he frame each player is caught in a problem of self-reference without being able to determine a unique strategy. Hence we have the co-ordination problem despite the salience of a Pareto optimal outcome.[8] The "We frame", by contrast, when it arises as a possibility under common knowledge, does not allow an individual player even to *conceive* of the possibility that it might not be rational for her to do her part under the best

---

[7] Some proposition *p* is common knowledge in a game if (i) each player knows that *p*, (ii) each player knows that each player knows that *p*, (iii) each player knows that each player knows that each player knows that *p*, and so on. It is the assumption that there is common knowledge that each player is working within an I/he frame of reasoning that renders Nash equilibrium thinking more convincing as a way for each player to play the game. For argument to this effect, see Chapman (1998b, 464-66).

[8] See Gilbert (1989) and (1990) for more detailed versions of this argument. Gilbert's various papers, emphasising the importance of introducing the idea of a "plural subject" (or the "We frame") into game theory to solve certain sorts of coordination problems, are now usefully collected in Gilbert (1996). Also see Sugden (1993, 73-75) for an economist's presentation of the same argument.

possible profile of strategies because the other player might not be doing his (perhaps, self-referentially, because he is waiting for her to do hers, and so on). Such individualistic I/he thinking ("What if *he* isn't? What then should *I* do?") is simply not available under the "We frame". Where it might be said that the "I/he frame" and, more specifically, the players common knowledge of it, incorporates a form of *intersubjective* rationality, and leaves open those characteristically recursive iterations of rational rethinking across the individual players, the "We frame" is more *objective* and, accordingly, more restrictive of each player's thinking (and rethinking) about possible strategic choices. Under the "We frame" each player asks only what is best for the group *as a group*, and then goes on (again, unthinkingly, unreflectively, *uncontingently*, at least in the I/he-sense) simply to do *what it is* (categorically) that the best group strategy S requires of her. She does all this, in other words, without any reconsideration of whether the other players in the group are also doing their individual parts in the overall scheme.

Bacharach (1998) has argued effectively that an objectively restricted We frame, available at least as a possibility for the players, can be important not only for achieving Pareto optimality in co-ordination games, but also (sometimes) for achieving joint cooperation in the PD game as well. Given this argument from Bacharach, the particular question that arises for the purposes of this paper is whether there is any reason to think that the obligation to talk about choices or strategies, or, in Warneryd's terms, the obligation to send messages about them, serves only to frame the choices of the interlocutors under an intersubjectively rational and accessible conceptual scheme like the "I/he frame", or whether, more strongly, such communication also imposes something of the disciplining effect of an objectively rational We frame as well. If it is the latter, then we are that much closer to understanding why it could be that sending messages about one's strategy choices in the PD game, and in particular why sending messages about the possibility of cooperating there, might actually induce greater cooperation in the way that Warneryd has suggested. We would be closer, in other words, to accepting the idea that there could be a connection between what we say and what we do in the PD game, a connection Warneryd has captured (but not argued for) in the idea of a partially transparent strategy.

Now the shared understanding that comes with an effective communication between interlocutors must surely presuppose at least a common (or overlapping) conceptual scheme, that is, one which is intersubjectively accessible. This much seems certain. Without that there would be no real possibility of communicating anything in particular at all. But in the actual communication (not mere existence) of this shared understanding there is likely to be much more than this. For in the very use of language to articulate the shared meaning, there is the necessity to order one's thoughts, and more specifically one's thoughts about one another's strategic choices, under the aspect of a shared language which itself must *transcend* the momentary interaction of the two interlocutors. After all, it is not open to the parties to invent a completely private and local meaning for their particular interaction. At some point the words they use to capture the shared significance of their interaction for each other ("Exactly *what* are *we* doing within this overall profile of strategy choices? Is it *S* or something else?") are words that they must take as given and, ultimately, bring *to* that interaction from the outside. The words and their meaning cannot (or, at least, cannot all) arise *out* of the interaction, for example, by agreement, since that would beg the question as to how the meanings of the words that form the basis for this meaningful agreement were themselves agreed upon.[9]

But then this must mean that the parties to such an interaction, at least when they become inter*locutors* and not merely inter*actors*, are ultimately forced, at least in part, into the objectivity of a "We frame". For when one player communicates an understanding of what she is doing by way of publicly accessible meanings, she must at some point order her particular action s_i under the aspect of S, that is, as something that she does *categorically* for the other.[10] We might say, again provocatively, that this simply is *what it is* for each player to do his or her part under the profile S of strategies where S is now understood, not merely intersubjectively (as would be the case if the players merely had to glimpse a private and momentary understanding of one another's behaviour), but objectively as well (where the words, and their meanings, which make up the communication must be brought *to* the interaction and, therefore, transcend its moment).

---

[9] This restriction would apply, for example, to the two judges who formed a majority in the earlier breach of contract example. It simply is not open to these two judges to say to others that, while it might appear that they have no conceptual views in common, the reality is that they share their own *private* understanding of the wrong in "breach of contract" and that the defendant has not run foul of it. The problem is that the words they use to rationally articulate a set of reasons for their view must ultimately, i.e., either at this level or at some more rudimentary one, make use of *publicly* available meanings of "contract" and "breach" (or the components thereof) to support their particular understanding. And it is to this which the majority must finally fall prey. The example only shows how there can be a deficiency of publicly available reasons at an early and obvious opportunity, where, for example, the most basic building blocks of "breach" and "contract" are in play. But other legal examples would show that purely private understandings of more nuanced legal concepts, even when such understandings are shared by the very judicial majority which has been responsible for developing the legal concept in question, are not sufficient to resist the disciplining effect of public (or objective) reason; see, e.g., *Mutual Life & Citizens Assurance Co. v. Evatt* (1971) A.C. 793 (P.C.) (where Lord Reid and Lord Morris, in an opinion which dissents from a court majority's interpretation of one their own earlier judgements, say "We are unable to construe the passages from our speeches cited in the judgment of the majority in the way in which they are there construed.") The law typically relies on a public understanding of the words chosen to express a particular legal meaning; the private understanding of the original framers of the law has no privileged status.

[10] While the player does action s_i *categorically*, that is, under the aspect of category S as a form of collective action, she need not do the action *absolutely*. In other words her commitment to do the action under the aspect of S might be defeasible or subject to revision. For discussion of the difference between a categorical and an absolute commitment to action, see Chapman (1998c, 1507), and for further discussion of the relevance of this difference for the theory of games, see Chapman (1998b, 455).

We are now in a position to summarise at least the basic steps of an argument that there might actually be partially transparent social interactions, as modelled by the PD game, in the way that Warneryd has suggested. The first step is to realize that certain conceptual schemes or frames make some issues more salient, and some choices more accessible, to us than others. Choices or issues outside the frame are, quite literally, inconceivable. And, in some sense, the inconceivable, while not impossible, is very hard to do. Second, some of these frames highlight certain forms of interactive reasoning, say, in the PD game, and (maybe just for a moment) make other forms of interactive reasoning in that game inaccessible. For example, the "We frame" suggests the rational question "What should *we* do?" or "What do I do when *we* do S as best?" and makes it inconceivable for a player to ask the question posed by the "I/he frame" "What if *he* doesn't do his part in S? Should *I* do my part then?" This lack of access to the questions posed by the "I/he frame", as Bacharach has shown, can be very useful to the achievement both of rational co-ordination in co-ordination games and rational cooperation in the prisoner's dilemma game. Third, and finally, the argument has been that the obligation to talk about or, perhaps more particularly, to offer reasons for ones choices under some strategy (or, in Warneryd's terms, to send messages about one's willingness to cooperate in the PD game) has the effect, if only for a moment or at some point in the verbal exchange, of putting a player into the very "We frame" that Bacharach has shown can be so productive of co-ordination and cooperation. This is because in the obligation to talk about what one is doing there is the need to organize one's conduct, if only in the mind's eye, under the aspect of categories of thought, say S, which are objective, public, or given to the interaction precisely in the way that the "We frame" demands. The words, at least if they are to communicate a shared understanding from one player to the other, cannot themselves be second guessed by the interaction, as they would be in the characteristically infinite regress of the "I/he frame". This has the effect of usefully reducing the range of opportunity for a player to engage in rational reconsideration, thereby making co-ordination and cooperation easier to achieve.

Thus, the connection between "saying" and "doing" is not that "Saying will make it so". That, properly, will always be a suspect claim for any causal decision theorist. Rather, the claim is that some "doings", while still available in the strictly causal sense, simply do not bear thinking, much less talking, about. This too can make such "doings" very hard to achieve. Not impossible, of course; there will always be some slippage between what we say and what we do. In Warneryd's terms there is only likely to be partial rather than full transparency. But doing and saying are not completely unconnected either, and Warneryd, Bacharach and others have done a service to our understanding of rational social interaction, even the sorts of rational social interaction commonly modelled as a PD game, in providing an interpretation of this connection under the guise of strategies made partially transparent through messages which are at least accurate to some degree.

References

Bacharach, M. (1997): 'We' Equilibria: A Variable Frame Theory of Cooperation; unpublished paper presented at the Seminar on Cooperative Reasoning, St. John's College, Oxford.

Bacharach, M. (1998): Players' Representations and the Theory of Games with Multiple Identity; unpublished paper (short version), Institute of Economics and Statistics, University of Oxford.

Binmore, K. (1994): *Playing Fair*, Cambridge, London: MIT Press.

Chapman, B. (1998a): More Easily Done Than Said: Rules, Reasons, and Rational Social Choice; *Oxford Journal of Legal Studies*, 18, 293.

Chapman, B. (1998b): Law Games: Defeasible Rules and Revisable Rationality; *Law and Philosophy*, 17, 443-480.

Chapman, B. (1998C): Law, Incommensurability, and Conceptually Sequenced Argument; *University of Pennsylvania Law Review*, 146, 1487-1528.

Danielson, P. (1991): Closing the Compliance Dilemma: How It's Rational to be Moral in a Lamarkian World; in: P. Vallentyne (ed.), *Contractarianism and Rational Choice*, Cambridge, New York, Melbourne: Cambridge University Press, 291-322.

Gauthier, D. (1986): *Morals by Agreement*, Oxford, New York: Oxford University Press.

Gilbert, M. (1989): Rationality and Salience; *Philosophical Studies*, 57, 61-77.

Gilbert, M. (1990): Rationality, Coordination, and Convention; *Synthese*, 84, 1-21.

Gilbert, M. (1996): *Living Together*, London, New York: Rowman and Littlefield Publishers.

McClennen, E. (1990): *Rationality and Dynamic Choice*, Cambridge, NewYork, Melbourne: Cambridge University Press.

Sugden, R. (1993): Thinking as a Team: Towards an Explanation of Nonselfish Behavior; *Social Philosophy and Policy*, 10, 69-89.

Tilley, John J. (1996): Prisoner's Dilemma from a Moral Point of View; *Theory and Decision*, 41, 187-193.

Tuomela, Raimo and Miller, Kaarlo (1988): We-Intentions; *Philosophical Studies*, 53, 367-389.

Warneryd, K. (1997): Rationality, Transparency, and Evolutionary Selection; Stockholm: Economic Research Institute, Working Paper Series in Economics and Finance, No. 167.

Comment on Bruce Chapman

Thomas S. Ulen[11]

1 Introduction

One might say that there are two core questions of political philosophy: How should society organize itself, including its governmental institutions? And how might society induce its citizens to comply with both its explicit legal commands and its implicit norms? Among the many remarkable achievements of John Rawls' *Theory of Justice* was its providing a single answer to these two questions by reviving the notion of a social contract among rational decisionmakers. The institutions of a liberal constitutional democracy[12] might be imagined as the result of an agreement struck among rational decisionmakers who were, at the time of the formation of the agreement, operating without explicit knowledge of what position they or their progeny would occupy in the future society. Presumably, rational citizens who inherited this political culture from the founding generation would adhere to the social contract thus struck.

Despite the great influence of Rawls' social contract theory, there has been a nagging doubt among scholars about the willingness of rational decisionmakers to continue to honor the original contract and to comply with newly developed norms.[13] Some scholars have noted that social cooperation is like a prisoner's

---

[11] I should like to thank Prof. Dr. Manfred Streit, Director of the Max-Planck-Institute for Research into Economic Systems, Jena, Germany, for his hospitality during the Summer, 1998, and Dr. Uwe Mummert of the Institute for his hospitality, including many fruitful conversations, during that visit. I also would like to thank my colleague Richard McAdams for his comments on an earlier draft of this piece.

[12] In *Political Liberalism* (1993) Rawls derived the political structure that he believed rational agents with deeply different fundamental beliefs would be able to agree upon.

[13] Clearly, Rawls and his commentators were discussing a social contract that specified the foundational governance structure and constitutional rules of a society, and one could easily argue that any subsequent legal command developed in accord with the original social contract would command approval and compliance. Those that did not would either not be passed, declared unconstitutional, or simply not be enforced. That is, the social contract might be understood to incorporate all subsequent legal actions in conformity with it. I leave aside, as beyond my scope, the possibilities of civil disobedience (practiced on the ground that the law was not legitimate under the social contract, even if the authorities say that it is) and political disagreement (including genuine differences of opinion about whether some legal act is consistent with the original social contract).

dilemma in the sense that although both parties would be better off if they cooperated with one another, each party has an irresistible compulsion to defect from social cooperation. The puzzle posed is, then, "Why do rational agents cooperate with social norms and legal commands, as we know they, by and large, do?"[14]

Bruce Chapman's chapter in this volume - "Rationally Transparent Social Interactions" - approaches one of these questions regarding social life from a new perspective. Using standard concepts of game theory, Professor Chapman offers a new explanation of why rational citizens will opt for social cooperation.

In this brief comment I shall first lay out my understanding of Professor Chapman's argument and then offer a critique.

2 Chapman's Argument in Brief

Chapman's central concern is to explain why there should be social cooperation among rational actors. The issue is of a puzzle because, although we know that people *do* cooperate in social settings, one is hard pressed to explain why rational actors should do so. Let me tentatively characterize "social cooperation" as adherence to the customs and mores of one's society - *e.g.*, to the unwritten but vital rules of good conduct, such as being polite; leaving tips for waiters and waitresses in a distant city; picking up and returning a pen that someone nearby has dropped rather than ignoring or stealing the object; and rendering aid to an injured or distressed stranger. The puzzle is that each of these situations looks to be a non-repeated prisoner's dilemma and that for rational decisionmakers defection, rather than cooperation, is the dominant strategy in such a game. Thus, a visitor to a distant city should not leave tips, reasoning that she is unlikely to return to this establishment and therefore does not need the good will or favorable remembrance of the waiter or waitress; or one should walk quickly by a stranger who has collapsed on the street, reasoning that the costs of inconvenience, notoriety, and, possibly, liability from negligently helping far outweigh the reasonably anticipated future benefits, discounted to present value; or one should not overlay one's inquiries to a stranger with politeness - *e.g.*, by saying, "Thank you" - on the calculation that there is no reason to covet the good opinion of that stranger.

Everyone recognizes that rational actors might cooperate in *repeated* prisoner's dilemmas because there is a positive return to establishing a reputation as a trustworthy partner.[15] But in the mill run of one-shot social interactions, rational choice

---

[14] A developing strand of the subsequent literature has incorporated consideration of the legitimacy and ability-to-command-respect to be accorded to informal rules - called "social norms" - that no one seems to design consciously. See, e.g., McAdams (1997). I mean my comments here to cover both social contract and social norms, unless I distinguish them explicitly.
For an important attempt to address these issues, see Young, (1998).

[15] See, e.g., Axelrod (1984).

theory has difficulty in explaining why rational actors would choose social cooperation, rather than individual maximization through flaunting of social customs and mores.

Others have heretofore explored social cooperation in game theoretic terms, reaching different conclusions and enjoying varying success.[16] Ken Binmore, for instance, is skeptical that any cooperative behavior can be explained in a one-shot prisoner's dilemma.[17] At the other end of the explanatory spectrum, David Gauthier famously argued that rational individuals might adhere to moral codes as the result of a strategy of conditional cooperation with the code, the condition being the adherence of others to the same moral code.[18]

Professor Chapman takes up this issue of social cooperation in one-shot prisoner's dilemmas and argues that rational agents may be induced to cooperate rather than to defect by means of "transparency." By "transparency" he seems to mean (I may have misunderstood him) the ability of the actor to give others a rational, coherent, and believable justification for cooperating with him. Other rational actors will be far more inclined to interact cooperatively if those with whom they might cooperate are transparent, in this sense.[19]

A second important aspect of transparency, according to Professor Chapman, is being able to convince other rational players to perceive the game as a cooperative rather than a non-cooperative game. For instance, if a rational actor perceives a game from an "I" frame, then he is likely to focus on finding a strategy that maximizes *his* payoff. He asks, "What is best for me to do?" And that focus will inevitably lead him to recognize the dominance of defection. In contrast, however, if the rational actor perceives the game from a "We" frame, then she may seek for

---

[16] For a superb general introduction that stresses evolutionary game theory, see Skyrms (1996).

[17] Binmore (1994). Incidentally, the theoretical arguments to the contrary notwithstanding, the experimental evidence is overwhelming that people tend to divide the cooperative surplus in an arm's-length ultimatum bargaining game equitably. See Korobkin and Ulen (forthcoming).

[18] Gauthier (1986).

[19] The transparency argument draws heavily on Warneryd (1997). That article is a critique and reformulation of Gauthier's game-theoretic argument for rational cooperation with moral codes. Warneryd, according to Professor Chapman, makes three central criticisms of Gauthier. First, making a player's strategy conditional on another's strategy means that there is a logical incoherence in the account: no one can define his strategy set until someone else has defined his set. There is no defined "first mover," and as a result, there is no way in which social cooperation can begin. Second, individuals are not "fully transparent to each other." At best they are partially transparent, a point to which I return in section 3 B of my comment. Third, the evolutionary argument in favor of cooperation (which Warneryd contends works, if at all, only in the long-run - in the sense that natural selection will favor adherence to moral codes only to the extent that that is a more successful strategy than other evolutionary strategies) does not work because a mutant might appear who mimics the behavior of a trustworthy cooperator but really is not. In short, there is no evolutionarily stable strategy.

strategies that maximize *joint* payoffs among all the games-players. And that focus is far more likely to lead her to consider cooperation as the best strategy.[20]

3 A Critique

My critical remarks will be of two different kinds. First, I shall raise some questions about Professor Chapman's article within the scope of the article itself. That is, I shall raise questions suggested within the four corners of his article, seeking to confine myself to matters that he has raised but not, in my opinion, sufficiently clarified. Second, I shall raise questions from outside the scope of the paper, suggesting an alternative explanation for social cooperation that, although outside the scope of his analysis, might provide a productive means of looking at the problem.

A An Internal Critique

At the heart of Professor Chapman's explanation of rational cooperation in a one-shot prisoner's dilemma is "transparency." I am not convinced that I fully understand that term's significance, but I believe that it centers on the rational actor's ability to make his motives evident to other actors - particularly to signal his willingness to cooperate and his trustworthiness. Although he recognizes and raises the problem that many rational actors would like to "pass" as transparent cooperators, he does not, I believe, lay enough stress on this problem. Let me be clear that I take this to be a particular problem in one-shot prisoner's dilemmas or social interactions that might develop into long-standing relationships. In a one-shot prisoner's dilemma or in the first play of what might become a continuing relationship, a prudent not to say "rational" decisionmaker will surely presume that the other person is *not* fully trustworthy, regardless of (or perhaps in proportion to) that person's protestations of his trustworthiness.[21] That is, transparency even what Warneryd calls "full transparency" does not become evidently valuable unless it is confirmed through repeat transactions or in some other compelling manner. Until such time as believing that transparency seems warranted, rational decisionmaker may not fully cooperate. Alternatively, they may not deal, in so far

---

[20] Professor Chapman borrows the "I/We frame" from Michael Bacharach (1997).

[21] Note that I am suggesting a slight variation on the general theme of Chapman's article. Namely, I am calling attention to the fact that a rational agent may prudently recognize that he may be disappointed if he relies upon another social actor whom he does not know well and may, therefore, take steps - *e.g.*, insurance against the other party's failure to perform - to prevent being disappointed or made sport of at the hands of the other potential cooperator.

as they are able, only with those whom they know well and can, therefore, trust.[22] When legal commands become sufficiently well defined, then in some circumstances one can substitute reliance upon legal enforceability for prudent self-insurance or full or partial transparency.[23]

Chapman seems to be aware of some of these problems. One passage in his chapter considers whether transparency and pre-game communication really have any meaning or are merely "cheap talk." And he well recognizes that there are situations in which it is extremely difficult to give a coherent justification for one's intentions or understanding.[24] And Professor Chapman also has an extended discussion of the problems of unconditional, conditional, and reciprocal cooperators. Nonetheless, I sense that there is something more troubling about this problem of believably signaling one's willingness to cooperate than either Chapman or Warneryd seems to believe. I return to this point from an entirely different angle in the next section.

My sense is that it is vain to hope to find a purely rational strategy for cooperating in a one-shot prisoner's dilemma. I strongly suspect that rational actors, both in theory and practice, do not credit others' trustworthiness until they have strongly credible evidence for that trustworthiness, whether from reputation, consanguinity, dependable legal protection, or a performance bond. And in those circumstances where repetition or performance bonds are not possible, I prefer to find a non-rational basis for collaboration, as I shall indicate.

Finally, let me turn to the matter of variable frames. I recognize the clear significance of the distinction between the "I"/"We" frame. But what I do not find in Professor Chapman's article is an account of the deliberations that a rational actor goes through in deciding which frame to adopt in different situations. I take not much more from his account than that one acts individualistically when one looks at a game from the "I" frame but cooperatively when one looks from the "We" frame. What one wonders is how a rational actor constructs the frame. Is it merely an act of will? If so, then social cooperation results from nothing more than rational actors' resolving to cooperate rather than to defect. But surely there's more to it than that. From a practical standpoint one would like to know what institutional arrangements or social norms could induce the "We" frame and dis-

---

[22] This is the familiar practice of dealing within the extended family or clan that some societies may adopt where there is a primitive system of enforceable legal claims against strangers.

[23] This, of course, is Sir Henry Maine's famous dictum that social and legal progress occurs in the form of the substitution of contract for status.

[24] To illustrate this point, Chapman invokes an example from law. Suppose that a three-judge panel must decide whether the defendant breached a contract and is liable for damages to the plaintiff. Two of the judges believe that the defendant ought not to be held to have breached - one, because she believes that the defendant ought to be excused from performing what is a valid contractual promise; the other, because he believes that although the defendant breached the contract, the agreement was not validly formed. A majority of the judges might reach the same conclusion - in favor of the defendant - but not be able to articulate a common ground for their holding.

courage the "I" frame. The distinction is clearly important, and there is much more to be done on this topic. I suggest a direction of inquiry for resolution of this matter in the next section.

B   An External Critique

I shall make only two brief points about matters that are external to Professor Chapman's critique but that, I believe, should figure prominently in the discussion of social cooperation.

First, Professor Chapman's formulation of the problem of social cooperation pays insufficient attention, for my taste, to the beneficial effects of social norms. The literature on social norms is growing rapidly within the field of law and economics. Although there is no clear consensus on what role social norms have in inducing efficient behavior and in interacting with explicit legal commands, there is, nonetheless, widespread recognition that norms play a tremendously important and generally under-appreciated part in compelling good behavior. I would suggest that the answer to many puzzles of socially cooperative behavior is to be found in people's predisposition to comply with what they take to be the prevailing social norms and not in ever more sophisticated rational strategies.

I recognize that I am invoking the possibility of social norms as a *deus ex machina* to explain why rational agents might cooperate when purely rational calculation suggests they ought not to cooperate. In so doing, I may be said simply to have invoked a tautology rather than to have provided an explanation. And, finally, I know that this method of explaining cooperation is "outside the box" of rationality to which Professor Chapman confined himself. All that may be true, but I strongly suspect that we even those of us who pride ourselves on our ratiocinative powers comply with social norms far more often and far more reliably than we would care to admit. In a sense, we substitute the heuristic of social cooperation for rationalizing about how to act. Perhaps we do that in order to save on our having to calculate afresh in each new situation; perhaps we do so because we have a strong desire to think of ourselves as good people and that good people are cooperative; or perhaps we cooperate because, as social creatures who thrive in group settings, we simply want others to think well of us.[25] For instance, one certain method of being well regarded within one's group is to practice the habit of cooperating with others, to be dependable and without artifice, and to be generous. And the converse is true, too: a certain method for eliciting ill favor is to act selfishly in dealings with members of one's group, to be undependable and artful rather than honest and straightforward.

I concede, again, that these possibilities lie beyond the scope of Professor Chapman's chapter, but I find them such powerful possible explanations for common behavior that lies beyond the assumption of pure rationality that I would

---

[25]   This notion - that people desire the esteem of others - is a very important element in my colleague Richard McAdams' explanations for the power of social norms. See McAdams (1997). See also Pettit (1995, 1996).

argue for their receiving more consideration in any discussion of cooperative behavior, but particularly of cooperative behavior that defies rational justification.

Second and pursuing the matter raised in the previous paragraphs, I find the evolutionary approach to be a powerful and, to my mind, persuasive beginning at looking at some of the deeper issues of social norms and social cooperation.[26] I take it that one of the most significant aspects of the evolutionary account is that in some sense - though not all senses - it relies on unconscious motives, rather than rational or transparent or reflective, deliberative motivation for action. For example, when we lie or are embarrassed, we often give tell-tale clues to others through blushing, nervous tics, and the like. None of us wants to give away these signs, and some of us seek to cultivate an ability to behave brazenly so as to hide our lies and embarrassments. But most of us cannot. These and other unconscious devices not only make it easier for others to assess our worthiness as reciprocal cooperators, they also induce most of us to behave in a socially desirable fashion so as to avoid being embarrassed by unconsciously revealing our perfidy. I am no expert on these matters, but in almost every social interaction that I have - as a parent, teacher, colleague, and sometime public official - I am aware of how powerful these unconscious inducements to cooperation are. To relate these matters to a topic that Professor Chapman relies upon, consider how powerful evolutionary forces working through social norms and conventions may be in inducing rational agents to adopt the "We" frame rather than the "I" frame.

4 Conclusion

Professor Chapman's chapter in this volume wrestles with as important a topic as there is in the social sciences today the bases of social cooperation. His insights into the role that transparency may serve in inducing cooperative behavior among rational actors are sharp and provocative. If, in the end, I am not persuaded that rationality in one-shot prisoner's dilemmas can ever induce cooperation, I nonetheless recognize the force and importance of the arguments he marshals in defense of his position and am grateful that his thorough and serious scholarship induces me to try to clarify a position that I had only dimly perceived that I held.

References

Axelrod, Robert (1991): *The Evolution of Cooperation,* New York: Basic Books.
Binmore, Ken (1994): *Playing Fair,* Cambridge/Mass: MIT Press.
Frank, Robert (1988): *Passions Within Reason,* New York: Norton.
Gauthier, David (1986): *Morals by Agreement,* Oxford: Clarendon Press.

---

[26] See Young (1998), Skyrms (1996) and Frank (1988).

Korobkin, Russell B. and Thomas S. Ulen (1999), Law and Behavioral Science: Removing the Rationality Assumption from Law and Economics, *California Law Review* (forthcoming).

McAdams, Richard H. (1997): The Origin, Development, and Regulation of Norms, *Michigan Law Review*, 96, 338-433.

Pettit, Philip (1996a): The Virtual Reality of Homo Economicus, *The Monist*, 78, 308-329.

Pettit, Philip (1996b): Functional Explanation and Virtual Selection, *British Journal for the Philosophy of Science*, 47, 291-302.

Rawls (1993): *Political Liberalism,* New York: Columbia University Press.

Skyrms, Brian (1996): *Evolution of the Social Contract,* Cambridge: Cambridge University Press.

Warneryd, Karl (1997): "Rationality, Transparency, and Evolutionary Selection," Stockholm Economic Research Institute, *Working Paper Series in Economics and Finance*, No. 167.

Young, H. Peyton (1998): *Individual Strategy and Social Structure,* Princeton: Princeton University Press.

Verstehen, Ideal Types and Situational Analysis for Institutional Economics[1]

John Finch

1 Introduction

This paper is a critical analysis of the potential for application of situational analysis principles to institutional economics. It may seem a little odd to write of the *potential for application*. The three related subjects of *verstehen*, ideal types and situational analysis date to debates between Menger and the German Historical School of the late nineteenth century, prior to Weber's attempts at unifying scientific and historical analyses, and were developed further by Schütz (Craib 1992, Giddens 1976, 1977, Weber 1947). Interest in situational analysis has recently been re-invigorated by Langlois, who, in a series of papers, has developed an argument that situational analysis should be adopted as a methodological basis for institutional economics (Langlois 1986a, 1989; Langlois and Csontos 1993). Situational analysis necessarily involves a commitment by researchers to principles of *verstehen* and to forming ideal types of situation and agent. *Verstehen* and ideal types can be recovered in much economics research, but a commitment to situational analysis involves explicit consideration of these issues in forming theoretical propositions or explanations. The recoverability of principles of *verstehen* and forming ideal types of agent and situation from established economics theorising is emphasised in Langlois and Csontos's (*ibid.*) argument that institutional analysis unite, or at least clarify relations between, institutional economics and neoclassical economics. This paper includes historical analysis prior to discussing contemporary applications.

A critical controversy within situational analysis concerns the nature of rationality assumed of agents in forming theoretical propositions and explanations. The

---

[1] This paper has benefited from discussions with and comments of Stavros Drakopoulos, Robert McMaster, Gerry Steele and participants at the International Symposium on Cognition, Rationality and Institutions, hosted by the Max-Planck-Institute for Research into Economic Systems in Jena. Professor Manfred Streit's editorial advice has further improved this paper. Finally, Professor László Csontos provided both pertinent methodological criticism and generous encouragement in his role as discussant. It is a great sadness for me that we were denied the opportunity to continue our discussions in the weeks and months after meeting in Jena. Errors and omissions in fact and interpretation are the author's responsibility.

aim of situational analysis is to understand or predict actions of typical agents acting in typical situations. This requires that social scientists somehow identify a typical situation and a typical agent. A principle of parsimony is established in that typical situation and agent are both formed with just enough information so as to allow prediction and understanding. Social scientists may work at different levels of abstraction and with different ambitions for generalising predictions and explanations. Hence, controversy regarding rationality assumed of agents: how much detail do we need to know of agent's rationality and cognition, and also of particular situations, in order to formulate theoretical explanations and theory-based conjectures or predictions? Situational analysis is though a unique method for social scientific inquiry in that it recognises that we are concerned with agents who act, that is consciously make decisions in pursuit of objectives based on agents' own theories or mental constructs and motives. These cognitive artefacts of conscious decision-making are unavailable to the casual observer. *Verstehen* establishes that social scientists can consider motives and mental constructs through introspection and possibly through dialogue and ethnomethodological research as well.

The main argument of this paper is based on a division of approaches to implementing situational analysis. One technique of situational analysis is single exit modelling, the aim of which is to provide theory-based conjectures that are, in principle, empirically falsifiable.[2] I argue that single exit modelling is a narrow interpretation of situational analysis that places scientific ambition ahead of interpretative ambition. The consequences of aligning situational analysis with the scientific methodology of single exit modelling are outlined, as are possibilities for broadening objectives to consider the development of institutions. The latter involves a focus on matters of ontology ahead of matters of epistemology.

The paper is organised as follows. To begin with, the main terms situational analysis, ideal types and *verstehen* are investigated. It is not clear that these terms have meanings that have remained constant as social sciences have developed. Following this, implications of adopting situational analysis for the practice of new institutional economics are pursued. *Verstehen* was initially seen as a scientific research method that could combine the essential subjectivism of the social milieu with the predictive ambitions seen in natural sciences. Situational analysis is reviewed in this context. Scientific ambitions are questioned within the context of contemporary understandings of what it is to do science, of the supposed separation of contexts of discovery/investigation and of justification. Continuing the theme of contemporary science, a further area of investigation concerns the nature

---

[2] Langlois (1997) draws attention to Popper's argument that situational analysis, or situational logic in Popper's terms, should be *the* method for social science as it is consistent with methodological principles of individualism, generalisation and falsification. Caldwell (1991, 13-17) provides some support for this interpretation from a review article on Popper and economics: "situational analysis is a powerful and fruitful method for social and other sciences, but that it need not be considered the only viable method" (*ibid.*, 17).

of knowledge to which situational analysis aspires: is it appropriate to predict outcomes which are caused by simple deterministic laws or principles, modelled or deduced by abstraction?

2 Situational Analysis

Situational analysis represents the application of *verstehen* principles (see below) to causal modelling abstracted from typical social situations in which an agent makes or is coerced into making a choice, that is in which an agent acts. Recent papers by Langlois (1986a, 1989) and Langlois and Csontos (1993) have provided fresh impetus to the search for a grounding in social scientific method for institutional economics. Situational analysis, also known as situational determinism and commonly associated with the technique of single exit modelling (Latsis, 1976), combines the subjectivity of rational motivated human action with the requirement that theories be capable of prediction or explanation in principle realistic enough to be tested in the course of empirical application. Langlois' contribution to the discourse is an important one: he has clarified the nature of rationality assumed of agents whose decision-situations are the subject of situational analysis, and the outcome of which institutional economists seek to predict. This has further drawn attention to the relationship between behavioural and neoclassical approaches to economic theorising, a relationship in which new institutional economics either exists between or unites.

Two aspects of situational analysis are set out in this section, by way of explaining what it is. First, it is argued that situational modelling aims to establish or verify causal scientific laws. Second, philosophical variety is added by the different roles that can be established for agents and for institutions. A discourse on institutions is necessarily a discourse on human action and interaction.

Situational analysis easily translates into single exit modelling because the researcher abstracts from typical observed social situations in which agents make decisions regarding action (see ideal types, below) and recreates a model in which a typical agent is coerced into making a particular decision (Latsis 1976, Langlois and Csontos 1993). Coercion, in the abstract, is a co-determination of an agent's preferences and knowledge, and also of the institutional environment of rules, custom and other social institutions. Note that this single exit modelling approach to theorising can, at its most abstract, explain the methodological individualism (or social atomism) common in neoclassical economics. By concentrating on an individual with constant and well-defined preferences and assumed perfect information, solutions can be determined with reference only to budget constraints. But this is not the aim of institutional economics. Institutional theorists often seek degrees of realism.[3] Institutions are introduced into theoretical modelling and, according to Langlois, have the following role:

> [I]nstitutions ... are ... interpersonal stores of coordinated knowledge; as such, they serve to restrict at once the dimensions of the agent's problem-situation and the extent of the cognitive demands placed upon the agent (Langlois 1986a, 237).

The above description of institutions as having a restrictive role is unnecessarily one-sided; perhaps the definition is influenced by concerns to protect ambiguously defined concepts of agents' free-will. Other writers (Giddens 1984, Hayek 1982, Hodgson 1988, Loasby 1976, 1991) have emphasised the essential co-ordinating, rather than just restricting, aspect of social institutions, especially where agents' dependence on tacit knowledge forms a significant basis for theoretical explanation (Nelson and Winter 1982, Polanyi 1967).

Different philosophical positions can be entertained within situational analysis, depending on a theorist's choice of theory of rationality for the agent. Langlois and Csontos (1993) raise some interesting issues around this matter, to do with how economists may go about introducing theories of psychology or cognition into causal and deterministic explanations. The main argument of Langlois and Csontos's paper is that where Latsis (1976) proposes situational analysis as a means of furthering and formalising behaviouralist theory, situational analysis can be better served by replacing an emphasis on realistic accounts of agent's decision-making processes with more detailed accounts of institutions, especially constraining aspects of institutions. There are many issues involved in Langlois and Csontos's argument. The behaviouralist perspective is criticised for being unnecessarily detailed and unnecessarily realistic in attempting to include details of rule-following behaviour of individuals, given scientific ambitions of generalisation. It is not clear whether the objection is strictly to do with method, *as in do we need accurate descriptions if our aim is prediction and verification?* It is also philosophical. The view of agents as rule-followers compromises cherished notions of free-willed action that are found in Weber and also Mises (Langlois 1986a, 1986b). Langlois and Csontos perform a neat operation in arguing that rules are located in environmental institutions, and are thus separated from the agent's decision-making which can now remain free-willed.

---

[3] Langlois and Csontos (1993, 114-118) provide a thorough account of the role of realisticness in theory, contrasting the necessity of theory to be abstract and hence generalisable with a desire that theories should be realistic, especially in its behavioural postulates. They argue that: "[T]he requirement of *Verstehen* ... speaks to what is still only an ancillary explanatory function of well-chosen behavioural postulates. The function is ancillary in that it is subservient to the role of the behavioural postulates in the larger explanation of economic phenomena. All other things equal, we want assumptions that are 'more realistic' in the sense of understandability, i.e. in the sense of meeting the Weberian requirement of *Verstehen*. But all other things are not always equal. In general, there is a trade-off between the realisticness of the behavioural postulates in a theory ... and the general applicability of that theory to a wide range of economic phenomena." Langlois and Csontos (1993, 116).

Langlois and Csontos's neat operation reunites the two themes of this section, institutions as constraints and theories of agency. Langlois (1986a) and Langlois and Csontos (*op cit.*) further this reunion by describing situation constraints which pre-exist the agent's entry into the situation, and system constraints which evolve in the course of that agent's involvement in the situation. Both types would seem necessarily to be reproduced or transformed over time, but, if adopting single exit modelling, our focus remains on the situation due to an interest in predicting the outcomes agents' actions. Further discussion of situational modelling depends upon detailed investigation of ideal types, as these are typical both for researchers who theorise in terms of situational analysis, and also regarding theories of how agents can conceptualise decision-situations.

3 Ideal Types

Ideal types are a necessary component of situational analysis and modelling. Ideal types refer to both researcher's and agent's cognitive processes of categorising phenomena as similar or different. Langlois and Csontos's (*op cit.*) rejoinder to Latsis's behaviouralism is that many situations do not require a detailed, thickly-rational, description of the agent, and that more or less detailed descriptions of situation and system constraints (the institutional environment) may be required to support uniquely predicted decision outcomes or exits. Ideal types require more or less detail depending on the level of generalisation expected of the sought-after causal law of determination. In part, the nature of idealisation supports the nature of empirical generalisation that can be expected from undertaking situational analysis. Ideal types are familiar in economics discourse, dating from Marshall's (1961) ideal-type - and hence theoretical representative - firm which has been related as an abstraction of Marshall's detailed empirical research into industrial organisation (Groenewegen 1995, Loasby 1989, 1991, Marshall 1919, O'Brien 1990)[4]. Ideal types are the subject of more detailed discussion later in the paper, when the application of situational analysis is considered. For now, the historical development of the concept is explained.

The emphasis which is placed upon ideal types by Langlois is consistent with Weber's scientific ambitions for discovering and verifying laws that determine social phenomena. Langlois (1989) draws attention to the phenomenological sociology of Schütz, in which forming ideal types is established as both a method for social science theorists, and as a psychological or phenomenological theory of how agents can be expected to categorise knowledge of everyday environments (Schütz 1964, 1971, Schütz and Luckmann 1974). To quote Langlois:

---

[4] Marshall employed his concept of the representative firm as a step from empirical analyses of firms exhibiting different growth rates with different managerial abilities to theoretical modelling of a static firm in competitive equilibrium (Lazonick 1991, 150-155).

For Schütz as for Weber, the method of situational analysis was animated by the construction of an ideal type; a simplified theoretical artefact that would help explain a more complex reality (Langlois 1989, 280).

Schütz's work addresses both matters of epistemology, as in how social scientists can be expected to form second-order ideal types, and ontology or phenomenology, as in how agents themselves go about categorising and deciding on necessary detail in forming the first-order ideal types which are subsequently interpreted by social scientists. Citing Schütz raises questions concerning the suitability of the scientific model upon which Weber undertook the type of intellectual endeavour, and which Langlois recommends be undertaken in the furtherance of institutional economic theorising. Different approaches to situational analysis can be distinguished by different commitments made by theorists to interpretive principles of *verstehen*. *Verstehen* is the third related aspect of this paper, different interpretations of which are investigated in the following section,[5] and drawn upon in establishing an agenda for discussion of the prospects for undertaking situational analysis as a method for institutional economics research.

4 Verstehen

Verstehen underlies much of Langlois' discussion of situational analysis and institutional economics and he promotes a Weberian interpretation of *verstehen* as a research method. Versions of *verstehen* contribute either to an interpretation of situational analysis as single exit modelling, or to a broader interpretation of situational analysis that is pursued in this paper. If social science is to explain observed social phenomena with reference to human action, explanations must refer to human intentions, motivations, and theories of the world. These are of course unobservable. The alternative is to explain observed outcomes or social phenomena in positivist or instrumentalist terms and necessarily without reference to subjectivity and human action. This implies either that subjectivity is unimportant, or that human *action* can be reduced to observable and environmentally determined *behaviour*.[6] Weberian *verstehen* is incorporated into the single exit modelling method of situational analysis:

> [The] method of situational analysis [is] ... an attempt to grapple with the problem posed for theory by free will. Since humans have free will, their conduct is inde-

---

[5] Interpretations include that made in Langlois (1989).

[6] Behaviour here is described from the perspective of a social scientist observer, and it is argued that there are no grounds for distinguishing action from behaviour from this perspective. From an agent's perspective, a criterion for distinguishing between action and behaviour can be identified by the presence of conscious reflection and planning in the case of action, and in subconscious rule-following, that is, following previously learned rules and procedures in the case of behaviour. Of course, action may involve the agent in choosing among feasible routines in a given situation, or choosing to modify elements of routine practice.

terminate; but theory demands determinateness: assumptions must lead to conclusions. Situational analysis compromises by creating this kind of 'conditional' determinateness. We create a situation for the human subject in which there is only one plausible or reasonable - or 'rational' - course of action. We create ... a single-exit model. This technique is very much an interpretive enterprise. ... [W]e must place ourselves in the shoes of the agent. And this involves the technique of understanding or *verstehen* (Langlois 1989, 280).

Langlois adopts the phrase *situational analysis* to describe this approach to interpretive social sciences. Latsis (1976) describes a similar approach as *situational determination*, which Langlois and Csontos (1993) avoid as it distracts from the subjectivity of agency. *Situational logic* is also used. All these versions can adopt *single-exit modelling*.

The paper has so far concentrated on *verstehen* as developed into a social scientific technique of theory formulation. Development and critique of situational analysis depends on considering other interpretations of *verstehen*, and of other methods of conducting social scientific enquiry. Schütz occupies a pivotal role in developing notions of *verstehen* and interpretative social science. The development spans exclusive concerns with mimicking natural scientific epistemology circa late nineteenth century, to considering ontological issues of how social science should respond to its subject matter being essentially different from that of natural science. This was hinted at in the previous section, and is elaborated below.

Schütz describes three roles for *verstehen*: "1) as the experiential form of common-sense knowledge of human affairs, 2) as an epistemological problem, and 3) as a method peculiar to the social sciences" (Schütz 1971, 57). In its first role, *verstehen* encompasses first-order typifications of agents in interpreting others' actions; in attributing motives and intent to what would otherwise be merely observed behaviour. Schütz (*ibid.*, 56) argues that this is not synonymous with introspection because such rules and conventions of interpretation are established in the public domain as social institutions. The development of these rules and conventions can be explained in a manner consistent with Menger's categories of organic and also pragmatic institutions, with explanations of the former comprising invisible-hand explanations. Hence, following Schütz, *verstehen*, the private perceptions and ways of interpreting others' actions, can be influenced to some extent by norms and rules helping to co-ordinate actions. Agents entertain theories of others' actions and understanding of rules and customs, and these theories combine knowledge of the what would I do in this situation type with knowledge gained from a shared culture. Knowledge is also gained from imitation of innovative practices. This is reflected in Loasby's discussion of Kelly's theory of personal constructs, and in Harré and Gillett's exposition of the *discursive turn*[7] in psychology (Harré and Gillett 1994, Kelly 1963, Lane *et al.* 1996, Loasby 1991).[8]

---

[7] *Discursive turn* refers to the rise in constructivist theories in social science, and is reflected in ethnomethodological research techniques. Introspection is no longer seen as the only way to assess agents' motivations and mental constructs as these are seen

Langlois and Csontos are wrestling with *verstehen* as an epistemological problem in their exposition of situational analysis employing single exit modelling. Langlois and Csontos construct their second-order typifications on the first-order typifications of actors involved in every-day activity and common-sense interpretation through introspection. Langlois and Csontos pursue *verstehen* as an epistemological problem, and so are interested in establishing testable conjectures formulated in single exit modelling simulations. Attendant objectives of realisticness and empirical verification of behavioural assumptions may be achieved incidentally. This is one version of *verstehen*; based on introspection. A more general point of *verstehen* is that social scientists must somehow approach the subjectivity (and intersubjectivity) of agency by attaching motive and intent to human action. Otherwise social scientists can only understand what they observe; that is action which, with no access to agents' motives, can be categorised as behaviour. Langlois and Csontos argue that *verstehen* is an important secondary aim of their situational analysis, the primary aim of which is to provide causal and determinate laws and predictions (*op cit.*, 116). This epistemological claim follows from interpreting *verstehen* in Weber's pre-Schützian terms depending on introspective insights of social scientists. Once considerations are broadened in recognition of epistemology and methods of social sciences, Langlois and Csontos's situational analysis is *verstehen* in its epistemological guise, as pointed out by Schütz, rather than an ancillary objective of single exit modelling.

The third of Schütz's roles for *verstehen*, as a method for social sciences, is a combination with either the first role of ontology or the second role of epistemology, and both are promoted as methods uniquely for social science research. An example of *verstehen* as method for social sciences is single-exit modelling. Note though that single exit modelling relies on *verstehen* as introspection, at least in designing refutable conjectures.

5 Situational Analysis, Subjectivity of Action and Intersubjectivity of Institutions

Discussion of the likely fruitfulness of situational analysis, as formulated in Sections II, III and IV above, as a research method for institutional economics begins with further consideration of the suggested analysis of agency, formulated

---

as being socially formed with reference to inter-subjective standards that are publicly available.

[8] The references cited in support of the phenomenological approach to verstehen are capable of both interpretavist and realist interpretation, the latter is discussed in Section VII. The realist approach explains social institutions and customs as analogous to structures and forces in physical sciences, as existing independently of social scientists' inquiries. An interpretative approach explains rules, customs and institutions as shared practices which, nevertheless, exist as agents' theories and mental constructs.

through introspection or *verstehen*. *Verstehen* is the means to the end of deducing theories expressed as causal laws and not an end in itself. It also ensures the free-will of the ideal-type agent, whose particular ideal situation is being modelled because agency is not reduced to stimulus and response behaviourism. The relationship between the ideal-type agent and ideal-type situation requires further investigation because it is not clear what is meant by free-will, and it is not clear why the relationship should be causal and deterministic, apart from the social scientist's desire to produce a refutable conjecture. *Verstehen* can be seen as a means to achieving the ends of scientific laws, sought by neoclassical economics theorists since the 1930s (Mirowski 1989) and sought for social science by Weber at the end of the last century. Giddens explains:

> The process of interpreting the meaning of social action, as employed by social observers, should be undertaken with the aim of meeting the same standards of precision and verifiability as are sought in natural science. The empathic 'reliving' of an experience is important for understanding, particularly of conduct ..., but it is rational action which can be understood and described with the greatest degree of certainty in the correctness of interpretation. ... [T]hat no one can capture the experience of another fully is not important ....(Giddens 1977, 180).

The introspective technique of *verstehen* is only possible through the shared social background of researcher and actor (Hayek 1952, 23), but little guidance is given as to how the introspective technique of *verstehen* is to be executed such that data can be arrived at with similar precision and verifiability as that analysed in the natural sciences (Abel 1953). Indeed, Hayek is highly critical of such attempts to mimic natural science, terming this *scientism* (Hayek 1952, Steele 1993) regardless of attempts to imbue observed behaviour with motivation and intent through introspective *verstehen*.[9] Situational analysis as single exit modelling aims to be both objective and positivist rather than objective and subjectivist (Bernstein 1983, Hayek 1952, Sayer 1992). That is, once introspection is undertaken, situational analysis as single exit modelling continues following a natural science canon of conjecture and refutation.

Verstehen beyond the technique of situational analysis provides detail about the forming of subjective data, which is the object of social science research. Ironically, this is drawn from Schütz's phenomenology:[10]

> 'Hermeneutic phenomenology' ... breaks with the subjectivism characteristic of the earlier phase of development of phenomenology. (Schütz never managed to complete the break.) From this perspective ... language is essentially a social or public phenomenon grounded in forms of life: the self-understanding of the individual can only occur in terms of 'publicly available' concepts (Craib 1992, 102-109).

Furthermore:

> This is very different from the philosophical schema within which Weber worked, and cuts across the assumptions of methodological individualism, since the locus of the creation of meaning is taken to be the standards or rules of the collectivity rather

---

[9] Without access to an actor's motives and intentions, all that can be observed is motiveless behaviour, behaviour as in stimulus-response behaviourism.

[10] See also Prendergrast (1986).

than the subjective consciousness of the individual actor, the latter ... presupposing the former (Giddens 1977, 175).

Giddens's argument exhibits similarities with that of Langlois and Csontos's (1993) in that individual action presupposes existing standards and rules of conduct that are available to agents. However, where Langlois and Csontos argue that rules of conduct, such as satisficing suggested by Simon (1976), should be understood as system constraints within an environment of rules and institutional practices, Giddens is arguing that rules are socially constructed. Social scientists - as well as other agents involved in reproducing and transforming a situation - do not rely merely on introspection. They have access to agents and can participate and discuss, negotiate and create meanings which describe actions, intentions and motives. Action cannot easily be separated from external system constraints - institutions which exist prior to action and persist during and beyond an episode of action - and situation constrains - practices which emerge during the episode of action - which form the institutional environment.

Further problems in applying situational analysis in furtherance of institutional economics arise from classifying whether social scientists can attribute the term *act* to all observed behaviour (Harré 1979). This is a complicated issue. It is from this conundrum that Langlois tries to escape with his version of situational analysis in the first instance. Laws require determination, or at least causal explanation, but human action must be free-willed. If action is caused by something, then how can the act be said to be free? Russell (1953) addresses part of this issue, that of free-will. He argues that fear of causal laws in constraining free-will are misplaced and relate more to illegitimate coercion, of getting people to behave in a way that they would not do in the absence of duress.

> [E]ven if we admit the most extreme claims of determinism and of correlation of mind and brain, still the consequences inimical to what is worth preserving in free will do not follow. The belief that they follow results ... from the assimilation of causes and volitions, and from the notion that causes *compel* their effects in some sense analogous to that in which a human authority can compel a man to do what he would rather not (Russell 1953, 405).

Free-will becomes an imprecise concept, and one can question whether it is worth going through analytical contrivances of locating cognitive enterprises within institutional constraints in order that it should be meaningfully preserved as part of institutional economics discourse.

Preserving free-will as attributed to agency is more important for legalistic and justice-centred analysis rather than in the case of scientific causal explanation. It is a fundamental precept of Hayek that individuals are held to be responsible for their actions, if not necessarily the outcomes of these actions. Outcomes are frequently interpreted as unintended consequences of the pursuit of plans and strategies (Steele 1993). Agents can play a role in causing events, and can give accounts of their actions which have been caused by preceding events. Agents can also be held responsible for causing outcomes by failing to act, if failing to act is seen as negligent and unreasonable compared with the predicted actions of a typical agent in a similar situation.[11] Failing to act is synonymous with continuing to behave in a manner lacking self awareness and self reflection. Standards of negligence and unreasonableness are established in common law (action is not only subjective and is not understood only in terms of an actor's intents, it is also intersubjective and assessed by others in terms of established codes of behaviour). Hayek captures this in distinguishing between conscious and non-conscious mental processes, and also in admitting many intermediate forms of mental events between the fully conscious and the non-conscious (Hayek 1952, 133-34).

Pitkin (1972) further distinguishes scientific causal explanations and legalistic and judicial notions of cause and human action. If all behaviour is to be understood as action, an individual should be able to provide explanations in terms of motives and intentions which are consistent with observed behaviour. Pitkin questions this established argument by pointing out that actions vary in the degree to which the actor invests them with intention and motivation: "With actions as with crimes in our legal system: some are contingent on the relevant intention, while others hinge on the objective consequences" (*ibid.*, 255). Pitkin argues that in categorising observed behaviour as action, identification is both descriptive and performative, or *quasi-performative*, that is descriptive and imputative (*ibid.*, 262). To act is to be responsible for making something happen. Acting is also descriptive of being a causal factor in making an event happen: "[t]he issue is not evaluation but responsibility" (*ibid.*, 263). Where Langlois assumes for the purposes of modelling that all behaviour can be interpreted as constrained action, Pitkin seems to be arguing that the social scientist's interpretation should be made in the light of the consequences of describing something as action or behaviour. It depends on the questions being investigated. Behaviour reproduces established norms, be these situation or system constraints. Action may involve conscious critical evaluation of established norms, of experimentation, of putting theories or mental constructs at risk. Action can result from old modes of behaviour being recognised as no longer adequate or reliable.

This section has undertaken to highlight the complex relationships between subjective action, intersubjective institutions and the possibility of causal explanations of such action. The objective of securing an agent's free-will is important in situational analysis. *Free-will* focuses our attention on the rationality assumptions assumed of action, and also avoids our ideal type agent being coerced into following rules which prevent the agent from otherwise doing something more preferred in the absence of such coercion. It was concluded that causal explanations are legitimate, that free-will is an ambiguous term and is likely to be something of a distraction. Further, scientific causal explanations may differ from legalistic or judicial explanations of cause (*the facts of our grammar*, Pitkin 1972, 267). These issues are explored further in the following section, in which the re-

---

[11] Langlois (1997) discusses the relative nature of rationality assumptions in terms of being adequate and appropriate given the nature of the situation. Imputative judgements can refer to situational analytical mental models in establishing the reasonableness of an act, or of a failure to act.

lationship between the agent and the institutional environment is assessed in terms of controversies concerning separability of contexts of discovery in theory formation and evaluation.

6 Contexts of Discovery and Verification

Two arguments are explored in this section by way of identifying consequences of the single exit modelling application of situational analysis. First, situational analysis as single exit modelling is interpreted as a short run model or method of prediction-generation consistent with the neoclassical convention. Second, and following on, links between a short run interpretation and a distinction made by Langlois (1986a) between a theory of knowledge and a theory of psychology are investigated. The distinction is itself a continuation of the arguably undue concern with preserving agents' free-will in undertaking single exit modelling (as discussed in the previous section). Both arguments can be related to an overall concern with the possibility of separating contexts of discovery and of verification in describing a theory-based proposition and then undertaking empirical analysis of the proposition. The imposition by the researcher of short run conditions and also the subsuming of psychology (and also cognition) into publicly available and hence institutional theories of knowledge may be of little significance if we are concerned with empirical analysis of testable conjectures.

It is argued here that single exit modelling is suited to short run theorising because of an emphasis on agents' constrained decision-making, and a subsequent relative neglect of interaction between intersubjectively established institutions and an agent's perceptions of culturally established norms and practices. Situation constraints exist prior to any action in any situation in which an agent is acting. From this, it could be interpreted that situation constraints are general to that society, at least common across different types of situation. These are taken as fixed so cannot be altered by interactions within the situation. System constraints evolve over time within a particular type of situation, so are specific institutional sets of customs, rules and practices which an agent would need to understand prior to undertaking any action within that situation.[12] An agent only acts once in single exit modelling and we aim to understand or predict the outcome of this act rather than understand, explain or predict the effect of action on existing system constraints, that is, on actions of others involved in the situation. All this is a con-

---

[12] Following Hayek, agents are assumed to posses theories or mental constructs, and draw on these with differing degrees of consciousness. System constraints can be expected to be mundane and constant across time, so do not require considerable conscious thought, taking them into account can become a matter of habit. Situation constraints can change within a particular situation through interaction among agents, and because these develop require an agent to posses and update a mental model or construct in order that plans for action can be formulated, exercised and evaluated in review.

sequence of a single exit modelling interpretation of situational analysis. It can be concluded is that an agent's actions serve to reproduce rather than transform the status quo. A long run approach to situational analysis would instead focus on explaining how reproductions or transformations of the set of routines, practices, cultural norms and institutions is or can be achieved.

Another interpretation of situational analysis is that it addresses action in situations characterised by equilibrium, that is equilibrium in terms of all agents being fully aware of the implications of their actions and the actions of all others so that actions mutually reinforce expectations (Loasby 1991, Hahn 1973).

That situational analysis in its single exit modelling guise lends itself to short run analysis, with short run theoretical propositions, is consistent with subsuming theories of psychology into necessarily intersubjective theories of knowledge. Decision-making is guided by previously established general and specific norms and patterns of behaviour, subject to the agent's objectives. Single exit models have institutions, and also rationality assumed of the agent, but cognition and psychology are seen as: (i) unnecessary detail given the objective generating theory-based propositions imbued, introspectively, with intentions; and (ii) a potential threat to the agent's free-will, complicating prediction and, from its proponents' perspectives, introducing unwarranted coercion - through rule-following behaviour - into the model.

Langlois' and Csontos' (1993) placing of an individual's routines of thought involved in cognition into the complex of system and situational constraints in single exit modelling may provide an example of what Tooby and Cosmides (1992) criticise as the *standard social scientific model*. The critique is made from the perspective of what Tooby and Cosmides call *evolutionary psychology*. Their discussion concerns the possibility of culture and the status of individuals in interpreting, reproducing and transforming that culture. The standard social scientific model is portrayed as seeing culture as solely an environmental phenomenon that individuals somehow learn, but learn by accumulating ways of doing things through the environment.[13] Hence, the social environment comprising culture - or sets of intersubjectively established institutionalised practices - determines individual action and the mental processes of cognition are passive. Tooby and Cosmides could classify the technique of situational analysis within their standard social scientific model. Langlois and Csontos argue, in a development of Latsis's (1976) situational determinism, that thicker representations of an agent's rationality could be replaced by a more detailed institutionalised or environmental theory of knowledge. Tooby and Cosmides argue that both these approaches deflect our attention from cognitive processes, with the Langlois and Csontos approach doing this to a greater extent.

---

[13] Tooby and Cosmides argue that describing an individual's accumulation of knowledge and know-how is too loosely and too inaccurately described as learning. *Learning* is a short-hand term which obscures complex cognitive processes involved in forming, evaluating and reviewing mental constructs.

Does the imposition of short term analysis, and the subsuming of theories of psychology and cognition into a theory of knowledge, really matter? This question draws attention to the main issue of this section: can contexts of discovery and verification be separated? An underlying argument of Tooby and Cosmides's article is that social sciences should become more integrated and mutually consistent with one another. This is not to argue that microeconomics or institutional economics should reduce to psychology, or for that matter, that psychology and cognition should reduce to neurology. Rather, different subjects within social science should be mutually consistent, such that implied psychological or cognitive concepts which can be recovered from economic theory should have some basis in psychology. Mutual consistency is already apparent in areas of economics research. Behavioral theory, such as Nelson and Winter's (1982) Schumpeterian theory of economic change, refers to Simon's bounded rationality. Loasby's (1986, 1991, 1993, 1994) work on the attainment of equilibrium through coordination of agents' actions refers to Kelly's (1963) theory of personality, which develops notions of individuals' personal constructs or interpretive frameworks. Steele (1993) argues that Hayek's economics can be better understood if read in conjunction with his psychological work, and in this Hayek seems to be arguing along similar lines to Tooby and Cosmides:

> [A]ll experience in the widest sense ..., causes, and all memory is based on, the creation of connections between physiological events represented by stimuli. [Rather than] ... the 'storage' theory of memory, ... with every experience some new mental entity representing sensations or images enters the mind or the brain and is there retained until it is returned at the appropriate moment (Hayek 1952, 105).

If the technique of situational analysis were developed into a long run theory, it may provide a framework for explaining the transformation of situation-specific institutions, and the relationship between individuals' cognition, rationality and the intersubjectivity of evolving institutional arrangements.[14] More precisely, situational analysis can be developed within a real-time framework, distinguished in a lucid manner from operational-time concepts of short and long run by Langlois (1992). Langlois argues that this allows for learning, although in the light of Tooby and Cosmides's argument, learning - like free-will - is too inaccurate a phrase to capture the cognitive processes involved in such adaptations of mental constructs and processes.

By imposing the short run conditions of unchanging situation and system constraints, and subsuming psychology and cognition to environmental and institutional theories of knowledge, proponents of the technique of situational analysis as

---

[14] Marshall's explanation of the long run has arguably been too strictly interpreted in some versions of economic theory, so as to preclude the possibility of learning and acquiring greater competence and dexterity in performing with a given vintage of technology. Marshall's short and long run analytical devices are though examples of economists conducting something like single exit modelling by closing off exits from typical situations. In the absence of real world system closure, economists can assume that one factor of production is variable in the short run, and that all factors are variable in the long run, given the constraint of unchanging technology.

single exit modelling are achieving predictions of action/situation outcomes at the expense of explaining how institutions are transformed over real time. The technique of situational analysis distracts attention away from empathic *verstehen*, and from the processes involved in forming and transforming first order typifications of agents, and second order typifications made by researchers, as explained by Schütz.

7 Method, Causality and Determination

This section makes tentative suggestions of what situational analysis could be like, free of single exit modelling. So far it has been argued that situational analysis, as undertaken within new institutional economics, has been advanced towards objectives of providing testable conjectures in an institutional setting by promoting institutions and rationality at the expense of cognition. It has been argued that single exit modelling focuses on short term explanations or predictions by adopting assumptions of typical individuals' conduct grounded upon *thin* rationality. It has also been argued that causal explanations of individuals' actions are quite consistent with seeking explanations at the cognitive level of individuals' pursuing objectives in action through rule-following behaviour. Rule following does not compromise free-will, or, more accurately, that individuals should pursue plans in the absence of unjust coercion. Having established the legitimacy of both rule-following as a necessary component of cognition, and of the possibility of causal explanation, the nature of causal explanation is discussed. First, it is argued that causal explanation is not synonymous with deterministic explanation. Second, it is argued that the new institutional model, together with the Schützian principles of first order and second order typifications, can be combined with techniques of *retrodictive explanation* as pursued as a component of critical realist social science research method (Bhaskar 1978, Sayer 1992).

The first argument is drawn from Mirowski (1989) who argues that economists' attempts to adopt the methods of physical sciences in testing theoretical conjectures are being undertaken according to an outmoded model of science. Similar points are made in Drakopoulos (1994) and Drakopoulos and Torrance (1994). The single exit modelling approach to situational analysis for new institutional economics arguably conflates causation and determination. Hence, generalisations of causal - although not deterministic - processes are provisionally accepted in terms of probabilistic relations, as set out, for instance, in quantum mechanics. Situational analysis, through single exit modelling, seeks theories that are both causal and deterministic. It does this by subsuming cognition and psychology into a theory of knowledge and intersubjectively available institutionalised rules, customs and practices, and by seeking predictions by isolating a typical agent's action from a typical situation comprising situation and system constraints. While it is debatable whether social science explanation should so slavishly adhere to the best practices which have evolved in physical sciences, situational analysis is based on a model of scientific method and it has yet to be established that this method is anything other than one of many appropriate scientific methods.

The second argument of this section is connected to the first. The critical realist argument (Bhaskar 1978, 1979) posits the possibility of naturalism - the combination of natural and social scientific epistemology - on the basis of an ontologically-grounded explanation of scientific endeavour. The basic realist argument is that physical science research is fundamentally interventionist in what are otherwise naturally open systems. Intervention requires system closure and manipulation of the object of scientific inquiry such that conjectured causal relationships can also be tested. Manipulation blurs the distinction between contexts of discovery and explanation. Manipulation is required because scientific rules are explained in terms of the tendencies of objects to interact in certain ways, and are not explained in terms of empirical observations of conjectured causes and effects. Tendencies may not be realised and observed (the co-presence of cause and effect), but just because cause and effect are not necessarily available for empirical observation, does not invalidate rules in terms of tendencies of the objects of enquiry.

Transferring realist explanation of physical science into social scientific explanation is again open to question, but the consequences can be explored for the situational analysis approach. In the absence of the possibility of imposing system closure in social scientific explanation, realist explanation in social science is sought in terms of *retrodiction* (Bhaskar 1978, Sayer, 1992). Retrodiction pursues explanation in terms of asking what must be the state of the world (institutional and also cognitive) such that an observed event can be possible. This is comparable with the intellectual endeavour required in undertaking single exit modelling, given that the agent is assumed to be rational and that analysis takes place by fixing situation and system constraints of the typical situation. A realist argument would seek explanations of chains or interactions of events and of tendencies. Social scientists manipulate situation and system constraints by deploying *ceteris paribus* clauses. Single exit modelling involves imagining hypothetical conditions of closure.

However, even if it is accepted that single exit modelling can be construed as a social science analogue of Bhaskar's critical realist explanation of what it is to conduct natural science experiments, ontological issues cannot be ignored. To interpret situational analysis narrowly as single exit modelling depending on introspective *verstehen* is too narrow an interpretation of interpretive social scientific inquiry. Other research questions could include how ideal types are formed, including a theory of knowledge, and studying evolution of customs, norms and conventions through actions of agents.

8 Concluding Remarks

This paper has sought to investigate the suitability of situational analysis as a method for conducting research within institutional economics. The main model of situational analysis is taken from Langlois and Csontos (1993), which itself follows articles by Langlois (1986, 1989). These argue that situational analysis should be the method for new institutional economics, and indeed is consistent at the limit with neoclassical economics explanation. Theoretical conjecture or explanation is sought in situational analysis through the technique of single exit modelling, in which the researcher closes off decision-exits from an action-situation through manipulating the institutions, the system and situation constraints of the situation, in a theoretically consistent manner.

Two criticisms are made of situational modelling, as explained by Langlois and Csontos. First, that concerns with preserving the free-will of the agent should not dominate. Second, that these concerns lead researchers to locate what would be subjective and cognitive mental processes instead in the social/cultural environment of the situation being analysed. This has the effect of negating many of the insights of Schütz, in terms of how (phenomenologically) agents form typifications of other agents and of the rules and customs of different situations, and how (epistemologically) researchers in turn form second order typifications of situations and agents in forming testable conjectures. *Verstehen* is thus relegated in importance in the Langlois and Csontos approach such that situation outcomes are codetermined by assumptions about the agent's rationality, and the nature of the cultural/institutional environment. Situation analysis is easily suited to, so can become dominated by, the pursuit of explanations in the short run. We cannot easily adopt the technique to explain the transformation of institutional customs and conventions, and cannot easily provide explanations of the functional significance and role of these customs and conventions. A possible development of situational analysis is to pursue analysis by following the critical realist approach of retrodiction.

References

Abel, T. (1953): The operation called *verstehen;* in: H. Feigl. and M. Brodbeck (eds.), *Readings in the Philosophy of Science*, New York : Appleton-Century-Crofts Inc., 677-87.

Bernstein, R. (1983): *Beyond Objectivism and Relativism*; Science, Hermeneutics and Praxis, Oxford: Blackwell.

Bhaskar, R. (1978): *A Realist Theory of Science;(*2nd ed.*)*, Brighton: Harvester Press.

Bhaskar, R. (1979): *The Possibility of Naturalism. A Philosophical Critique of the Contemporary Human Sciences*; Brighton : Harvester Press.

Caldwell, B. (1991): Clarifying Popper; in: *Journal of Economic Literature*, 29, 1-33.
Craib, I. (1992): *Modern Social Theory. From Parsons to Habermas;* (2nd ed.), London: Harvester Wheatsheaf.
Drakopoulos, S.A. (1994): Economic method and the scientific philosophy of contemporary physics; in: *Journal of Interdisciplinary Economics*, 5, 37-53.
Drakopoulos, S.A. and Torrance, T.S. (1994): Causality and determinism in economics; in *Scottish Journal of Political Economy*, 41, 176-193.
Giddens, A. (1976): *New Rules of Sociological Method. A Positive Critique of Interpretative Sociologies*; London: Hutchinson.
Giddens, A. (1977): *Studies in Social and Political Theory;* London: Hutchinson.
Giddens, A. (1984): *The Constitution of Society. Outline of the Theory of Structuration;* Cambridge: Polity Press.
Groenewegen, P. (1995): *A Soaring Eagle. Alfred Marshall 1842-1924; in:* Edward Elgar, Cheltenham.
Hahn, F. (1973): *On the Notion of Equilibrium in Economics;* Cambridge: Cambridge University Press.
Harré, R. (1979): *Social Being. A Theory of Social Psychology*; Oxford: Blackwell.
Harré, R. and Gillett, G. (1994): *The Discursive Mind*; London: Sage Publications.
Hayek, F.A. (1952): *The Sensory Order. An Inquiry into the Foundations of Theoretical Psychology*; London: Routledge and Kegan Paul Limited.
Hayek, F.A. (1982): *Law, Legislation and Liberty. A New Statement of the Liberal Principles of Justice and Political Economy*; London: revised three volume edition, Routledge.
Hodgson, G.M. (1988): *Economics and Institutions. A Manifesto for a Modern Institutional Economics*; Cambridge: Polity Press.
Kelly, G. (1963*): A Theory of Personality. The Psychology of Personal Constructs*; New York, London: W.W. Norton and Company.
Lane, D., Malerba, F., Maxfield, R. and Orsenigo, L. (1996): Choice and action; *Journal of Evolutionary Economics*, 6, 43-76.
Langlois, R.N. (1986a): Rationality, institutions and explanations; in: Langlois, R.N. (ed.), *Economics as a Process. Essays in the New Institutional Economics*, Cambridge:Cambridge University Press, 225-55.
Langlois, R.N. (1986): Coherence and flexibility. Social Institutions in a world of radical uncertainty; in: Kirzner, I.M. (ed.*), Subjectivism, Intelligibility and Economic Understanding. Essays in Honour of Ludwig Lachmann on his Eightieth Birthday*, Basingstoke and London: Macmillan, 171-191.
Langlois, R.N. (1989): What is wrong with old institutional economics (and what is still wrong with the new); in: *Review of Political Economy*, 1, 270-298.
Langlois, R.N. (1992): Transaction cost economics in real-time; in: *Industrial and Corporate Change*, 1, 99-127.

Langlois, R.N. (1997): Rule-following, expertise and rationality: a new behavioral economics?; in: manuscript, Department of Economics, University of Connecticut.

Langlois, R.N. and Csontos, L. (1993): Opitimization, rule-following, and the method of situational analysis; in: Mäki, U., Gustafsson, B. and Knudsen, C. (eds.), *Rationality, Institutions and Economic Methodology*, London: Routledge, 113-132.

Latsis, S.J. (1976): A research programme in economics; in: Latsis, S.J. (ed.), *Method and Appraisal in Economics*, Cambridge: Cambridge University Press, 1-41.

Lazonick, W. (1991): *Business Organization and the Myth of the Market Economy;* Cambridge: Cambridge University Press.

Loasby, B.J. (1976): *Choice, Complexity and Ignorance. An Enquiry into Economic Theory and the Practice of Decision-Making*; Cambridge: Cambridge University Press.

Loasby, B.J. (1986): Organisation, competition, and the growth of knowledge; in Langlois, R.N. (ed.), *Economics as a Process. Essays in the New Institutional Economics*, Cambridge: Cambridge University Press, 41-58.

Loasby, B.J. (1989): *The Mind and Method of the Economist. A Critical Appraisal of Major Economists in the Twentieth Century*, Aldershot: Edward Elgar.

Loasby, B.J. (1991): *Equilibrium and Evolution. An Exploration of Connecting Principles in Economic*, Manchester: Manchester University Press.

Loasby, B.J. (1993): Institutional stability and change in science and the economy; in: Mäki, U., Gustafsson, B. and Knudsen, C. (eds.), *Rationality, Institutions and Economic Methodology*, London: Routledge, 203-221.

Loasby, B.J. (1994): Organisational capabilities and interfirm relations; in: *Metroeconomica*, 45, 248-265.

Marshall, A. (1919): *Industry and Trade. A Study of Industrial Technique and Business Organisation*, London: Macmillan and Co. Limited.

Marshall, A. (1961): *Principles of Economics*, ninth (variorum) edition, London: Macmillan and Co. Limited, for the Royal Economics Society.

Mirowski, P. (1989): *More Heat than Light. Economics as Social Physics, Physics as Nature's Economics*; Cambridge: Cambridge University Press.

Nelson, R.R. and Winter, S.G. (1982): *An Evolutionary Theory of Economic Change*, Cambridge, Massachusetts – London: The Belknap Press of Harvard University Press.

O'Brien, D.P. (1990): Marshall's industrial analysis; in: *Scottish Journal of Political Economy*, 37, 61-84.

Pitkin, H.F. (1972): *Wittgenstein and Justice. On the Significance of Ludwig Wittgenstein for Social and Political Thought*, Berkeley, Los Angeles – London: University of California Press.

Polanyi, M. (1967): *The Tacit Dimension*, Doubleday and Company Inc: Garden City.

Prendergrast, C. (1986): Alfred Schütz and the Austrian School; in: *American Journal of Sociology*, 92, 1-26.

Russell, B. (1953): On the notion of cause, with application to the free-will problem; in: Feigl, H. and Brodbeck, M. (eds.), *Readings in the Philosophy of Science*, New York: Appleton-Century-Crofts Inc, 387- 407.

Sayer, A. (1992): *Method in Social Science. A Realist Approach*, 2nd ed., London: Routledge.

Schütz, A. (1964): *Collected Papers II. Studies in Social Theory*, Martinus Nijhoff: The Hague.

Schütz, A. (1971): *Collected Papers I. The Problem of Social Reality*, third unchanged edition, Martinus Nijhoff: The Hague.

Schütz, A. and Luckmann, T. (1974): *The Structures of the Life World*, London: Heinemann.

Simon, H.A. (1976): From substantive to procedural rationality; in: Latsis, S.J. (ed.), *Method and Appraisal in Economics*, Cambridge: Cambridge University Press, 129-148.

Steele, G.R. (1993): *The Economics of Friedrich Hayek*, London: Macmillan.

Tooby, J. and Cosmides, L. (1992): The psychological foundations of culture; in: Barkow, J.H., Cosmides, L. and Tooby, J. (eds.), *The Adaptive Mind. Evolutionary Psychology and the Generation of Culture*, Oxford - New York: Oxford University Press,19-136.

Weber, M. (1947): *The Theory of Social and Economic Organization*, London: William Hodge and Company Limited.

Comment on John Finch

László Csontos

The Logic of Deductive-Nomological Explanations and Situational Analysis[*]

John Finch's paper is a comprehensive discussion of the methodological status of the interrelated concepts of *Verstehen*, ideal types and situational analysis in the context of the debates on the methodological underpinnings of institutional economics. While I basically agree with most of his conclusions, I strongly disagree with him when he argues that „we cannot easily adopt the technique [of situational analysis] to explain the transformation of institutional customs and conventions, and cannot easily provide explanations of the functional significance and role of these customs and conventions" (Finch 26f.). I think the relationship between situational analysis and standard models of explanation in the social sciences deserves further, and a more thorough discussion. In what follows, first I am going to offer a brief conceptual analysis of two types of deductive-nomological explanations, and then, by way of an illustration, I will proceed to highlight the role of situational logic in supplementing these types of explanatory arguments.

Standard models of bounded rationality (or of neoclassical economics, for that matter) seem to be closely connected with what the philosophy of science calls the methodology of deductive-nomological (D-N) explanation. I would like to argue, however, that (1) D-N explanations, as they are commonly used in the social sciences, are necessarily incomplete, and, moreover, (2) this unavoidable theoretical incompleteness of D-N explanations can be eliminated by situational analysis.

D-N explanations[1], like scientific explanations in general, seek answers to "Why?" questions. From a methodological point of view, however, we have to distinguish between different classes of "Why?" questions. Since "Why?" questions referring to the acts of human individuals belong to the realm of intentional explanations, to the most important subtypes to be considered here are the fol-

---

[*] Reprint of László Csontos' oral presentation at the Symposium. Due to his sudden death he was not able to elaborate further on his comment. We are grateful to Emilia Berényi for granting access to his notes.

[1] What follows is a modified version, tailored to the methodological needs of social scientists in general and economists in particular, of the accepted view on the logical structure of D-N explanations in the philosophy of science. (see Braithwaite 1953, Hempel 1965; Nagel 1961, Popper 1959, 59-62 and Scheffler 1963, 25-31; Stegmüller, 1969).

lowing: (A) "Why does such and such an empirical regularity hold?" or, more precisely, "why is such and such a proposition (R_0), describing such and such an empirical regularity, true?" and (B) "Why did such and such an event (E) occur?" or, alternatively, "Why did such and such a state of affairs come about?"

We may baptize the standard answers to questions of the first type "D-N explanation of empirical regularities" (D-N_R) and answers to questions of the second type "D-N explanations of events" (D-N_E). In order to state the argument as clearly as possible, I want to take a closer look at the logic of D-N_R and D-N_E explanations.

From a formal point of view, explaining an event or empirical regularity in this context is equivalent to deducing the proposition describing the event or empirical regularity in need of explanation (the so-called *explanandum*) from other, appropriately chosen, propositions. The methodological differences between the two subtypes of D-N explanations result from differences between the "appropriately chosen" propositions constituting the *explanans* or explanatory premises of the respective explanations.

When we are trying to explain an empirical regularity, then R_0 is to be deduced from two sets of generic propositions representing empirical regularities. Whereas the first sets consists of propositions (L_j) that are more general than R_0 (the *explanandum*) itself, the second set includes propositions (R_i) that are same level of generality as R_0.

In the case of D-N_E explanations, however, the explanans incorporates not only general but also singular propositions referring to particular circumstances that constitute initial or boundary conditions for the occurrence of E, the event question. Symbolically, we are dealing with the following two subcases:

Empirical regularities.

$$\frac{L_1, L_2, \ldots L_j, \ldots L_m}{R_1, R_2, \ldots R_i, \ldots R_n}$$
$$R_0$$

Events.

$$\frac{R_1, R_2, \ldots R_i, \ldots R_n}{C_1, C_2, \ldots C_j, \ldots C_m}$$
$$E$$

where L_j and R_i are general propositions (law-like statements) describing either empirical generalisations or observed empirical regularities and differing only in their level of generality; C_j is a singular proposition describing one of the initial or boundary conditions for occurrence of the explanandum; R_0 is a generic proposition representing an empirical generalisation or an empirical regularity requiring explanation; and E is a singular proposition describing an event, the occurrence of which is to be explained.

Since theoretical science (like theoretical, as opposed to applied, micro- or macroeconomics) are not much concerned with the explanation of specific events or the genesis of a particular state of affairs, I will focus on the underlying logic of D-N_R explanations.

Suppose, for the sake of argument, that we make the following empirical generalisation: "Every firm has a hierarchic internal structure" (R_0). Suppose further that this sweeping (but in all probability rather well-founded) generalisation arouses our scholarly curiosity, so that we want to find out: Why is it the case that R_0? Suppose, finally, that as a partial and oversimplified answer to this "Why?" question we put forward the following argument.[2]

Every firm faces production problems the solution of which involves "team production" (R_1).

Where team production is involved, the measuring and monitoring of individual effort by the members of the group is technologically infeasible or prohibitively costly (L_1).

If the measuring and monitoring of individual effort by the members of a group is technologically infeasible or prohibitively costly, then the original, loose and informal, organization of the group will be supplanted by a hierarchic internal structure (L_2).

Consequently, every firm has a hierarchic internal structure (R_0).

Now, this explanatory argument, as it stands, is clearly defective in several respects. The logical structure of premises is not clear enough to ascertain whether the deduction is correct, and on a closer scrutiny it might turn out that it is not so easy to find confirming empirical evidence for some of the propositions included in the *explanans*. Although these are distinct possibilities, however, they have nothing to do with the basic deficiency or built-in methodological flaw of D-N explanations in social science. Such explanations are methodologically flawed, I would argue, because, without having fundamental laws to support them, they are essentially incomplete.

By the essential incompleteness of D-N explanations I roughly mean this. Putting aside the issue of confirming evidence, our acceptance of R_0-like propositions, i.e. propositions put forward as describing allegedly general empirical regularities, depends crucially on explanatory premises that are part of a larger theoretical structure. If our explanatory premises were not embedded in a larger theoretical structure we could not make a distinction between well-founded and *ad hoc* explanations.

Assume now that the argument put forward in defense of R_0 meets the above methodological requirement. But why did we accept the explanatory premises, R_1, R_2, ..., R_n, in the first place?

---

[2] See Alchian and Demsetz 1972, 777-795 and Williamson 1975, 49-56.

Or, returning to our quasi-hypothetical example: Why should we accept, let's say, L_1 or L_2?

Although one is tempted to argue that the explanatory premises should be accepted only if they seem to be well-founded in empirical facts, and, more importantly, if they could also be deduced from other, appropriately chosen propositions describing more general empirical regularities, this answer clearly will not do. And it will not do for two simple reasons.

First, notice that on closer scrutiny the suggested argument proves to be equivalent to the following methodological prescription: if doubts arise as to the theoretical status of your explanatory premises, try to construct new, systematic - but at the same time more general - $D-N_R$ explanations for them. But what about the explanatory premises involved in these new $D-N_R$ arguments? Of course, at least in principle, they could also be deduced from more general propositions, and these latter from even more general ones and so forth until we get to fundamental laws that require no further explanation. Since there are no fundamental laws in the social sciences, by following the suggested methodological algorithm - and this is the first point I want to make here - we are bound to get entangled in an infinite regress of successive deductive-nomological arguments, that is, we shall have to climb higher and higher on the ladder of more and more general D-N explanations.

Moreover, and this is my second point, even if we assume that the foregoing methodological argument could be applied successfully, that is, even if we hit upon fundamental laws in the explanatory process, the intentional and motivational background of the relationships described by the explanatory premises would still be opaque and thus the sequence of $D-N_R$ explanations would still remain essentially incomplete in the social sciences.

To follow this line of argument to its seemingly logical conclusion and to dispense with D-N explanations altogether, however, would be equivalent to taking the easiest but least promising way out of a methodological quagmire. Rather than doing this, I would like to argue that D-N explanations have a proper place in the social sciences, provided they are augmented by situational analysis.

This situational analysis of L_1 and L_2 for instance, might be accomplished in two steps. First, we could try to show that the situation underlying team production is structurally similar to the situation underlying a multiperson Prisoners' Dilemma game, and then we might proceed to show how simple hierarchies emerge as organizational or institutional innovations serving to stabilise a Pareto-optimal but originally unstable outcome.

Since in clear-cut SL models there is a complicated but – and this seems to be decisive – theoretically fully specified and transparent relationship between motivation and individual or collective outcomes, situational analysis, superimposed on D-N explanations, is not only functionally equivalent methodological substitute for fundamental laws, but also provides for the sorely needed reduction of empirical regularities to individual motives and intentions. Thus, by adding situational logic models to C-N explanations we can kill three methodological birds with one stone. First, the essential incompleteness of "pure" D-N explanations can be eliminated in a theoretically and methodologically satisfactory manner. Second, since the introduction of situational analysis into D-N models helps clarify the intentional or motivational background of empirical regularities, D-N explanations cum situational logic can be shown to have a rock solid foundation in the principles of methodological individualism. Finally, situational analysis is vindicated again as being a powerful and indispensable tool of explanation in social science.

References

Alchian, A. and H. Demsetz (1972): Production, Information Costs and Economic Organization; *American Economic Review*, 62 (12), 777-795.

Braithwaite, R. B. (1953): *Scientific Explanation*; Cambridge/England: Cambridge University Press, 342-350.

Hempel, C. G. (1965): *Aspects of Scientific Explanation*, New York-Toronto: The Free Press.

Nagel, E. (1961): *The Structure of Science: Problems in the Logic of Scientific Explanation;* New York, Chicago, San Francisco, Atlanta: Harcourt, Brace & World.

Popper, K.R. (1959): *The Logic of Scientific Discovery;* London.

Scheffler, I. (1963): *The Anatomy of Inquiry: Philosophical Studies in the Theory of Science;* New York.

Stegmüller, W. (1969): *Wissenschaftliche Erklärung und Begründung;* Heidelberg, New York: Springer.

Williamson, O. (1975): *Markets and Hierarchies;* New York: The Free Press.

Learning and its Rationality in a Context of Fundamental Uncertainty

Hansjörg Siegenthaler

Introduction

Suppose we define a "context of fundamental uncertainty" as a situation in space and time in which a relevant number of individual actors loose confidence in their ability to interpret the signs of the outer world and to anticipate future events: What can be said of learning processes taking place in such a context? We would like to explore the idea that these processes lend themselves to an approach which puts them in an evolutionary perspective, which models evolution as a communicative process, and which attributes rationality not to individual action but to special traits of communicative structures.

The focus of our inquiry will be on learning processes, not on the particular context, to which we refer. If it is possible to say something useful on these processes even for a context of fundamental uncertainty, it should be possible a fortiori to say something useful on learning processes for a context of lesser complexity. And usefulness would depend on our ability to describe, in an observer's perspective, those elements of an environment, past and present, which help an individual actor to get straight his thoughts on future outcomes of his decision and to bring him closer to a true picture of the world. "Truth" in our present context may well be defined in a pragmatist tradition as it gets revitalized right now by American philosophers like Hilary Putnam (1995), who quite recently referred to William James and to his definition of the "true": 'The true ... is only the expedient in the way of our thinking ... Expedient in almost any fashion; and expedient in the long run and on the whole of course ...'."[1] This concept of truth is closely related to an economist's understanding of rationality. We think that learning processes opening up an avenue to the "true" deserve to be qualified as "rational". What can be said on these learning processes? And why should we address the question at all?

Economists hesitate to answer the last question in the affirmative for very different reasons. Some of them are true "realists" who believe in an intrinsic ability of individual actors to grasp the world quite adequately despite of sporadic elements of "rational ignorance" to the effect, that the professional economist's

---

[1] Putnam (1995), p. 8, in an essay on William James. Emphasis ought to be laid on the qualifications expressed in the second half of the quotation of course.

model of the world is available, as a matter of principle, to entrepreneurs and householders alike. This believe leads to an identification of reality perceptions of individual actors with professional reality perceptions within economics as a scientific discipline. And learning theories tend to converge with the methodology of economics. On the other hand many economists are true "skeptics" who find it quite difficult to assume that reality perceptions are adequate to their task except by chance. So they t-end to reserve the concept of "rationality" for the outcome of evolutionary processes governed by the rules of institutionalized markets. It is our primary goal to question both positions of "realists" and " skeptics" on the basis of one central argument: Individual learning adds to the rationality of decision-making if it gets adequately embedded in a communicative process and if this process is adequately institutionalized. This paper occupies the middle ground between skepticism and "realism", a middle ground well trotted of course. It tries to show that reality perceptions and their rationality decisively depend upon identifiable features of a social context within which learning processes evolve.

It does so with special regard for some peculiarities of "fundamental uncertainty" for reasons alluded to before. These reasons are quite independent of the historical relevance of a highly stylized typification of the "context of fundamental uncertainty". We happen to take this relevance to be very high indeed. But it is not our ambition to convince the doubtful reader because our main argument is independent of an answer to the question of historical relevance. Suffice it to say that to our knowledge it is possible - and worthwhile - to identify within the process of modern economic growth and institutional change exceptionally severe depressions every twenty years or so, at least in the cases of Swiss, American and British history with which we are reasonably familiar. This sequence of great depressions meets the chronology suggested by Simon Kuznets (1965) and his students. It accords with facts established by Friedman and Schwartz (1963). It is confirmed by Solomou's (1988) pertinent statistical study.[2] These phases of severe depressions invariably coincided with major discontinuities in the development of institutions and cognitive frameworks of individual agents. They exhibit a kind of a clustering of those behavioral traits one would expect to show up in a situation we just referred to as a "context of fundamental uncertainty". They could serve as a testing ground for our theoretical suggestions to be developed in this paper; they would serve this purpose very well if we were to address them seriously.[3]

Our paper is structured as follows. Section 2 highlights an implication of our definition of "fundamental uncertainty": the difficulty to explain, in an observer's perspective, what actors happen to decide. This difficulty suggests an evolutionary approach, and it rises the question, whether such an approach can be expected to

---

[2] We follow the periodicity pattern proposed by Kuznets and his followers without sharing their explanatory framework. The set of variables they take into consideration is likely to be too narrowly defined. See e.g. Siegenthaler (1981).

[3] Among the economists addressing them as a testing ground for theories developed within the field of political economics, see Higgs (1987).

be adequate to the task. Section 3 starts from the proposition that an evolutionary approach makes sense if and only if it is possible to distinguish factors making for variation and factors making for selection. It refers to methodological falsificationism which offers a normative model of a communicative process fulfilling these requirements. It applies this model to learning processes outside the realm of science and points to some of the difficulties one has to cope with when one tries to realize such an application. Section 4 elaborates the concept of "fundamental uncertainty" and its behavioral implications. It emphasizes the impact of "fundamental uncertainty" on the use of words, and it highlights the importance of "institutionalized experience" as an input in the process of mutual understanding and verbal communication, justifying the idea that this importance conveys to the "institutionalized experience" selective authority. Section 5 deals with factors making for variation outside the realm of science. It suggests the idea that individual actors produce their theories as hypothetical constructs and confront them continuously with "institutionalized experience". They discard them if they fail to conform with "institutionalized experience". They start to rely on them if they do conform with "institutionalized experience". This distinction between a social process leading to the institutionalization of experience and an individual learning process leading to cognitive schemes or cognitive frameworks may be strongly contested on many grounds. So some arguments are put forward to meet possible objections. Section 6 concludes with a rather brief examination of an institutional framework which is likely to sustain a process of communicative and evolutionary learning adequate to its task. It adds an argumentum ad personam and hopes to gain some respectability by quoting James Madison, who anticipated our conclusions two hundred years ago not only by what he did, but also by what he said.

Economic Crisis and Uncertainty

People were fundamentally uncertain in the context of great depressions referred to above. They found it difficult to interpret what was going on around them. They found it difficult to anticipate the outcome of whatever they tended to initiate. In the words of Walter Lippman in a widely read article in 1932:

> "A demoralized people is one in which the individual is the prey of his own suspicions. He trusts nobody and nothing, not even himself. He believes nothing. He sees only confusion in himself and conspiracies in other men. That is panic. That is what comes when in some sudden emergency of their lives men find themselves unsupported by clear convictions that transcend their immediate and personal desires."[4]

Now if in the context of crisis and uncertainty the individual actor looses confidence in all those cognitive rules which hitherto served to relate expectations to observable facts, i.e. to model future outcomes of present actions, the historian as

---

[4] Quoted from Steel (1980, 290).

an observer of what he did, finds it rather difficult to interpret what he did. To the extent that an actor's rationality fails to be grounded in mental models held to be reliable, the ex post explanations of a historian appear to loose their explanatory potential; what seems to be left is nothing but the description of surprising events. Very surprising events indeed, when one considers what happened in terms of institutional or ideological change. Events which as a rule came to be commented upon by contemporaries as extraordinary even in a long term perspective, and quite often the frame of reference for contemporary comments was looked for not in history of the modern world but in the history of mankind of at least two thousand years.

Does it make sense to place these very unusual events in an evolutionary perspective? It is fair to say that a major change in institutions or in the mental models of individual actors will meet some sort of a test of survival. But it is a moot question just which authority finally decides upon the outcome. Variations in structure do not meet unambiguously definable efficiency standards, which would be responsible for a final selection of structural solutions. Inefficient solutions may prevail for centuries.[5] So the evolutionary approach fails to provide the observer with an opportunity to relate the change to observable facts of an identifiable environment. The predictive power of the evolutionary approach seems to be weak: Perestroika came as a surprise.

So much on the phenomena one encounters when starting to go into the problems of communication and to look for the explanatory potential which might be implied in modeling communication as an evolutionary process <u>sui generis</u>. Let us try to outline the approach to be pursued.

Communication and Institutionalized Experience

We would like to start from the proposition that it makes sense to model communication as an evolutionary process if it is possible to clearly distinguish between factors making for variation and factors which make for selection.[6] It should be possible to identify elements in verbal communication which are related to variation on one hand and elements which are related to selection on the other hand, elements which represent the environment within which communication develops. And the elements of this environment responsible for selection should be observable, in principle at least, in advance, quite independently of the outcome of the communicative interplay.

---

[5] Not every challenge induces what one might call an adequate response. This statement is an element of the main implications of North's (1981) theoretical approach.

[6] In economics it seems possible to attribute to the market the role of an environment as a selective authority. The identification of suitable objectives for this selective authority obviously raises problems (Witt 1996, 6-13) . In our case both sides of the coin - variation and selection - create difficulties.

How is one to proceed to achieve the desired result, viz. the separation of factors of variation and factors of selection and identification of the factors of selection as elements of an environment existing independently of the outcome of the communicative interplay? We all are familiar with the model of a communicative process which fulfills these requirements quite adequately.[7] This model stands in high regard with scientists of many disciplines and is held to be of considerable prescriptive value. I am referring to the model of social learning supposedly or hopefully ruling the actual behavior of members of our profession: We produce variation in our hypothetical descriptions of reality. We confront these descriptions with facts, so that the facts select among our hypothetical ideas. These facts - and that's where the communicative process comes in - are supposed to get established in ways which guarantee intersubjectivity. Let me assume that we all agree with Popper's concept of "facts" as mental constructs which are themselves open to debate so that the establishment of the very facts of the world is the outcome of a communicative procedure.[8] Experience does not count for itself. What counts is experience agreed upon by the members of the scientific community. I would like to call this kind of experience "institutionalized". It acquires, once agreed upon, the quality of something we have to meet in what we are doing, something we have to obey when framing our mental models. In fact, even the procedures by which this kind of institutionalized experience get produced tend to become institutionalized. Consider the national income statistics compiled by the OECD. If someone wished to modify them, he must initiate a debate which may or may not lead to a new convention. But individually he is not supposed to tinker with them, he certainly is not entitled to adjust them to the particular investment theory he confronts with the data. Institutionalized experience thus precedes, ideally, the statistical testing of a particular hypothesis. It commands the authority to reject whatever ideas are not logically compatible with it. It commands selective authority. It makes up part of the environment within which our ideas are put on trial. It is not the world itself within which our ideas are put on trial, not the real world. It is a world agreed upon, agreed upon, to repeat it, in order to secure intersubjectivity. It is a very poor world, a world devoid of whatever experience does not lend itself to the procedures considered to guarantee intersubjectivity, devoid of experience which e.g. introspection might produce. It is a poor world, but a world carrying all the authority of something agreed upon according to a procedural consensus.

---

[7] We are referring to the methodology of falsificationism. See Popper (1934/71), Gadenne and Wendel (1996).

[8] See Popper (1971, 18-21) . - The concept of a communicative procedure seems to be implied in Popper's discussion of what constitutes a "Basissatz" (20 f.): Propositions, not experience pure and simple constitute the relevant selective authority. And since Popper rejects the idea of propositions of a last resort, so that propositions always require justification, the preliminary acceptance of a proposition must be the outcome of a social convention.

Let me now come back to the issue of everyday communication taking place in the context of a crisis: does it make sense to apply an evolutionary approach to this everyday communication and to identify, within the process of everyday communication, elements of variation and elements of selection just as I sought to identify such elements within the standard procedure of scientific research? My answer to this question will be that it makes sense indeed, that it is feasible to identify institutionalized experience in everyday communication, that this institutionalized experience does provide an environment responsible for the final selection of outcomes. This answer is crucial for my whole argument. So let me spend some time on its development.

At first glance, of course, all the odds seem to point against its validity or even its plausibility. Competing ideas seem to meet a demand which is not defined by identifiable elements of an environment preceding the outcome of the communicative procedures themselves. All kinds of influences might gain importance, might acquire what we called "selective authority". So we really appear to be left with what we learned from good old history: that personality matters in times of crisis, that persuasion relates to vitality much more than to argument, that the gifts of an able orator may count for far more than the niceties of mental models. Hence, it is impossible therefore to predict the outcome of the struggle of ideas. It is very interesting to see that during the last few years in the debate of professional historians the voice of those authors who resolutely reject anything resembling theory in the least has gained dramatically in importance. Things happen to happen, ideas emerge, Jelzin has so far survived, he may continue to survive, he may fail in his objectives: In any case, what will remain is a tremendously interesting story. Let us tell the story and forget about explanations, they are of no avail. In the early days of Perestroika, one eminent representative of German historiography who was a devoted adherent of history as a social science reacted to the events with the statement: "Well, we thought we were on the way to an analytical understanding of the process of historical change, now we feel that we do not understand anything at all".

This digression into the field of arguments and sentiments of those historians who take it for granted that in the last resort irrationality is the driving force behind history points to the core problem with any attempt to integrate the events originating in the choice of individuals unable to rationally choose their ideas in an evolutionary perspective: If the acceptance or rejection of ideas is not firmly grounded in experience, it is quite unclear in what sense experience could possibly develop into a selective authority. I would like to suggest that it is possible to meet this core problem by analyzing the characteristics of communication in the specific context of fundamental uncertainty. In order to explore these characteristics, I have to return once more to the notion of "fundamental uncertainty" and to show that rational individual choice tends to favor the institutionalization of experience not despite of, but because of "fundamental uncertainty".

Fundamental Uncertainty

"Uncertainty" may be defined as a state of the world in which individual actors find it impossible to attribute a reasonably definite probability to the expected outcome of their choice. Among the authors who were involved in the development of this concept - and who delimitated it against the notion of risk - was Keynes. In his General Theory and in his famous article of 1937, in which he discussed some of the reviews of his book of 1936, he made use of a third notion besides "risk" and "uncertainty" (Keynes 1936, 1937) a notion which makes part of everyday language and which is still in use in the British newspapers, namely the notion of a "state of confidence". Keynesianism discarded this notion altogether, together with everything referring to the more enigmatic elements in Keynes' views on long-run expectations. When Mark Stohs (1980) confronted the concept of a "low state of confidence" with that of "uncertainty", he believed he had discovered that Keynes used these concepts synonymously. I disagree with Stohs. Although to my knowledge Keynes did not explicitly discuss the difference between the two notions, he clearly implied a difference of crucial importance. In his 1937 article he spoke in a marvelously accurate metaphor of "pretty polite techniques" guiding the individual actor's attempts at getting his long run expectations straight. "Pretty polite techniques" guide the actor's attempts at the development of long run expectations, but they do so only if the actor regards them as trustworthy. If he does not trust them he discards them. When he discards them he finds himself without long-run expectations. Future events become uncertain in this case, to be sure. So a lack of confidence in one's "pretty polite techniques" is of course a sufficient condition for "uncertainty". But it is not a necessary condition, since "pretty polite techniques", even if trustworthy, may not, in conditions of an informational overload for instance, guarantee the certainty of expectations. For this reason let me suggest a concept of "fundamental uncertainty" which is analytically related to a lack of confidence in the mental models an actor applies when forming his expectations.[9]

What happens when an individual actor looses confidence in the cognitive foundations of his views of the world? In order to put my argument in a clear-cut context which leaves no room for ambiguities, let me assume a situation in which the actor is "fundamentally uncertain" to the extent that he completely resigns with regard to his ability to interpret the signs his environment is emanating, that even the words of his counterparts lose their definite meaning, that semantic rules become a problem, that all the relationships between what he perceives to exist and what he expects to happen tend to become frail and tenuous. In such a situation strategic behavior is out of the question. This applies to behavior in general, it applies to the use of words in particular. If an actor communicates in a context of fundamental uncertainty, he does not pursue, as a rational being, a goal which would be worthwhile to be pursued only if the effects, which his choice of words

---

[9] See Siegenthaler (1993, 84-106) for a more substantial discussion of "fundamental uncertainty" and of the role of confidence. - See also Luhmann (1973).

might produce, were known. These effects are not known under conditions of uncertainty. It is not worthwhile, therefore, to play strategic games with words. It is irrational to cheat. Lies do not serve a useful purpose.[10] But if it is irrational to cheat for reasons which refer to a common context and not to the idiosyncrasies of people involved in the communicative process going on, it is irrational also to assume that any one else of those involved is cheating. Unless communication breaks down completely the subjective rationality of all the players wants them to attribute truthfulness to what happens to be said by others. This in turn motivates attitudes of mutual empathy, a readiness to expect that the utterances of others convey something intelligible and that they are likely to contribute to the clarification of things one wants to have clarified in the first place.[11] Empathy is likely to entail a generalized consistency assumption, the assumption that my partner's thinking is consistent. This assumption helps me to infer, from what I understand, the ideas conferred by words which my semantics still fail to decode. Now this inference draws by necessity on things which participants feel to have in common. Let me call these things "communicable experience": reality representations to which reference can be made in a common language. "Communicable experience" furnishes the common ground on which participants build up their ideas on what participants seem to believe. The indispensability of this common ground tends to enforce a high degree of faithful adherence to "communicable experience" once it becomes repeatedly referred to. And this faithful adherence amply justifies the belief that "communicable experience" gains, in the process of its institutionalization, "selective authority".

Reference made to common experience does not furnish the clue to the cognitive rules which bridge the gap between the past and the future. The individual actor who rationally decides upon the use of scarce resources has no advantage over the economist who seeks to model rational behavior. Just as any member of the scientific community who confronts his ideas with experience is unable to deduce them from experience, the entrepreneur or the politician is unable to become any wiser from past experience with regard to the future unless he develops a theory; this theory overdraws past experience. But it necessarily refers to past experience, and it remains to be seen in what respect it does so. I maintain that, in the context of fundamental uncertainty in which the reconstruction of semantics draws upon the resources of common experience, this experience becomes institutionalized in much the same way as common experience in the scientific community becomes institutionalized according to the device of intersubjectivity. Communication within the context of fundamental uncertainty tends to produce shared

---

[10] This attributes to fundamental uncertainty what Habermas (1981) postulates on ethical grounds. It may be that fundamental uncertainty has a stronger impact on the souls of human beings than mere exhortation.

[11] With all due caution we would like to suggest that this attitude of mutual empathy might be covered, at least to some extent, by the concept of "charity" as used by Donald Davidson in his attempt to identify conditions of mutual understanding, see Davidson (1984).

experience and to follow the rule of intersubjectivity not as a norm set by professional agreement, but as a device dictated by psychological necessity: the actors find it very difficult to put faith in their own experience as long as they fail to be reassured by a confirming resonance or acceptance among their counterparts. Hence they suppress personal experience, they deny it that kind of selective authority which shared experience is likely to demand. Institutionalized experience is therefore highly selective and rather tenuous when set against the richness of the total of individual experience. I think that the poverty of shared experience should command considerable attention in any attempt to interpret those communicative procedures in which new cognitive rules emerge: Institutionalized experience tends to be poor even within large heterogeneous groups, all the more so within small homogeneous groups.

Social Learning as an Evolutionary Process

So far we have tried to show that, in a context of fundamental uncertainty, communicable experience tends to become institutionalized because it serves as an indispensable input in the production process of communication. And we attributed to this institutionalized experience a kind of selective authority which people correspondingly try to comply with in their endeavor to model the world and to make sense again of available information. We did not refer to "variation", to the crucial element in an evolutionary framework, which makes for redundancy and diversity and constitutes the objective of our "selective authority". Needless to say, it makes no sense to place a communicative process in an evolutionary perspective unless it is possible to separate the substance of what is varied in this process from "institutionalized experience", i.e. from our "selective authority". Is such a separation feasible at all? If it is feasible: does it add to our understanding of social learning in a context of fundamental uncertainty?

Let us begin again with a reference to the premises of methodological falsificationism. Among these premises, the clear-cut distinction between factual evidence agreed upon within a scientific community and individually designed hypothetical constructs expected to meet these facts looms very large. This distinction may provide a first approximation to the solution of our problem at hand. It may also be useful because of its very ambiguities which point to some of the necessary precautions to be taken.

As suggested earlier, "institutionalized experience" may be treated with good reason as an analogon to the conventionally defined facts in science. What is the analogon to the individually designed hypothetical constructs outside the realm of science?

A likely candidate must be considered to be the tentative and preliminary results of what we would like to call "fundamental learning".[12] "Fundamental learning" involves a change in cognitive rules, a change in the rules which govern individual information processing. We referred to these rules in our discussion of "fundamental uncertainty" above, and we defined "fundamental uncertainty" precisely in terms of a lack of confidence in such rules. And to this lack of confidence we sought to attribute the particular characteristics of those communicative processes leading to the institutionalization of experience. For very good and very conventional economic reasons, we would like to suggest that fundamental uncertainty also makes for fundamental learning, so that the institutionalization of experience and processes of individual fundamental learning tend to go hand in hand and to concentrate on rather short periods of time: Pervasive fundamental uncertainty removes the all important obstacle to fundamental learning by dramatically lowering its opportunity costs. The opportunity costs of fundamental learning might be measured in terms of efficiency differentials between routine learning with given cognitive rules and learning with rules exposed to imminent change. These differentials are negligible in a context of fundamental uncertainty; there is no routine left worth while worrying about.

Falsificationism applied to everyday learning predicts the preliminary outcomes of fundamental learning - new mental models designed to establish the cognitive foundations of rational choice - to get confronted with communicable evidence agreed upon within the relevant social networks. New mental models in this sense become involved in an evolutionary process in which institutionalized experience plays, as mentioned before, the role of a selective authority. Whatever individual fundamental learning produces in terms of variety undergoes a process of social selection before it affects individual decision-making in the realm of economics or politics. The application of falsificationism to everyday learning is, however, open to criticism, in part to criticism advanced against falsificationism in general, in part to that advanced against a possibly misdirected application. We would like to address just one of the pertinent problems. Does it make sense, one might ask, to talk of "institutionalized experience" as if it could emerge without new cognitive rules being safely established already?[13] If it is true that a context of fundamental uncertainty motivates both individual fundamental learning and the social construction of "institutionalized experience": Why not go back to Berger/Luckmann (1970) and treat both facts and theories as the common result of one and the same social process?

---

[12] For an early presentation of this concept see Siegenthaler (1989, 218 ff.) . It closely corresponds to the "fundamental elements of learning" discussed by Dosi and Marengo (1994, 160) .

[13] For a critical stance and advanced by the sociology of knowledge and by communication theory see e.g. Heintz (1993), McCloskey (1994). Heintz refers to Ludwik Fleck (1993) and to his concept of a "Denkstil", which emerges from communicative processes taking place within scientific communities and which decisively impinges upon the social construction of "scientific facts".

The following tentative and sketchy remarks will not suffice to convince the doubtful reader of the relative merits of an evolutionary approach. But they may be able to draw attention to the issues one would like to address:

First, the pertinent literature is not without support for the crucial distinction between "institutionalized experience" on one hand and preliminary outcomes of fundamental learning as highly conjectural mental models on the other hand. Remember Reinhart Koselleck (1992), who wants us to treat the space of available experience ("Erfahrungsraum") and the range of expectations ("Erwartungshorizont") as two separate aspects of the human mind, without expectations being reducible to experience.[14] Foucault (1970) includes in his analysis of human discourse both a narrative of events as individual cultural constructs put into language and a systematic exploration of the rules which constrain these events. He clearly distinguishes between elements of variation (events) and elements of selection (constraints). These eminent philosophers and historians both took it for granted that an adequate treatment of human discourse and cultural change crucially depend on an analytical separation of fortuitous variation and of path-dependent selective authorities, although neither of them made the slightest reference to an evolutionary approach.

Second, our distinction can of course be treated as an element of a meta-theory governing ideas and learning processes of individual actors and social groups quite safely even within the context of fundamental uncertainty. The scientific observer will have a very hard time indeed if he wants to deconstruct this element of conventional belief systems. Individuals want to treat the facts of past experience and the results of their conjectures at two different levels. They believe in factual evidence even if they find it very difficult to figure out future outcomes. And they want their conjectures to meet the "facts" as well as possible.

This seems to overlook, at first sight, all the insights which we gained from Ludwik Fleck (1935/94) and his constructivist followers: "Facts" and their elaboration depend upon theoretical premises shared by members of communicative networks. If there is consistency between "facts" and "theories" it is a result not of a matching process within which "institutionalized experience" selects its appropriate theories, rather it is a result of a concomitant and mutual adjustment of new additions to the stock of both theoretical and factual knowledge. But even if this were an entirely convincing description of knowledge production we still would have to allow for the deeply rooted feelings of all of us who try to defend our "facts" against the objections of our adversaries. Our defence, and this seems to be the crucial point, does not start from a relativistic assumption to the effect that we would peacefully admit the coexistence of factual incompatibilities. Whatever the theoretical inspirations of our factual assertions might be we want our "facts" to meet any competitive pressure which rival assertions could bring upon them. "Facts" get socially institutionalized as something which commands authority for

---

[14] Koselleck (1967) does not hesitate to interpret the dualistic nature of the relationship between "Erfahrungsraum" and "Entscheidungshorizont" as an anthropological fact.

everybody. And whenever they fail to command this authority they produce debates, arguments, justifications, with the result of a restitution of authority or else of a common rejection of the factual assertion. Of course the debate may go on and on for fairly long periods of time. Our thesis does not exclude such a lengthy debate. But it excludes peaceful acquiescence in factual incompatibilities.

Third, economics is also in favor of the distinction. "Institutionalized experience" as something to be shared with others is not the stuff which people want to privatize. Outcomes of individual fundamental learning, on the other hand, may convey a comparative advantage one might want to preserve.

Last but not least: The distinction and its affinity to an evolutionary perspective gives access to heuristically fruitful explorations into the field of social learning. It allows for very rich descriptions of both collective and individual components of this process. It makes for compatibility of ideas, stressing the importance of communication for institutionalized experience and of theories which allow for individual innovation. And it points to some of the reasons for individual and collective failure to measure up to the tasks of fundamental learning. Historians are keen to explain success stories, but they also want to explain historical disasters. They must welcome therefore an approach which allows for mistakes. In the final section of our paper we will focus on some systematic reasons for misdirected learning activities.

Concluding Remarks

In section 4 we already took into consideration what seems to be the most important of them: The loss of relevance of individually-held experience in the context of fundamental uncertainty when individual actors no longer trust the elements of their experience not shared with others. The poverty of shared experience affects the selective impact which our "selective authority", i.e. precisely this shared or institutionalized experience, may have on the outcome of fundamental learning. The poverty of shared experience gives new ideas too much free play. It is not an impediment to the mushrooming of these ideas, but it makes it difficult to suppress what later might turn out to be the misleading ones. The selective authority shifts too early - and quite uneconomically - from institutionalized experience to the forces of markets.

Let us therefore put forward the hypothesis that final results of fundamental learning tend to improve ceteris paribus with growing richness of institutionalized experience. What makes for richness? Our arguments lead us straight back to John Stuart Mill (1859) and his followers, who stressed and discussed the importance of the existence of a plurality of opinions, of free speech and free press, of an uninhibited communicative interplay among agents.[15] At the same time, these argu-

---

[15] See Ritter (1995, 236-240) and Popper (1994, chapt. 2).

ments want us to modify the liberal framework within which parts of the relevant discussion was carried on. Plurality of opinions and social heterogeneity, even within very large social networks, do not guarantee by themselves richness of institutionalized experience. At least they do not guarantee such richness when it counts most: in a context of fundamental uncertainty. In this context, to say it again, people find it very difficult to tolerate the plurality of opinions, they fall back on shared experience, and individually-held experience loses its relevance. What helps in such a situation is not plurality as such but rather social differentiation combined with communicative integration of all the different social groups: communication across the boundaries of social groups. Most promising seems to be a two-stage process with, first, shared experience becoming institutionalized within clearly delineated groups or networks and, second, with people of fairly strong convictions challenging other people of equally strong but quite different convictions in an open debate.

This two-stage model seems to accord very well with some of the historical facts crucially important for social learning in, e.g., American, British and Swiss history. Think of social movements mushrooming during the crisis of the 1830s or 1890s in the United States e.g.: grass-roots movements in both cases became the locus of individual attachment to clear-cut convictions.[16] What emerged in the first phase of the process was a plurality of specific and not particularly rich packages of institutionalized experience as the truly distinguishing feature of social groups, of the new charities of the nineties, the new women's clubs, neighborhood associations, and, not to forget, German Turnvereine among the immigrants.[17] But in a second phase, some peculiarities of American communicative structure allowed for a debate which clearly crossed the frontiers of all these special groups. These peculiarities were nicely described by Alexis de Tocqueville. When he addressed the activities of the previously mentioned social movements which emerged during the thirties, he stressed the fact that, unlike European political factions, they entered the field of ideological rivalry not with the intention to gain power pure and simple but to convince their adversaries in a battle of ideas. This fact he related to the unlikeliness of rising within due time to a position of hegemonic power.[18] But it seems to me that since the 18th century the virtues of an evolutionary process of communicative procedures granting a perpetual confrontation of ideas with a plurality of institutionalized experience were well understood in many quarters in the United States. And such an understanding sustained the very process to be understood.

---

[16] We tried to demonstrate that a context of fundamental uncertainty makes it easier for social movements to overcome the free rider problem, quite in contrast to a proposition of game theory, treating certainty of expectations as an important condition of cooperative behavior; Siegenthaler (1989, 1993). - For an account of the American depression of the 1890's along the lines of our argument see Siegenthaler (1995).

[17] Siegenthaler (1995).

[18] Tocqueville (1835-40, new ed. 1951, 198 f.).

This leads to our final result. In a context of fundamental uncertainty, rationality has to be looked for not in the process of individual learning but in the peculiarities of the structure of communication which govern social learning as an evolutionary process. We have stressed the importance of institutionalized experience as a selective authority, of social groups within which institutionalization of experience takes place, and of an open debate going on among citizens of very different social groups sure of themselves and sure of what they consider to be their experience.

James Madison, one of the truly outstanding American Founding Fathers of the late 18th century, and many of his contemporaries with him, would have followed our arguments with sympathy. He was a devoted adherent of a falsificationist approach to the problems of fundamental learning, and he was an experienced practitioner of the art of translating historical tradition into a visionary concept of a world to be created and of a constitution, which could be expected to meet the problems of a new world. And he was quite outspoken when he had an opportunity to explain the arcana of this art to his readers. Intimately familiar as he was with constitutional history he raised the question whether his knowledge of the past made him any wiser with regard to the problems of the day. And in number 37 of the Federalist papers he gave the answer: "It has been shown, that the other confederacies which could be consulted as precedents ... can ... furnish no other light than that of beacons, which give warning of the course to be shunned, without pointing out that which ought to be pursued."[19] History does not point to the future, but it provides experience, which throws the full weight of a selective authority against those mental constructs "to be shunned". However, Madison was certainly not plagued by post-modern skepticism with regard to the self-evident validity of everything he wanted to treat as "historical experience". This experience threw the light of beacons, and the beacons were there to be reckoned with. No doubt about the beacons. We hesitate to join him in his overly positivistic attitude towards the concept of "historical experience". Beacons are not just there, they have to be constructed. We tried to outline a communicative process which we would like to hold responsible for this very construction.

References

Berger, P.L. and T. Luckmann (1970): *Die gesellschaftliche Konstruktion der Wirklichkeit. Eine Theorie der Wissenssoziologie;* Frankfurt/Main: Fischer.

Davidson, D. (1984): *Inquiries into truth and interpretation;* Oxford: Clarendon.

Dosi, G. and L. Marengo (1994): Some Elements of an Evolutionary Theory of Organizational Competences; in: R.W. England (ed.), *Evolutionary Concepts*

---

[19] Cook (1961), The Federalist No. 37, January 11, 1788, p. 177.

in Contemporary Economics, Ann Arbor: University of Michigan Press, 157-178.

Fleck, L. (1935/94): *Entstehung und Entwicklung einer wissenschaftlichen Tatsache. Einführung in die Lehre vom Denkstil und Denkkollektiv;* edited with an introduction by L. Schäfer and T. Schnelle, stw 312, Frankfurt/Main: Suhrkamp.

Foucault, M (1970): *Die Ordnung des Diskurses;* Inaugural lecture at the Collège de france, December 2nd, Paris.

Friedman, M. and A.J. Schwartz (1963): *A Monetary History of the United States*, Princeton, NJ: Princeton University Press.

Gadenne, V. and H.J. Wendel (eds.) (1996): *Rationalität und Kritik*; Tübingen: Mohr.

Habermas, J (1981): *Theorie des kommunikativen Handels*; 2 vols., Frankfurt/Main: Suhrkamp.

Heintz, B. (1993): *Die Herrschaft der Regel: Zur Grundlagengeschichte des Computers;* Frankfurt/Main: Campus.

Higgs, R. (1987): *Crisis and Leviathan. Critical Episodes in the Growth of American Government;* Oxford: Oxford University Press.

Keynes, J.M. (1936): *The General Theory of Employment, Interest, and Money;* London: Macmillan.

Keynes, J.M. (1937): The General Theory of Employment; *Quarterly Journal of Economics*, 51, 209-223.

Koselleck, R. (1967): Historia Magistra, Magistra Vitae: Über die Auflösung des Topos im Horizont neuzeitlich bewegter Geschichte; in: H. Braun and M. Riedel (eds.), *Natur und Geschichte*, Stuttgart: Kohlhammer, 196-219.

Kosseleck, R. (1992): *Vergangene Zukunft. Zur Semantik geschichtlicher Zeiten;* stw 757, Frankfurt/Main: Suhrkamp.

Kuznets, S. (1965): Long Swings in Population Growth and Related Variables; in S. Kuznets, *Economics Growth and Structure. Selected Essays*, New York: Norton, 328-378.

Luhmann, N. (1973): *Vertrauen: Ein Mechanismus der Reduktion sozialer Komplexität;* 2nd extended ed., Stuttgart: Enke.

McCloskey, D.N. (1994): *Knowledge and Persuasion in Economics;* Cambridge: Cambridge University Press.

Mill, J.S. (1859/1956): *On Liberty;* Indianapolis, New York: Bobbs-Merrill.

North, D.C. (1981): *Structure and Change in Economic History;* New York: Norton.

Popper, K.R. (1934/71): *Logik der Forschung;* 4th ed., Tübingen: Mohr.

Popper, K.R. (1994): *The Myth of the Framework. In Defence of Science and Rationaliy;* London, New York: Routledge.

Putnam, H. (1995): *Pragmatism: An Open Question;* Oxford: Blackwell.

Ritter, U.P. (1995): Die Evolution von Wirtschaftssystemen, das Interdependenztheorem und die Poppersche Falsifikationsidee; in: A. Wagner and H.-W. Lorenz, *Studien zur Evolutorischen Ökonomik III*, Schriften des Vereins für Sozialpolitik, Bd. 195/III, Berlin: Duncker & Humblot, 227-242.

Siegenthaler, H. (1981): Ansätze zu einer generalisierten Interpretation langwelliger Wachstumsschwankungen und ihrer sozialen Implikationen im 19. und frühen 20. Jahrhundert; in: H. Kellenbenz (ed.), *Wachstumsschwankungen: Wirtschaftliche und soziale Auswirkungen (Spätmittelalter bis 20. Jh.)*, Stuttgart: Klett-Cotta, 1-45.

Siegenthaler, H. (1989): Organization, Ideology and the Free Rider Problem; *Journal of Institutional and Theoretical Economics*, 145(1), 215-237.

Siegenthaler, H. (1993): *Regelvertrauen, Prosperität und Krisen: Die Ungleichmäßigkeit wirtschaftlicher und sozialer Entwicklung als Ergebnis individuellen Handelns und sozialen Lernens;* Die Einheit der Gesellschaftswissenschaften, Bd. 81, Tübingen: Mohr.

Siegenthaler, H. (1995): *Wege zum Wohlstand: Das Beispiel der USA, der Schweiz und Brasiliens;* in: W. Fischer (ed.), Lebensstandard und Wirtschaftssysteme, Frankfurt/Main: Knapp, 173-212.

Solomou, S.N. (1988): *Phases of Economic Growth, 1850-1973: Kondratieff Waves and Kuznets Swings;* Cambridge: Cambridge University Press.

Steel, R. (1980*): Walter Lippmann and the American Century;* Boston: Atlantic Monthly Press.

Stohs, M. (1980): Uncertainty in Keynes' General Theory; *History of Political Economy*, 12, 372-382.

Tocqueville, A. de (1835-40/1951): *Oeuvres, papiers et correspondance, Tome I: De la démocratie en Amérique;* edition définitive publiée sous la direction de J.-P. Mayer, Paris.

Witt, U. (1998): Evolutionary Economics and Evolutionary Biology; in: P. Koslowski (ed.), *Developmental Systems, Competition, and Cooperation in Sociobiology and Economics*, Berlin: Springer.

Comment on Hansjörg Siegenthaler

Horst Hegmann

Fundamental Learning and Implicit Knowledge

The facts on which we base our utility maximizing calculations are not just a given reality, but the result of human interaction. Nobody can privately create this reality. Reality, to use the words of Berger and Luckmann (1960), is a social construction. For Hansjörg Siegenthaler it is the result of shared cognitive rules for selection, classification and interpretation of information.[20] Using such rules society creates a stock of common knowledge "institutionalized experience", on which individuals can base their attempts to maximize utility.

As an economic historian Siegenthaler distinguishes phases of routine and phases of crisis in history. In phases of routine everyone acts on a given stock of institutionalized experience. He uses a set of established cognitive rules to separate false propositions from true ones. In phases of crisis there is a need to reconstruct these rules, in order to cope with new problems in an appropriate manner. Thus a crisis leads to a situation of "fundamental uncertainty". Individuals then are not only forced to look for better instruments to realize given aims in a given reality, they also rebuild the foundations of that reality, in order to be able to maximize utility again. Siegenthaler's distinction here is closely analogous to Thomas Kuhn's differentiation between research within a paradigm and a change of paradigm (Kuhn 1962)[21] or to James Buchanan's choice of rules as compared to choices within rules (Buchanan 1990).

Siegenthaler argues that in a situation of fundamental uncertainty a collective process of fundamental learning through communication is needed. It is feasible because in such a situation nobody has enough orientation to have an incentive to cheat. The general approach of Hansjörg Siegenthaler looks very fruitful to me, there seems however to be a serious flaw in his argumentation. My comment will concentrate on that issue. In the first of three parts I will show that even within a

---

[20] In his 1993 book *Regelvertrauen, Prosperität und Krisen* Siegenthaler distinguishes the two types of learning as follows: "Der erste betrifft den Erwerb, die Einübung und Modifikation von Regeln der Auswahl, der Klassifikation und Interpretation von Informationen, der zweite die regelgebundene Selektion und Deutung der über erreichbare Informationen zugänglichen Erfahrung." (Siegenthaler 1993, 33)

[21] For an explicit reference to Kuhn see also Siegenthaler 1993, 128n.

situation of fundamental uncertainty there is room for opportunistic misrepresentation. There is danger that the basis for collective efforts to engage in "fundamental learning" will be destroyed too early. In the second part I will propose a modification to Siegenthaler's approach, which should repair this structural defect. In the third I will apply the modified approach to conflict resolution in a pluralist setting.

1 The production of "institutionalized experience" and the danger of opportunism

In Siegenthaler's view communication in a fundamental sense is a process not of exchanging but of producing information. Only intersubjectively shared information seems to be sufficiently trustworthy to base individual action upon. Knowledge of this kind pre-supposes what Boudon postulates for beliefs as compared to preferences: we expect them to be the same for others (Boudon 1996, 128). The result of communication is a pool of common knowledge, a view of the world, which is shared by all members of the communicating group. The socially constructed worldview is much poorer than each individual one but it provides a secure basis against which to check the validity of individual conjectures. We may call such a pool of common knowledge the culture of a group. Such a culture is not determined but only influenced by the material circumstances of its members (Siegenthaler 1993, 56). Siegenthaler identifies two inputs to the productive process of culture. The first is mutual trust. He reduces it to a "consistency assumption" which means the expectation that other participants in the process will follow the rules of logic. Siegenthaler can reduce trust to consistency because in a situation of fundamental uncertainty nobody has the opportunity to cheat (see also Siegenthaler 1993, 182). Fundamental uncertainty therefore can be interpreted as an extremely radicalized version of Rawls' *veil of ignorance* (Rawls 1988, 136n). In a situation of fundamental uncertainty nobody knows where he is, who he is, or what he can do. The only interest left is orientation.

The second input to the process of fundamental learning is what Siegenthaler calls "communicable experience". In his 1993 book *Regelvertrauen, Prosperität und Krisen*, he identifies the crisis itself as the core of the communicable experience needed (Siegenthaler 1993, 184n). To cope with a crisis may indeed be the only common interest of those communicating. Therefore, so Siegenthaler claims, it is irrational for each individual to cheat in a situation of fundamental uncertainty.[22] If uncertainty creates low cost situations, fundamental uncertainty

---

[22] For a somewhat more cautious interpretation see: "Das Ergebnis (der Kommunikation) nimmt auf Erfahrung Bezug, ist aber nicht durch Erfahrung bestimmt. In ihm gewinnt eine neue Welt Gestalt. Das spürt der beteiligte individuelle Aktor, und

leads to zero-cost situations. Here individual rationality and utility-maximization are indeed meaningless. But this is only a limiting case. Fundamental uncertainty and secure expectations are just the two extremes in a whole range of possibilities. If we want to speak of communication in any meaningful way, the communicating individuals will soon leave the state of fundamental uncertainty and move towards established rules on how to look at the world. Each step of producing a new intersubjective reality will increase the scope for a free ride.

It is very improbable that all participants remain in a state of fundamental uncertainty for the whole time of communication. Let's imagine we are in a completely dark room and we are looking for a way out. We may start talking in order to make sense of our situation and try to orientate ourselves. In doing so the room brightens up to a certain extent. At one moment in time each of us reaches a point at which he may decide that there is enough orientation now and that it may be better to take a free ride on the efforts of the others from now on. The exact point of that decision will depend on the value of the communication itself. Therefore it depends on the trustworthiness of other persons in the room. Distrust therefore may destroy the atmosphere for cooperation at an early stage. In an extreme case, the process of fundamental learning will break down before even one single person is ready to switch. For this reason trust, as the first input in the production of institutionalized experience, is more precarious than Siegenthaler assumes.

This situation becomes even more difficult if not all participants in a communication process do indeed start from scratch.[23] Individuals always belong to different social groups. If just one group is dealing with fundamental uncertainty, the cognitive rules of others are left intact and individuals may join a disorientated group for instrumental reasons alone. Especially in the case of new social movements there is always at least a suspicion that this is true. (The widespread comparison of the early Green Movement in Germany with a water melon is a case in point. It was said that the new party was green just at the outside but red within.) Opportunistic misrepresentation in communication is not only possible on the level of routine learning, but also on the level of fundamental learning.

---

gerade deshalb vertraut er persönlichem Urteilsvermögen nicht ausschließlich. Fundamentales Lernen überfordert individuelle Rationalität, entzieht sich dem individuellen Nutzenkalkül, verweist den individuellen Aktor auf die prozedurale Rationalität kommunikatjven Handelns" (Siegenthaler 1993, S. 81).

[23] Siegenthaler himself himself takes this case only as a limiting one (Siegenthaler 1993, 186).

2   A modification of Siegenthaler's approach: replacing communication by practice

Because of the fact that even in a case of fundamental learning the danger of opportunism may destroy the conditions for collective action, we need another foundation for a group dealing with fundamental uncertainty. In restricting the production process of common knowledge to communication, Siegenthaler's concept shows a language bias which I think is responsible for its structural defect. If we keep the idea of producing "institutionalized experience" through human interaction, but replace communication by continuous collective action, the danger of opportunism will disappear. In acting together to solve a problem, the group in question develops a different kind of common knowledge. Whereas in communication everything is explicit, a common practice will produce implicit knowledge and the explicit parts make sense only with respect to the implicit ones.

Let us take a group of feminists for example. They are fighting what they perceive as sexual inequality. In doing so they create a stock of common knowledge, a culture of fighting male dominance. The implicit and explicit rules which mould such a culture are the unintended side effects of the collective effort to come to terms with a perceived problem. The implicit part is a *know how* without a corresponding *knowing that*. The explicit parts are verbal ones, but they make sense only in connection with the implicit ones. Individuals who know the rules can apply them and they can even control the application without being able to articulate them. These aspects of implicit knowledge as developed by Michael Polanyi [1964] move the concept quite close to that of the later Wittgenstein. The implicit parts of knowledge correspond to what Wittgenstein calls a *form of life*, with respect to which some *language game* makes sense (Wittgenstein 1958, I/23)[24].

The proposed modification of the process of fundamental learning has important implications. As long as we consciously know all the rules produced in a process of fundamental learning, we are always able to decide that at one point in time we can promote our emerging individual interests better by cheating than by continued cooperation. If our cooperative enterprise creates implicit knowledge however, we are no longer able to take such decisions. If rules of selecting, classifying and interpreting information remain implicit knowledge, they are not subject to opportunistic misrepresentation or misuse. Because of the fact that nobody follows these rules in a conscious manner, nobody can use them strategically, even in cases where he would like to do so. Nor are the *langauge games* as the explicit parts of knowledge easily abused because they make sense only in the context of a certain *form of life* (Wittgenstein 1958, I/23) and are therefore only partly understood by the members of the group. The opportunities to cheat are severely restricted. If institutionalized experience is implicit only, nobody can consciously try to change that institutionalized experience. The stock of institutionalized experi-

---

[24]   For an application of Wittgenstein to the social sciences see especially Winch (1965).

ence is therefore a touchstone for propositions which can not easily be manipulated. Here again it is not irrational to behave in an opportunistic manner, it is impossible, because participants lack an overall picture of the situation.

Implicit rules are not open to strategic misuse. For that reason group selection is possible (Hayek 1980, 34) and Vanberg is wrong in criticizing Hayek on that point (Vanberg 1986). Groups with "good" rules can do better than groups with "bad" ones, independent of the question of whether or not a degree of exploitation is present within the group. As long as nobody can improve his individual situation because he is not aware of the rules he is following, he is not able to change his behavior. Because of the fact that individuals, for informational reasons, are not able to maximize their individual utility, groups may work on rules which are not perpetually endangered by opportunism.

3   Conflict resolution in a pluralist society

A group with a common culture can solve internal conflicts by pointing to its stock of institutionalized experience. As far as this experience remains implicit knowledge, the argument will point to evidence. All members of a group sharing the same culture will find the argument compelling but nobody will be able to explain why. What they believe to be evidence is just that part of institutionalized experience which is internalized to the point at which it becomes impossible to question the foundations of the judgement. This creates no difficulties as long as only individuals with the same cultural background are interacting. As soon as they argue with strangers, this no longer holds true.

In his 1993 book Siegenthaler is quite explicit that within society there may be a whole range of different groups with different kinds of institutionalized experience (Siegenthaler 1993, 43). These different groups can be seen as a generalized version of a research program in the sense of Imre Lakatos (Lakatos 1978). In generalizing Lakatos' approach, we could also speak of life programs showing the same characteristics as Lakatos' research programs: they consist of teams of individuals working with a common methodology towards a common end. They are following a common set of rules from which no single rule can be isolated and evaluated on its own. The rules make sense only in a complex system of hypotheses consisting of a hard core of theoretical articles of faith surrounded by an elastic, protective belt of auxiliary hypotheses and a developed methodology (Lakatos 1978, 4). What insiders find compelling as an argument, having internalized the whole culture of their program, may seem to be utter nonsense to the outsider.[25]

Where we have different life programs dealing with each other, the institutionalized experience is not the same for everybody. Members of different cultures

---

[25]   For an application to problems of research see also Hegmann (1995).

will see different things as evident and they will not be able to figure out their differences. What besides power and persuasion can resolve conflicts here? To solve conflicts, the discussants cannot point to the "institutionalized experience" of their groups as in the case of a conflict within a group, because the institutionalized experience is not consensual for all conflicting parties. There may always be an occasion for cheating and even if nobody wants to, the mere suspicion is sufficient to destroy such cross-cultural communication from the beginning.

The problem could be solved however in the same way as before. If enough individuals perceive the lack of cross-cultural understanding as something important, they may well perceive it as a crisis. A danger of civil war may be its most salient example. In that case, they may start to tackle the problem, creating a practice of dealing with cross-cultural conflicts.[26] The longer they act together, the more common knowledge evolves and the more institutionalized experience can be used to check whether an individual step should be permitted or not. Sharing the new stock of common knowledge, participants in the process are able to make consensual judgements about whether certain arguments are well grounded in institutionalized experience. Members of different groups, sharing the common interest to solve conflicts between their groups will act together in the same way as they did within their groups. They develop a "culture" for dealing with cross-cultural conflicts, a set of partly implicit rules which are hard to consciously violate.

4   Conclusion

Between fundamental uncertainty and mere routine there is a whole range of informational states in which communication can take place. If communication aims at producing institutionalized experience, fundamental uncertainty will be increasingly replaced by a new common reality. The more communication there is, the less uncertain the world becomes and the more scope for opportunistic action emerges. In order to make Siegenthaler's concept work, we should replace communication by collective action, aimed at producing "institutionalized knowledge". Collective action is not in danger of being diverted through opportunistic misrepresentations right from the beginning. This also holds for cross-cultural conflict resolution in a pluralist setting. Dealing with the latter should be viewed as the product of institutionalized experience functioning as the higher authority to separate acceptable propositions of mediation from unacceptable ones. This modification should render Siegenthaler's very interesting approach more powerful than it already is.

---

[26]   For a somewhat similar argument concerning the emergence of justice in an international setting see also Homann (1994).

References

Berger, Peter L. and Luckmann Thomas (1966): *The Social Construction of Reality;* New York: Doubleday.

Boudon, Raymond (1996): The 'Cognitivist Model' a generalized 'Rational-Choice Model'; in: *Rationality and Society,* 8/2, 123-150.

Buchanan, James M. (1990): The Domain of Constitutional Economics; in: *Constitutional Political Economy,* 1, 1-18.

Elias, Norbert (1970): *Was ist Soziologie,* München: Juventa.

Hayek, Friedrich A von (1980): *Regeln und Ordnung, (Recht, Gesetzgebung und Freiheit;* (Vol. 1), München: Verlag Neue Industrie.

Hegmann, Horst (1997): Differing World Views and Collective Action - The Case of Research", *Constitutional Political Economy,* 8, 179-194.

Homann, Karl (1994): Ist der Begriff 'Gerechtigkeit' auf das Verhältnis zwischen Industrienationen und Entwicklungsländern anwendbar?; in: L. Schuster (Hg.), *Die Unternehmung im internationalen Wettbewerb,* Berlin: Erich Schmidt Verlag.

Kuhn, Thomas (1962): Postscriptum; in: Thomas Kuhn, *The Structure of Scientific Revolutions,* Chicago: University of Chicago Press 1970.

Lakatos, Imre (1978): *The Methodology of Scientific Research Programmes;* (Philosophical Papers Vol. I), ed. by John Worrall and Gregory Currie, Cambridge: Cambridge University Press.

Polanyi, Michael (1964): *Personal Knowledge;* New York: Harper Torchbooks.

Rawls, John (1988): *A Theory of Justice;* Oxford: Oxford University Press.

Siegenthaler, Hansjörg (1993): *Regelvertrauen, Prosperität und Krisen;* Tübingen: Mohr.

Vanberg, Viktor (1986): Spontaneous Market Order and Social Rules; in: *Economics and Philosophy,* 2, 75-100.

Winch, Peter (1965): *The Idea of a Social Science;* London: Routledge & Kegan Paul.

Wittgenstein, Ludwig (1958): *Philosophical Investigations;* Oxford: B. Blackwell.

Comment on Hansjörg Siegenthaler

Thráinn Eggertsson

Learning and its Rationality in a Context of Fundamental Uncertainty

Professor Siegenthaler's essay discusses some of the most difficult an important issues in social science, the behavior of actors in an environment of fundamental uncertainty, and the extent to which assumptions of rationality are helpful for analyzing such environments. The essay deals in an stimulating and imaginative way with perplexing problems, and my response primarily attempts to digest these interesting ideas by translating them into terms that are familiar to me. In the language of Professor Siegenthaler's essay, I will try to use the institutional experience of my tribe or social group – a rather peculiar sub-division of the econ tribe – to understand and evaluate the hypothesis he advances.

The main concepts of the paper are (a) fundamental uncertainty; (b) institutionalized experience; (c) individual fundamental learning (or individual hypotheses); and (d) shared mental models and cognitive rules. Fundamental uncertainty is said to arise, when actors cannot assign (subjective) probabilities to the expected outcomes of their choices. Individual fundamental learning is an response to states of fundamental uncertainty and attempts to build new rules of behavior, and institutionalized experience provides rules (institutions) for selecting new cognitive rules and mental models from competing individual hypotheses.

Let me now explore these concepts. In recent work, I have tried to understand changes in mental models by drawing on, and modifying, the old theory of economic policy (Eggertsson 1997a, 1997b, 1998). The old theory of economic policy is associated with Jan Tinbergen, and suggests a world populated by policy models, instruments, targets, and policy measures. The old theory of economic policy assumes that policy models only guide the behavior of a central authority, but, in line with recent developments in economics, I have suggested that the behavior of private actors is also guided by policy models. In fact, recent work in political psychology shows that experts and amateurs often think about complex social systems or policy issues in ways that are not qualitatively different (Denardo 1995). I use this approach to discuss how unexpected social outcomes often destroy people's faith in their policy models.

Professor Siegenthaler also refers to unexpected social outcomes to explain how situations of fundamental uncertainty emerge. In particular he draws on the notion that capitalistic economies experience exceptionally severe depressions about every 20 years. I would like comment here that the jury on long-term business cycles is still out, and it is unnecessary for the argument of the paper to enter that controversy. Anyway, it is unlikely that severe business cycles which occur fairly regularly about five times every century would by themselves create the radical uncertainty which the author describes so vividly. Major structural changes, driven by new technologies that uproot traditional industries and change geographic locations of economic activity clearly are major sources of upheaval, which may find strong expressions when they are reinforced by severe cyclical downswing in GNP. The drastic depression of the 1890s in the USA, mentioned in the paper, coincided with major structural changes and dislocations, which created a powerful cocktail.

Uncertainty is a permanent condition of humanity, although it need not be as radical as the author's definition of fundamental rationality. But uncertainty involves more than unknown probabilities; uncertainty can mean that elements in various choice sets are not known – potential instruments of action may be unknown, and also potential outcomes. Also, we must emphasize that the failure of social systems has a dynamic element, which doubtlessly can be analyzed as an evolutionary process. Economic systems are not stationary over time, they evolve, and the evolution in part involves repeated revisions of both private and public policy models, revisions which are driven by what the author calls fundamental learning. Various subjective and objective factors determine in which direction social systems move, whether it is in the direction of increasingly satisfactory outcomes, or whether performance of social systems deteriorates over time and they possibly crash. Dynamic decline, involving interacting policy models, characterized not only in the former soviet economies of Eurasia, but also various regulated industries in the West – although, in many instances, regulations have produced acceptable outcomes.

Fundamental or severe uncertainty arises when policy models fail. However, I find the radical uncertainty that the paper describes a little exaggerated. Fundamental uncertainty is seen as an environment where words lose their meaning, where it becomes irrational to cheat, and so on. Economic crises upset people, but most people do not lose their senses quite to this extent. I find it useful to see each person, or each social group, as relying on an whole range of specialized and layered policy models. Except in cases of severe mental illness, people do not lose all their policy models in response to an economic or social crises, uncertainty is seldom or never fundamental in the sense of this essay. Rather, according to my view, only a subset of policy models are knocked off, and others survive, and are used for rebuilding new models and for communicating with other actors.

The paper's use of the concept, institutionalized knowledge is fascinating; particularly the idea that institutionalized knowledge tends to be relatively poor because of the high cost of communicating experience. I was reminded of mainstream economics, which has strict standards of evaluation that the suppliers of new models in economics must adhere to before their constructs are taken seriously. In economics, institutionalized knowledge – the selection authority – reflects past model building, individual learning, which has gained acceptance, was been selected. I agree with the author that we can (and should) separate new hypotheses, new models derived from individual learning, from the selection mechanism of institutionalized knowledge. Although these two categories are intimately related, they are separated in time, which is a firm enough boundary.

When severe uncertainty arises, people seek new policy models. Various social interactions require shared policy models, but policy models can be useful without being shared. The paper does not emphasize this possibility. It certainly is true that policy models, which emerge through individual fundamental learning, must be communicated if they are to be shared, and, as the paper emphasizes, richness often is lost in attempts to communicate. But some policy models can be useful without being shared, for instance when actors play against nature und receive clear feedbacks. Also, in human interactions, actors sometimes benefit by keeping their cognitive rules secrete. Kuran's (1995) work on preference falsification is related to these issues. But Professor Siegenthaler is right, shared mental models are of primary importance.

I do not quite see why the paper wants to deny the claim that shared experience of social groups is an input in the process of developing mental constructs. I agree, of course, that shared experience lowers the cost of communication. I also agree that raw experience, brute facts without a theory, do not explain the present or predict the future. But surely, people who live in an polar region are more likely to develop theories concerning the problem of living with snow and ice than are typical social groups in Africa. Shared environments and experience is likely to stimulate similar individual hypotheses, mental models, and world views, and also lower the cost of communicating and sharing these views.

I agree with the author that we should pay much attention to the poverty of shared experience, when we try to understand the formation of shared mental models and the nature of institutional change. The poverty of shared or institutionalized experience, and the tyranny of this selection mechanism must be a fundamental factor in path dependence. Path dependence in institutional change means that only particular qualitative categories of mental models are selected. The paper suggests, and I think correctly, that the poverty of institutionalized experience implies that we always will have path dependence. Path dependence becomes severely perverse, however, when the selection authority systematically rejects large categories of models that are of great relevance for a particular social group in terms of its goals and environments.

The essay ends with an interesting discussion of which environments will limit the poverty of institutionalized experience (along with the perversity of path dependence), and strengthen the rationality of the authority which selects hypotheses and policy models in an uncertain world. The author makes the sensible claim that factors such as plurality of opinion, large social networks, free communications, and social variety by themselves do not guarantee an effective selection mechanism. These factors must be accompanied by appropriate social or political structures, which guide the selection process. The essay draws on De Tocqueville and argues that an ideal environment will constitute sub-groups with common interest and experience that first institutionalize their experience, and then, in a second stage of this process, attempt to communicate their ideas to members of other groups in the wider community, not to dominate but to persuade in good will, and to learn from others.

This vision of how to deal with uncertainty, and how to build effective social institutions, reminds me of the work of Professor Vincent Ostrom (1991), who emphasizes many of the same ideas: the importance of pervasive uncertainty (which Ostrom sees as prevailing not only when social systems crash, but always when we try to design complex social systems), the central role of language in communicating social change, the importance of open discussion within and between groups, a gradual process of learning, and the importance of institutionalizing experience, the virtue of gradualism, and the danger of large-scale social experiments.

On the last page of his essay Professor Siegenthaler mentions that in the opinion of De Tocqueville, Americans have or had a peculiar communication structure that allowed open debate between groups, whereas European political factions often enter the field of ideological rivalry primarily to gain power, and not to persuade, listen, and learn. It is, of course, a question of tremendous importance, how communication structures originate, how societies institutionalize their experience. We must ask, therefore: How do rational communication structures originate in an uncertain world? Professor Ostrom has theorized that the origins of rational communication of religious beliefs, beliefs that some cultures share, but not others. Of course, such a solution suggests another question: Why do religious beliefs vary? In his paper, Professor Siegenthaler does not deal with this question, which alone would require a separate essay, at least.

References

Denardo, J. (1995): *The Amateur Strategist. Intuitive Deterrence Theories and the Politics of the Nuclear Arms Race*; Cambridge: Cambridge University Press.
Eggertsson, T. (1998): Limits to Institutional Reforms; *Scandinavian Journal of Economics*, 100, 335-357.
Eggertsson, T. (1997a): When the State Changes its Mind. Discontinuity in Government Control of Economic Activity; in: H. Giersch (ed.), *Privatization at the Turn of the Century*, Berlin: Springer.
Eggertsson, T. (1997b): The Old Theory of Economic Policy and the New Institutionalism; *World Development*, 25, 1187-1203.
Kuran, T. (1995): *Private Truths, Public Lies. The Social Consequences of Preference Falsification*; Cambridge, Mass.: Harvard University Press.
Ostrom, V. (1991): *The Meaning of American Federalism. Constituting a Self-Governing Society*; San Francisco: ICS Press.

List of Authors

IRIS BOHNET is Assistant Professor of Public Policy at the John F. Kennedy School of Government, Harvard University.

THOMAS BRENNER is Research Associate at the Max-Planck-Institute for Research into Economic Systems, Evolutionary Economics Unit, Jena.

BRUCE CHAPMAN is Professor at the Faculty of Law at the University of Toronto.

LÁSZLÓ CSONTOS has been a Professor of economics at the University of Budapest.

THRÁINN EGGERTSSON is former senior research fellow of the Max-Planck-Institute for Research into Economic Systems, Institutional Economics Unit, Professor at the Faculty of Economics and Business Administration at the University of Iceland and currently Visiting-Professor at Columbia University, New York.

JOHN FINCH is Lecturer at the Department of Economics at the University of Aberdeen.

BRUNO S. FREY is Director of the Institute for Empirical Economic Research and Professor of economics at the University of Zürich.

HEIKO GEUE is former Research Assistant of the Economics Department at the University of Marburg. Currently he is an adviser for the German Federal Ministry for Research and Technology.

GERD GIGERENZER is Director of the Centre for Adaptive Behavior and Cognition of the Max-Planck-Institute for Human Development, Berlin.

GERNOT HANDLBAUER is former Research Assistant of the Department of Management of the University of Innsbruck and currently academic guest at the Institute of Industrial Engineering and Management at the ETH Zürich.

HORST HEGMANN is Assistant Professor at the Economics Department of the University of Hamburg.

STEFFEN HUCK is Research Assistant at the Department of Economics of the Humboldt-University, Berlin.

DANIEL KIWIT is former Research Associate of the Max-Planck-Institute for Research into Economic Systems, Institutional Economics Unit and currently working as an auditor.

JACK KNIGHT is Associate Professor at the Centre for Political Economy, Washington University, St. Louis.

BRIAN LOASBY is emeritus Professor of economics, University of Stirling.

RENATE MAYNTZ is emeritus Director of the Max-Planck-Institute for the Study of Societies, Cologne, and emeritus Professor of the University of Cologne.

UWE MUMMERT is Research Associate of the Max-Planck-Institute for Research into Economic Systems, Institutional Economics Unit, Jena.

ANDREAS ORTMANN is Research Scientist at the Centre for Adaptive Behavior and Cognition of the Max-Planck-Institute for Human Development, Berlin.

MARKUS PASCHE is Assistant Professor at the Economics Department of the University of Jena.

BIRGER P. PRIDDAT is Professor at the Department for Economics and Philosophy of the University of Witten/Herdecke.

EKKEHART SCHLICHT is Professor of economics at the University of Munich, Department for the Theory and Policy of Income Distribution.

HANSJÖRG SIEGENTHALER is emeritus Professor of the Socioeconomic Centre at the University of Zürich.

MANFRED E. STREIT is Director of the Institutional Economics Unit at the Max-Planck-Institute for Research into Economic Systems and Professor of Economics at the University of Jena.

THOMAS S. ULEN is Professor at the College of Law and at the Institute of Government and Public Affairs of the University of Illinois at Urbana-Champaign.

PIET DE VRIES is Assistant Professor of economics at the University of Twente, Faculty of Public Administration and Public Policy.